Love in a Tuscan Kitchen

Savoring Life through the Romance, Recipes, and Traditions of Italy

SAVORING LIFE THROUGH THE ROMANCE, RECIPES, AND TRADITIONS OF ITALY

SHERYL NESS
— THE CHEF'S WIFE —

Rochester, Minnesota

Neither the publisher nor the author is engaged in rendering legal or other professional services through this book. If expert assistance is required, the services of an appropriate competent professional should be sought. The author and publisher shall have neither liability nor responsibility to any person or entity with respect to any loss or damage caused, or alleged to have been caused, directly or indirectly by the information contained in this book.

These recipes are taken directly from the handwritten collection of Sheryl Ness. Any resemblance to commercial recipes in published books is a coincidence and shows good taste by both parties. Recipes and stories from other family and friends were invited and freely given for inclusion in this book, and for them we are extremely grateful.

Tuscan Dreams LLC
c/o Concierge Marketing
4822 South 133rd Street
Omaha, NE 68137

www.LoveInATuscanKitchen.com

Paperback ISBN: 978-1-7320194-1-6
Mobi ISBN: 978-1-7320194-2-3
EPUB ISBN: 978-1-7320194-3-0

Library of Congress Cataloging Number: 2018934313
Library of Congress Cataloging-in-Publication data on file with the publisher.

Printed in the USA

10 9 8 7 6 5 4 3 2 1

For Angiolino,

taken too soon from this earth, who is an angel watching over us now.

Contents

LIST OF RECIPES

INTRODUCTION

One of my early memories as a child was cooking together with my mom in our old farmhouse kitchen in Minnesota. The kitchen was where everything happened. She taught me how to cook traditional Midwestern comfort food on a regular basis. We had a small farm with land for growing corn, soybeans, and wheat, along with cows and pigs. In the summer there were always extra people around helping with the many chores of the season. This meant cooking for ten or more people some days.

Mom taught me the basics and then some. We cooked casseroles that could feed an army, baked bread, cookies, cakes, and roasted meats in the oven for hours. The most exotic thing we created was pizza from a kit that came in a box. The smell of the spice packet with oregano was one of my favorite parts of the pizza-making experience. I was her helper in the kitchen, mainly because I was the only daughter, but also because this got me out of doing the dirty work outside with animals and crops. I had two brothers, one older and one younger, who were outside every day with my dad caring for the farm.

My mom taught me that putting love and care into the food she created was important. This was how she expressed her love for others. This tradition was passed to me through her, and it is one of the reasons that I love the feeling and comfort of spending time cooking and being in the kitchen. When in the kitchen, everything else fades into the background, including deadlines, stress, and worry. What I did not realize was that this love of food and cooking would reveal a path to another country and into a Tuscan kitchen, where I would fall deeply in love with the chef.

I grew up and married in my early twenties, which ended in a divorce ten years later. In my thirties, I was on the fast track to launching my career as a nurse and manager. It was what I was expected to do, especially since I did not have a family or husband. After all, what else could there be?

As I was sitting in one of my time management classes that I was expected to take as an up-and-coming leader in a busy academic medical center, I learned something incredibly valuable. Usually these things are boring and a bit of a waste of time. The instructor during the class detailed the steps of goal setting one day.

He said, "If you want something to happen, you can't just think about it in your mind. It won't just magically occur. You have to first write it down, and be very specific. This will make the goal real. You can read it and see it on the paper. Next you need to write out the possible steps to achieve your goal. After this, you need to share it with others. Talk about it openly with others who can potentially help you achieve your goal. If you never put it out there, it will never happen."

For me this was a sort of epiphany. No one had ever told me that I could do something like this. Most of my goals in life so far had been at the direction or desire of others. It was like when I was a kid and finally learned that to catch a ball I had to keep my eyes wide open. Well, I thought about my goals, and I wrote down a few that I wanted to achieve in my career because, after all, that was why I was in the class.

Then, I thought, why not write a personal goal for myself? Something just for me. At the end of the list I wrote that day,

I wrote this one: take a trip to Italy. There it was in black and white. I had a very strong sense, almost a longing, that I needed to go to Italy. Perhaps this was because of the love and care the Italian culture also placed on food and cooking. I was intrigued by the stories I had heard from others. My hunger for living a full life was another strong motivator for me during this time.

So I did what the instructor that day had told me. I kept my list of goals close to me and started talking about them with others. One day I was having dinner with a group of girlfriends. Two of them had just returned from a hiking trip through Tuscany and mentioned how incredible it had been. As they described meeting the people along the way and the memorable food and wine they had discovered, my mind was racing.

I looked around and said out loud, "I've wanted to do this for a while now."

This came out of my mouth at the same time as Ann, a good friend, said it too. We looked at each other with excitement and said, "Yes, let's make a plan."

Ann and I decided we would go the very next spring, so we had a few months to plan. This would be a fun adventure, but I had never done any serious hiking, so I started to train on a regular basis walking and taking long hikes on the weekend. While walking, I started listening to Italian podcasts to get some experience with the language.

The experience was everything I had been longing for and more. Do you ever get a feeling that you've been somewhere before? Or that you feel a strong connection to a place, but you're not sure why? I have traveled many places in my life and had wonderful experiences. The feeling I had in Italy was something I had never felt before.

On that first trip to Italy in 2004, I kept thinking about how comfortable I was there. Everything around me gave me a feeling that I was at home, from the foods to the people and the unique landscape. I was falling in love.

I returned home to Minnesota and could not get the memories and experience out of my mind. I surrounded myself with things that reminded me of Italy, including pictures of the landscape of Italy, pottery, shoes, and scarves. I could not get enough. I even took cooking classes and learned more about the language, cuisine, traditions, and wines. The more I discovered, the more connected I felt to my inner self. I loved the escape and creative experience of Italian cooking and would get lost in reading the recipes and discovering more of the culture and traditions.

Eventually, I returned to Italy a few years later. I was hoping that it would not disappoint me. I had such high hopes that I realized the trip was at risk for letting me down. I loved it as much as I remembered, perhaps even more. Some people have near-death experiences, but I had what I might call a near-life experience on that second visit to Italy.

This time, I was traveling with another good friend, Cathy, touring with a couple from California, Pam and Sam Hilt, who create small-group immersion tours to Italy. They showed us their Italy—the places you would never find on your own. One of my favorite memories was the experience and deep emotions felt while sitting in a little square, in a tiny little village, in the middle of rural Tuscany, sipping a glass of local Chianti wine while watching the final match of the World Soccer Cup in 2006 when Italy won over France.

Cathy and I had just eaten one of the best meals of our lives in a tiny little restaurant in the village of San Gusme. The soccer match was being projected on an old white sheet that was hung in the square of the village so that everyone could watch and celebrate together. The drama, energy, friendships, passion, and culture from the local people were just swirling around me. In that instant, my world had changed dramatically. I wanted to somehow be a part of this culture, this place, and these people. It was a comfortable feeling of being at home.

After this experience, my mind was made up. I was tired of waiting for something to happen. I knew that life was short and that I was not about to let time just keep passing by without doing something to seek out my dreams. My philosophy about taking more chances in life changed. In my work as a nurse with people suffering from memory loss and Alzheimer's disease, I saw so many people as they aged and lost their memory and physical function.

How many times I heard these words from them, "I wish I had done more, took more chances, and not waited for someday to come along."

My life was missing something—true love and companionship. There were days when I thought maybe I should just give up and be happy with the status quo. I had good friends, a wonderful family, and a career. However, I wanted so much more. I felt as if I might never find it. That was until I followed my heart back to Italy for a third time in 2007. This time, Italy intervened and changed the path of my life forever.

This is my true story. It chronicles my journey starting in the year 2007 and continues for ten years. I first started writing about my experiences in Italy after traveling there. I did not want to forget any of the details of what I was experiencing. Then something incredible happened and Italy became my life. Eventually, this is where I found love and a life of complete contentment. So I kept on writing.

After a while, I started hearing this from others who knew me: "You need to write a book. Your story is incredible."

Each time I heard this, I thought that perhaps the story should stay with me, my own personal memories. I was not so sure I wanted to share this treasure of a life I had discovered.

People also remarked that I had been brave and taken a huge risk that they could never do. Then, I wondered, if I could write my story in a way that reflected the true experiences I had, it might inspire others as well. My story connects to the traditions, people, and foods I experienced along the way.

My hope was to encourage others to strive to find meaning and purpose in their lives and perhaps, in the process, discover what I had found—pure happiness. So here it is. My story of finding love in a Tuscan kitchen and the unfolding of the journey that led to a life-altering experience of living in a little village in Chianti.

1

The Past and Present Collide

Time is standing still. We are just celebrating the Nuovo Anno (New Year) here in our little village in Italy and it is 2011. On New Year's Eve in Italy, there are a few customs you must follow. As with everything, I am learning this as I go along.

My friend Giulia looked at me with an intense look and asked, "Do you have on your red underwear for good luck tonight?"

I replied, "I have no idea what you are talking about."

"It's a tradition here," she replied. "You must at the very least have on your red underwear on New Year's Eve. It means that you will live your life to the fullest in the coming year. It also is a prediction of continued love and passion for you. You want that, don't you?"

I panic. And as I ran back to our apartment to look for a pair of red underwear, I was thinking that I didn't even own a red shirt, so the best I could do was find some pink underwear, so I put it on and hoped for the best. I would later learn that the tradition of wearing red underwear has a strong connection in the Latin cultures. Red signifying blood, life, passion. It was not a surprise to understand this about Italian culture. My life in Italy had changed my perspective forever. At the moment, this was experiencing life to the fullest, with all of the passion and dimensions possible.

Tonight, my husband and I would celebrate the New Year, our first one together as husband and wife, but only for a few minutes at midnight with a kiss and a glass of prosecco together in the same kitchen where we originally met. His restaurant was packed with tables of friends, families, and a few locals celebrating together.

"Auguri amore mio, buon nuovo anno (Happy New Year, my love)," Vincenzo says to me as he looks up from cleaning up the last few dishes in the kitchen where he is the chef. His sous chefs are quickly finishing up their duties so that they too can head out to celebrate the New Year.

"Happy New Year, my love." I say, "We must kiss at midnight. For me, this is what I need for good luck." I reach over and kiss him and hand him a glass of prosecco. We clink glasses, take a sip, and kiss again, this time a little longer, lingering with our noses together.

"I'm almost done drying all of the wine glasses, and my feet are killing me," I told him. I finish the glass of prosecco and go back to my work cleaning the glasses.

As I take the last sip of prosecco, I think back to the past four years and how my life has unfolded here in this little village in Tuscany. I could feel my past and present colliding during a split second in the same kitchen that drew me in to ask about the recipe for a decadent chocolate cake that I loved. I knew instantly on that day four years ago, as I gazed into the warm brown eyes of this Italian man who is now my husband, that I was experiencing something life changing. It was almost as if I could see my future reflected in his eyes. I had a keen sense of falling headlong into a moment that would define my future, without control, and that I somehow knew him inside and out. Fate had brought us together for a chance at happiness.

The restaurant is owned by Vincenzo, my husband who is the chef, and his two friends, Marco and Aldo. Together, they opened up this charming paradise six years ago in the heart of Chianti. Tonight, for New Year's Eve they hosted a special menu, including recipes that Vincenzo will only make for the evening: pumpkin soufflé, handmade tagliatelle with mushrooms, and a steak with herbs and sauce that will make you want to take the last piece of bread from the basket and as Italians would say "fare la scarpetta," or mop up every last bit of sauce and clean your plate with it.

Reservations for the evening started arriving just after Christmas, from locals who love to celebrate here to others who plan to travel in from Rome and Florence to this little piece of heaven in history. It's also tradition to, at exactly midnight, eat lentils and zampone (a type of decadent pork sausage) to bring good fortune in the year to follow. The richness of the sausage and the coin shape of the lentils are symbols of having a rich and prosperous year to come. The traditions of the foods that are important to eat on the eve of the New Year have been long standing.

A glass of prosecco always welcomes in the New Year at midnight, with all of the families from the area celebrating with fireworks and greetings in the square rounding out the evening. Vincenzo is a purist as a chef. He believes in using traditional recipes that reflect hundreds of years of perfection. This is one of the reasons he is so successful. People come to his restaurant because they want to experience traditional and incredibly good food made with care.

I always try to help out at the restaurant for special occasions, and this was one of them. I am not a great waitress, but I do my best to help at the restaurant because I know how important food is to people and this culture, and I love to experience the celebrations that occur in this warm and welcoming space that instantly makes you feel at home.

I can barely feel my legs and feet; we've both been working all day. As I look in the kitchen, I see Vincenzo carefully mopping the floor and checking to make sure his kitchen is clean, prepped, and ready for tomorrow. We both finish up our work and close the heavy doors to the back entrance. The cool, fresh air hits me and reality sets in. As we walk home just a few feet across the square to our little apartment, I see that a few people are still practicing the age-old tradition of throwing old items out the window at midnight in order to start fresh with the New Year.

Carla, one of the neighbors, launches clothing and other items out her windows warning those below to be careful.

"Out with the old, in with the new," she yells with a laugh.

When she sees us, she says, "Are you coming to play bingo with us? This year the prizes are great."

I reply, "No, Carla, maybe next year. I'm so exhausted I can barely stand up anymore. I'm dead tired."

I have to admit, I would love to celebrate a little more and hang out with the locals, but I know that Vincenzo is ready for a hot shower and a foot rub, and so am I. Together we are speaking in Italian, as Vincenzo does not speak English. We have a quick laugh and a look at each other. We have another plan for this evening. Kisses and snuggle time in bed together.

Most of the village was gathering at the local Circolo, which is the Italian word for a local community club or gathering place with a coffee bar in the front and a large space in the back for community events with a stage to play the tombola or bingo into the night. The Circolo exists still today to preserve the culture and traditions of the local area.

It will be a wild and rambunctious night that will last into the wee hours of early morning. The tradition of the tombola is also well preserved in our little village. The priest and the locals all pitch in to gather prizes for the winners with everyone from young children to grandmothers purchasing as many bingo cards as they can manage to keep track of for the evening.

We reach our apartment and walk up the flight of stairs to the terrace that overlooks the main square as well as the restaurant. I can't help but reflect on the beauty of this place and the way I was drawn to it from the first moment my feet stepped inside.

As I look across to the restaurant, which is located in the lower level of an old palace in the middle of our little village, San Gusme, I think of its long history. The space was originally a stable and workshop back in the fourteenth century. The top floors had been where an extended family had lived. Now, the top floor was made into apartments where many of the local families lived. The outside of the building reflects the years of patchwork brick and stone repair and restructuring that had taken place as it transformed from a family palace to its current state.

Half of the old well is still visible inside the walls of the restaurant, with brick and stonework arches at such unique angles that it would make any architect swoon. At first it seemed as if it was a patchwork of mistakes, with brick covering some walls and stone mixed in on others. Down the middle of the restaurant is a large, open-arched ceiling, which is perfect to place long wooden tables to seat over twenty people. On either side of this are smaller arched nooks, perfect for small tables for two or four.

Tonight, the restaurant was full of locals and visitors celebrating with passion and hope for the New Year that had just arrived. On this New Year's Eve, I feel grateful that I am here in this place in time, with a man I love, experiencing life in a way I never imagined. I am amazed at the road that brought me here. I had experienced heartbreak and sadness along with a longing for something more in my life. I could not believe that I had finally found love. Sometimes I felt guilty or worried that it might be taken from me at any time. It felt like every minute of every day for the past twenty years was preparing me to take in and appreciate the happiness I felt in my heart.

On this same night, in my mind, I took myself back in time to about five years ago, when I had first eaten in this restaurant during my second trip to Italy. I remember sitting at the small table with my friend Cathy, looking around and thinking, this is an incredible place. I could almost feel the energy from the past and present coming together. I had the sensation that I had been there before, but I knew that I never had. I felt the summer wind swirl around me like a magical spell. For a time, I was truly mesmerized and thought to myself, what is happening around me? Why do I feel such a connection to this place? Is this real or is it a dream?

That day, I remember eating my meal very slowly because I did not want it to end. I will never forget the freshness of the tomatoes, the texture of the pasta and cheese, and the incredible flavors that harmonized together. The wine was bright and clean and tasted of cherries and figs.

The dessert was a hot chocolate cake that when I cut into it, my spoon found a heart of dark chocolate still melted and warm. It was paired with a custard-like homemade vanilla ice cream with a little swirl of raspberry and cream sauce next to it that seemed to have the shape of a free-form heart. Little did I realize at that point in time that the chef who created the food I ate that day would be my future husband.

On that particular visit, Vincenzo and I would not meet. Not yet. However, I felt as if maybe my spirit already knew that I was home. My subconscious had already made my choice for me. Later, my heart guided me back to the man I loved and this place I would call home.

That memory was from my first visit to this little village during a ten-day vacation in Tuscany. I felt a strong connection with the life and people in Italy. I noticed that they took time to greet each other warmly, with kisses and greetings that sometimes went on for ten minutes or longer. Children were playing with each other, not with their cell phones; teenage girls were laughing and walking arm in arm together, hugging and kissing and catching up. There was no fear of touching each other, talking, and taking the time to really be together. I could feel that connecting and friendship was important.

The physical beauty of Tuscany was also a strong element in my experience and stayed in my memory long after I had returned to Minnesota. The old cypress trees along the ancient noble roads stand tall as if to welcome you into their home. Around me I could see the hills and mountains, dotted with little villages. The beauty of terraced olive groves and many fields of grapevines are planted together as if to say that they belong to this place, to live together with the villages, the land, and the people. I could feel that the dimensions of Italy were many layers deep, including the culture, foods, and traditions old and new. I could see a horizon full of beauty unlike any other I had ever experienced. I was fascinated by this and knew that I was forever changed by the experience.

I returned home feeling as if I had left a secret lover in Italy that would be impossible for me to have in my life. I wanted the chance to be with my secret love, but at this point that seemed impossible. My family and my job were in Minnesota. As was my relationship that seemed to be on the road to nowhere despite my efforts to ask for more. Sometimes I felt empty inside. How could I tell my family, my work, and my boyfriend at that time that I wanted more out of life? It seemed selfish and bit unreachable, so I kept this thought in my heart only.

2

The Mystical Road to Tuscany

This memory of a secret love took me back to the road that had drawn me to Italy in the first place. After returning from that incredible vacation in Tuscany with my friend Cathy, I kept in touch by email with the woman who had organized our trip, Pam. She and I became instant friends. A few months later, Pam sent me a note and asked if I knew anyone who would be willing to come to stay with them during their busy touring season and watch over their two girls and their house and work a bit with their travel business—one that was growing and prospering more each year.

I had loved the experience of seeing the real Italy as she and her husband, Sam, had showed me. Their business (TuscanyTours.com) was focused on tours that gave you an immersion into the culture and traditions of Italy on a level that you would never find on your own as a traveler. The experience left me wanting more.

I thought about what she was asking and responded to her almost immediately. "What about me?"

She responded back. "Don't say that unless you're serious. We would love that."

I have to admit, I had no idea what I had just done. I instantly thought this was my chance to be with my secret love again, Italy.

All that came out of my mouth in response was, "Why not?"

You see, at that point, I had worked for over twenty years as a nurse for a major academic medical center. I worked while putting myself through university and graduate school, and become a successful leader and manager. I had played my life so far completely by the rules, as everyone expected me to do. I had focused on my career because that was all I had. I had been through plenty of disappointments including a failed marriage and a long-term relationship that never felt quite right. I had no children and no spouse, so my career and my work was everything—it defined every part of me.

However, I was constantly wondering to myself if this was all there was to life. I wanted to discover my place in the world that was comfortable for me. I felt like my roadmap so far had been designed by someone else. I wanted a life that allowed me to have new experiences and give me a deeper sense of meaning and belonging. I think my ancestors helped me along with this notion because it was a sensation that was very strong. I could not ignore it.

My great-grandfather was a ship builder from Norway and had sailed to nearly every continent. After all of these adventures, he packed up his wife and two little girls and sent them off to New York where they lived for three years while he returned to Norway to make enough money to return to America. He loved what America had to offer. Once he returned, together they took the train to the place where it ended at that time—North Dakota—where you could homestead land. There, they made their new life as farmers.

My grandmother (his little girl) was a big influence on me. She was one of the first women to go to formal nursing training in South Dakota and had a constant sense of adventure. When I was a kid, I remember that she would pick me up in her little pickup camper and we would go on weekend camping adventures. I attribute my sense of wanderlust to her family and the adventurous experiences of generations past. Surely it was in my DNA.

So here I was, like my grandparents before me, about to embark on the adventure of a lifetime. I boldly asked my employer for an unpaid educational sabbatical for six months to finish writing my original research I had done for my master's thesis and study for a teaching exam that I never had time to do when I was busy working. I was so tired of the daily rat race with continuous pressure to keep doing more.

After I asked for time away, my manager said, almost immediately, "No, I could never allow you to take that much time away."

I said, determined and without even blinking, "Well, then I think I need to quit my job, because I really need this time off. I can always come back to work again."

What had I just done? Did this actually come out of my mouth? When I thought about it later, I was amazed at how strong I had felt about this, and I was not giving up. My manager considered it and came back to me with a deal, a compromise. I could have three months at a time, as long as I came back for six weeks in between to work in the office.

This whole experience really got me to thinking: Why is it so hard to ask for time off during a long career? My manager at the time was so disappointed in me, I could tell. He had big plans for me to climb the ladder with him as my mentor. That was the expectation. However, this was not at all what I wanted. I kept asking myself why we keep working until it's too late to really enjoy our life. I think that this whole concept is wrong, but the only way to change it is to insist on what you need during your middle career years. For me (and probably for many others), this was the time when I needed a break the most.

Making the decision to travel back to Italy and spend this kind of time away from my family and job was not an easy one. So many questions were constantly on my mind. Was it a big mistake? Would I ruin my life? Ruin my career? It was time to leave my fears behind me. Returning to my secret love was the one primary goal clearly in focus. I couldn't wait to be back in Italy where my heart felt happy and content.

Night had descended on the little village of San Gusme as I arrived and started settling into my attic apartment above my friend Pam's office. There were many adjustments to make. The apartment was tiny, with a cement floor, a single bed, small table, and kitchen with a sink and a few cupboards all in one room. Behind the small table was a frosted window framed with black iron that opened to the inside and was full length. I could see that it was old and did not close well, as the light from the village was peeking through in many areas.

The only other room was a bathroom with a small shower, toilet, and sink. This room also held the water heater, which was small and attached to the wall. There was only one radiator in the bathroom and one in the main room. The stairs that led up to the apartment were so narrow and steep that it felt more like climbing up a ladder than a stairway. I had to unpack my suitcase little by little carrying items up the stairs to settle in.

The first night, I nearly froze to death because the windows were not sealed well and I had no idea how to turn on the heat. However, I was so tired that I feel asleep in five seconds.

The next morning, I woke to the sounds of the village around me and thought, where am I? Just then I heard the bell tower chiming seven bells. That's when I knew that the world around me had changed. As reality hit, I realized that I was snuggled under as many wool blankets as I could find in a tiny little bed in Italy. It was so small that if I turned over once, I might actually fall out of bed.

Off to a bit of a rough start, all was remedied when I got dressed and made a pot of coffee to start my day. I had arrived in the night darkness, so I was excited to go out and take in the place that I would call home for the next few months. This was the beginning of a new start for me. I had mixed emotions and many doubts about what I might discover about myself and this place that I had fallen deeply in love with from the moment I saw it a few years back.

The village of San Gusme is tucked into a curve of one of the wine roads of Chianti. Most people driving by might look up and see the walled village and think that no one lives there anymore, perhaps it is abandoned. It seemed a bit like a ghost from afar. The one-lane road that leads up and curves past the village to the mountains above it was probably a logging road at one time, as it travels up to the mountains and forests of Tuscany, which you can see tower above it.

The village is surrounded by a large vineyard that curves around the village like nature's wave of green and brown, following the contours of this ancient place. San Gusme was once a strategic outpost that protected Siena because of its location between Florence and Siena. It was high enough in the mountains to have clear views of the towers of Siena in the distance. What an incredible history this place held inside its walls. The name San Gusme was derived from a mispronunciation of Saint Cosmas to whom the nearby ancient parish church of Campi is dedicated. The village was founded in the late fourteenth century and has always been considered an ally of Siena.

Once you arrive, you have to leave your car outside in the little parking lot under one of the olive trees or near the ancient white fig tree that hangs over the wall of the village. From here, you can walk up and through one of the old doors or entries to the village. The main door that looks out on Siena has a scenic view of the surrounding countryside, framing it as you leave.

As I passed through the old door, I was instantly transported to another place and time—realizing that, for me, this was an ancient place, but so new to me at the same time. The village walls are made of old limestone and exposed red and terra-cotta bricks that have obviously been repaired and renewed through the centuries. Inside the doors, you walk on a rough combination of various colors of stone and cement tiles. I could see the little doors and stairways leading to the various apartments that surround the circle of the village inside, with brick-framed windows and terraces belonging to each level.

As I walked around that day, I discovered the people of the village for the first time. They became part of my family when I lived here, but in the beginning, it was all new for me.

Inside the village, everyone was getting their start to the day. It was alive and breathing already. I could see inside the little market where Gianni and his mother were greeting the first few customers as they do their shopping for the day. I encountered Tosca, a tiny little woman in a flowered dress about four and a half feet tall, with silver hair who must have weighed only about seventy pounds. She was carrying a small market bag with a sack of bread sticking out of it as she walked up the stairs to her little apartment on the top floor of the central palace. Tosca gave me a warm smile, but I could see that behind the smile she looked at me with sad eyes.

She greeted me with, "Good morning, dear," even though she did not know me yet. Later we would be very close and I wonder now, did she know this already?

Later on, I saw a man about sixty years old, Giancarlo, who was sitting on the bench, smoking a cigarette with his little granddaughter toddling around close to him. He looked to me as if he had had a tough life. He had suntanned skin with rough-looking hands and no extra fat to show on him.

He said in a loud voice while wagging his finger in the air, "No, no, where are you going?" to Martina, his granddaughter. She looked back and gave him a sneaky smile as if she wanted to escape.

He noticed me, but did not say anything. I could tell that he wanted to, but perhaps he thought I was just a visitor and would be gone by day's end. Giancarlo seemed to be at ease with the village, almost as if he were in charge. I could tell that perhaps he was waiting to see who he could talk to, or eager to catch up on the gossip for the day.

From the corner of my eye, I saw Remo just coming out of his cantina in his blue farmer's coat. He walked slowly and was bent over from years of work as he toted a metal trolley loaded with a couple of cases of his own Chianti wine in the traditional straw-covered bottles to his bar across the piazza. He stopped and regarded the village, looking around to see who was out. Seeing no one but me at the moment, he kept walking.

On the other side in the central piazza, an older woman with red hair who was named Nara had wandered out on the little terrace of her second-story apartment to water her geraniums. She gave them a big drink. So much that it drained down and poured onto the stone square below her. A cat that was nearby narrowly escaped getting a shower. She looked out across the piazza and seemed to be regarding it all as her own, almost like a queen. I could tell that this was her village. I instantly knew that she had lived in it for a long time. I wondered what that must be like, to be from this place and to call it home for so many years. To think of all of the changes that had taken place around it, still the village seemed to be lost in time, preserved in a way that was hard to explain with words.

In the distance, I heard children playing and dogs barking near the preschool, which has a small playground with the doctor's office on the other side. As I reached the far side of the village, I peeked out of the opposite door of the village and saw the small road winding up the mountain to the forest. Looking out and up, I could see that I was standing under ancient umbrella pines that seemed to be watching over the village.

In the garden was a terra-cotta statue of a strange looking old man who was made to look like he was peeing, with a fountain of water streaming out from under his hat. I thought to myself, good, this place seems to have a sense of humor too. A small tractor with a wagon was making its way up the winding mountain road with a load of wood in the back. It was early April, and the smells from the countryside waking up from winter were coming alive. I could smell wet soil, pine trees, and smoke from the distance.

As I walked around the circle, I encountered another older woman, whom I know now is Lina. She had bright red hair and a stern look on her face that showed that she had worked hard in her life and suffered a lot. She was looking out of the local coffee bar with a broom and swept out the doorway. She looked around the corner as if to check to see if someone was coming, but it was just me, and since she did not know me, she returned into the bar and back to her work.

As I looked inside, I could see that the local priest was sitting sipping on a coffee and smoking a cigarette. He looked very at ease and well taken care of. This was the bar I later called the church lady bar. Then, in a flashback, I remembered that this was exactly the place where my girlfriend and I had sat outside one year earlier to watch the soccer match being projected on a sheet just in front of the stone wall so that everyone in the village could watch together. I remember the slope of the stone was perfect to set up chairs so that we could all see well. The bar was lively that night with everyone out enjoying the cool summer air and the excitement of the soccer match between Italy and France. The memory instantly made me smile as I thought, I know this place already.

Just a few steps away from the church lady bar, I walked through the back door to the village; the wall around the back entrance seemed to be rustic and broken down. I wondered why it had not been fixed. Why would they leave it in such a state of disrepair? Later, I would understand why. This door looked as if it was not used much as it was very narrow. The view from this door looked out to the back of the village to the country homes that once were local share cropper farms, now probably someone's vacation home.

I regarded the picturesque vineyards and olive groves dotting the surrounding land and thought of the long walks that I could take. I watched a woman walking quietly on her own with a bouquet of flowers going in the direction of the cemetery. I think this was Tosca whom I saw before. Around every corner I saw the beauty and dimensions in a life that I had never known. The colors and landscape were so breathtaking, I wondered if it was real.

On the next turn, I was welcomed to the main piazza, with the old palace and terraces from the apartments where the locals live. The old church from the fourteenth century was also here. This was the church with the bell tower for the village. Its melodic song rang out during the day starting at 7:00 a.m. until 10:00 p.m. to designate each hour passing and once in between to mark the half hour.

As I looked to the corner, I could see the old tailor's shop with Vezio inside. Vezio was in his late seventies or early eighties. He was intent on his work at the moment and did not realize that I was peeking into his shop. He was bent over his sewing machine, perhaps creating someone's custom dress or suit. Later, I would realize that Vezio was a person who truly defines San Gusme. He was a true historian and caretaker of the village. He cared for its people and all of the treasures with his entire heart and soul. And he was a true treasure as well.

In the lower level of the main palace, I noticed a restaurant. It did not look like much from the outside, but once I looked inside, I could not believe my eyes. Arched brick and stone ceilings with centuries-old limestone outside. The polished terra-cotta tiles on the floor with little wooden tables and straw-covered chairs were seated around the restaurant. One

Main piazza of San Gusme with the church tower.

long table was situated down the middle with smaller tables located around the intimate little coves in the corners.

This was the place. I remembered the life-changing meal I had experienced on my trip one year earlier. That restaurant was exactly where I had a visionary, magical moment that had taken my breath away. I was mesmerized by this thought. How did I get back to this place?

Later, as I walked outside the village on my first hike, I noticed that the side ditches along the road were covered with wild poppies with their red flowers bending in the wind, raspberry bushes, little purple hyacinths, daffodils, and other wild herbs. This memory instantly brought me back to my childhood walking the country roads near our farm in Minnesota when wildflowers still grew along the road.

Each day was a new adventure in what I would see and find on my walks. The old road I was on traveled straight up for at least a mile, curving around and up the mountain before leveling out. About halfway up, I could stop and take a break at a little stone shrine with a local painting of the Madonna and Child along with a rosary hanging on top. I could see that someone (I wondered who) had left a little bouquet of flowers at the shrine not long ago as they were still fresh.

As I approached the top of the mountain, I was a bit winded, so I turned around to take a little break. I could barely believe my eyes.

Picture in your mind what I saw and you might also fall in love. Rolling hills of green and gold below me, the village of San Gusme nestled above the hills surrounded by ancient limestone walls with towering umbrella pine trees that looked as if they had been protecting the village since ancient times. I could hear the old bell tower from the village tolling at the moment. The sound echoed up the mountain and mixed with the sounds of the birds chirping and the sheep on the hill close by. The mountains in the far distance in the opposite direction had a cloudy, purple mist just covering them so that I was not entirely sure if the scene was real or a dream. In reality, the mountains were many miles away, but standing there at that moment, I felt as if I could reach out and touch them.

I honestly felt I could see the entire world from where I stood. The terraced hills of olive trees, the land covered with grapevines that followed every curve—just starting to wake up for the season. I could hear the farmers out cleaning up the olive branches and tying up the trailing vines so that they would grow along the wire. As I got closer, I could smell their little fires burning the cut olive branches, filling the air with a smell of the olive wood, smoke, and something else—a smell coming from the land itself, steeped in the deep traditions of this place.

These daily walks became a tradition for me. A way of connecting to this new place I was living in. Each day as I would leave for my hike, I would encounter someone from the village on their way back home.

One day, Vilma (Giancarlo's wife) saw me and said, "Where are you going?"

I responded, "Just out for a walk."

She looked at me and said, "You walk on purpose?"

"Yes, this is my way of relaxing a little and meditating," I responded. "Would you like to join me?"

She looked at me like that was the strangest idea anyone ever had. She responded, "I walk so much every day that my feet feel like they are going to drop off. I can't imagine walking more, or that it would help me relax."

After this, I would see her or Giancarlo on my way out of the village, and they would smile and shake their heads and say, "Walk, walk, walk," they would tease. I knew that they thought I was a bit crazy.

As the weeks went by, Vilma became curious about this idea of walking for relaxation. One day she said, "I want to go walking with you, but I can only go early in the morning before my grandchildren need me. They come home for lunch and then I watch them until the evening."

I was not the best at getting up early, but I replied, "Sure, when do you want to start?"

We agreed to meet at 6:30 a.m. a few days later to walk together. After she joined me, she finally understood the pure relaxation that occurs when you are walking for no reason other than to walk, relax, and take in your surroundings. As we walked, we mostly talked. Well, she talked and shared the gossip and news from the village. It was the perfect thing for me. I got to know more about the people and happenings, and I was able to practice my Italian, which at this point was not very good at all.

Vilma was never impressed with my language skills. One day, she told me that I spoke Italian like a Chinese person. I was devastated. Learning the language was one of the hardest things about this transition. Time would help, but I struggled with this daily.

3

Uncovering Easter's Surprising Treasures

My first days and months in our little village were spent during the time of Easter, which is one of the most widely celebrated holidays in Italy. The traditions are centuries old and continue to be practiced and embraced by young and old in the village.

The holiday season starts in the weeks before Martedi Grasso, or Fat Tuesday, where we celebrate with friends and eat decadently, followed by the weeks of Lent, which includes a special daily Mass, eating only fish on Fridays, and giving up sweets and indulgences.

During Easter week in San Gusme, the villagers organize a Good Friday processional, which starts at dawn—including carrying a statue of Mary on a pedestal and a large wooden cross, which follows the same tradition each year by walking up the path of the mountain road, stopping at an ancient church at one of the highest points to watch the sunrise, and moving through the woods to an old cross from 900 AD. Along the way, everyone says traditional prayers and sings songs. Villagers young and old from the area, who are able, take part in the walk. I was amazed at the physical strength and stamina of the women and men who were seventy or older in the group that day.

After the visit to the old cross, everyone stops for a little snack, which is packed in your own knapsack. I noticed that most consisted of ham or salami sandwiches made with the traditional Tuscan bread and big hunks of pecorino cheese. Most people finished their snack with either a little cup of vin santo or grappa.

Vin santo is a very special wine made in the Chianti region and is incredibly unique. The grapes are aged on the vine, placed on straw mats or hung to dry for weeks, and then pressed and aged in tiny little wooden casks for five to ten years. The wine was traditionally offered as a wine for Mass or used for those who were ill or needed healing. Now, vin santo is produced as special dessert wine that is given as a gift to those who are special to you and is especially treasured if it comes from a local wine producer with no label at all.

The Good Friday processional continues down through the steep and rocky mountain paths to the neighboring village where a formal Mass is held in the local church, and then everyone returns home on foot to San Gusme. The entire processional takes about three hours and starts at 5:30 a.m. It was a peaceful and meaningful way for me to experience my first Easter in Italy. This was symbolic of my new beginning in a place that I would eventually call my home and was my path to discovering tranquility and love.

The Saturday evening prior to Easter, a traditional evening processional is also held. This is led by the priest dressed in his finest holy robes, a few little girls from the village dressed as angels, and the deacons in their holy attire, as well as Mary on a pedestal and Jesus on the cross. A special band (uniforms and all) plays traditional religious dirges as they walk along with the villagers holding candles.

The only lights in the village are candles in every window with the path of the processional also glowing with candles along the road. Large bonfires of olive branches are set afire during this evening walk and give it a deeply spiritual feeling. The path that the villagers take follows the ancient traditions of passing by a historic noble house nearby to pay homage to the descendants who still live in the same villa. San Gusme is one of the last communities to continue this tradition in the area, so people come from all over the region to participate in the processional.

When Easter Sunday arrives, Easter Mass is held, followed by a traditional lunch with family and friends. Many people celebrate by going out together. The church bells ring throughout the day and everyone celebrates by exchanging beautifully decorated giant chocolate eggs with a surprise inside.

I'll never forget my very first chocolate Easter egg. It was about twelve inches high and made of some of the best milk chocolate I have ever tasted, and decorated with peach flowers and green accents. I did not want to break it open, but everyone insisted. Inside I found two little cupcake molds that I use to make cakes or muffins.

Later, I realized the incredible personal connection to the treasure in my egg—something to keep making cakes. It was perfect because of my love for baking. Every person picked out special decorated chocolate eggs to give their family members and close friends, both old and young. In the village, the local priest gave out chocolate eggs to all of the children of the parish. Once this happened, the village was high on chocolate, laughing and enjoying the celebration with the festivities that lasted into the evening.

Every season in Tuscany has special gifts to enjoy. Springtime brings a sense of freshness and awakening after the cold, dark winter days. March had been very rainy and cold, everyone told me, as was much of April, preparing the land for the hot days of spring and summer ahead.

On my daily walks, I noticed that the almond trees were among the first to show signs of spring with delicate pink blossoms against the brown of the landscape. Next, the olive trees started to produce the most tiny, delicate white flowers that would eventually become olives. The vines seemed to wake up suddenly. One day I saw only the sleeping brown of the grapevines and the next moment, the bright green leaves popped out and started to soak in the sunshine. The grass got greener and the fields of grain were being planted for the spring and summer wheat.

From the village and on my walks, I could see that the herds of sheep were also awake and happily grazing on the freshness of spring. I discovered new wild herbs I had never seen and asparagus growing alongside the road and in the forests. My favorite were all of the red poppies dotting the fields and along the roadside. Eventually much of the land became covered in red. It was spectacular. Later, the yellow broom brought fragrance and happiness to the area.

One of the things I learned about the Italian culture is that the people eat and enjoy everything in season, when the produce is fresh and available. This makes each season so special and unique. Everyone anticipated the foods from each season when they were ripe and delicious, only in their time. During this time, I remember the spring market was full of fresh asparagus, baby lettuce, green peas, zucchini, and strawberries.

Fruits and vegetables are eaten only fresh from the local countryside. Most in the area didn't shop at large groceries, but instead found their items at the weekly market just down the road from the village, or they would be shared from one to another if someone had a large garden.

One of my favorite dishes from springtime is a zucchini risotto with parmesan cheese and pistachios. Vilma first described this dish to me. One day, she knocked at my door with fresh, tender zucchini and so it was the perfect time for me to make risotto.

Risotto with Zucchini and Pistachios

1-2 small zucchini, halved and sliced thin
(or 1 cup of fresh vegetables, such as asparagus, mushrooms, peas)
4 tablespoons olive oil
1-2 vegetable bouillon cubes dissolved in boiling water (around 1-2 quarts)
1 cup Carnaroli risotto rice (Hint: use ½ cup for every two people)
½ cup white wine (cooking wine or regular white wine)
4 tablespoons butter
Salt (to taste)
4 oz. parmesan cheese (grated)
½ cup chopped pistachios (unsalted)

Assemble all ingredients and start by sautéing the sliced zucchini in olive oil for 5-10 minutes until lightly browned. Set aside.

Bring 2 quarts of water to boil. Add bouillon cubes to dissolve. You can also use canned, boxed, or homemade vegetable stock for this. Broth should be warm when adding to the rice as it is cooking. Keep the broth close to the rice on the stove in order to ladle it easily into the rice as it is cooking.

In a sauté pan, warm 4 tablespoons of olive oil over medium heat and add the rice. Stir 1-2 minutes until rice is slightly toasted. Next add the ½ cup of white wine and let the wine evaporate. As the wine evaporates, add one large ladle of broth and simmer the rice. Broth should cover the top of the rice. Keep the rice on medium to low heat to simmer while cooking.

Every 2-3 minutes, add another ladle of broth to the rice and stir. It's not necessary to stir constantly. Continue adding broth until the rice has cooked 10-12 minutes. This is the midpoint of cooking, and time to add the cooked zucchini.

Next, add in the cooked zucchini (or other vegetables) and continue stirring and adding broth every few minutes. Test the rice at around 20 minutes to see if it done. Normally, risotto rice takes a total of 20-25 minutes to cook. Mixture should be creamy, white, and tender (not hard inside) when you eat it.

Once the rice is cooked, take off the heat and add in 4 tablespoons of butter and 2 oz. of the grated cheese. Stir well and add salt to taste. If needed, add another ladle of broth depending on the consistency of the rice. It should be creamy, not runny and not too sticky.

Spoon into individual bowls or plates for serving, grate remaining parmesan cheese over the top along with 2 tablespoons of the chopped pistachios and a drizzle of extra virgin olive oil (if you prefer).

Serves 4.

Recipe note: Carnaroli or Arborio rice can be used to make risotto. You can find this in the dry goods area of the grocery store near other types of rice or in the Italian specialty area of the store.

May was warm and sunny in Tuscany. The grapes were starting to form on the vine, and the wildflowers kept surprising me on my daily walks. Along with the deep purple wild iris and poppies, I would see many big mounds of purple lavender, with the bees just humming on them, more of the yellow broom, bright and fragrant, wild rosemary and fennel, fig trees, and berry bushes everywhere.

One of my favorite walks followed a dirt road down through a small valley and then up through an ancient cypress-lined road to an old ruin from Villa Arceno—a collection of country houses with the land that has cultivated grapes for Chianti wine for years. At one time, the houses were owned by a noble family and caretakers. There are many houses in the area that are now vacation homes for those who want a house in Tuscany, especially during the hot summer months. Some are also rented out for vacation rentals. Each one had a unique stone exterior with maintained gardens of cypress trees, rosemary bushes, and lavender. Every house had a unique name that was posted on an old sign or carved into the stone around the house. This usually noted something unique or interesting about where the house was located or may have been traced to ancient history. Some of the names I remember were Arco al Poggio, which means the arc of the well, Arceno di Sotto, meaning below Arceno, Casa Nova, or new house, as well as San Giovanni, named after Saint John.

If you were a local, you knew the place by the name, not the street or road it was on. This was a common understanding—perhaps because the roads were not named or numbered when the original houses were built. This is a theme that I noticed all over Italy. Most of the time, if you understood the name of the place you were traveling to, that was on the directional sign, not street names or road numbers.

In the middle of the grounds is a large villa that was once a noble house surrounded with architecturally designed gardens ringed by old stone walls and its own little chapel. It was so hard to believe that it had been abandoned for years now. It was obvious that someone still cared for the gardens around the villa, but the larger gardens behind the stone walls had gone wild. I would have loved to have had the opportunity to see it in all of its glory decades ago. This became one of my most favorite walks.

Sometimes, I would even stop to talk to the trees along the way, which seemed so wise and welcoming. Approaching the trees, they did not seem real; however, as I got closer, the smell of sunshine and pine wafted up through my senses and, in their own way, sent me the message that they were real. My strength symbol had long been that of a tree, so it meant so much to me to be able to connect in this way.

Many of the houses I passed were now abandoned, and it made me wonder what they must have been at one time. Each time I would pass by, my thoughts would automatically dream of being able to someday restore one of these houses back to the beauty of a long-ago time.

I especially enjoyed one house that is not far from the village, nestled in the vineyards with old stone walls and archways that were falling down. I could picture what it must have been like to live there, with fruit trees in the garden and views of the Tuscan mountains in the distance. The top of the house has an old terrace that surely must reveal the most spectacular view of the countryside ever.

4

New Meaning for this Blond American

I had no idea that I would fall in love so many times over during my time in Italy. One of the primary reasons for returning to Italy was to help my friends with their travel business and occasionally be nanny to their two children. I had never had a chance to be a mom in my life, and always had a strong sense that I wanted this (very much), so this was my opportunity to be a second mom to two incredible young women.

I remember in the first few days asking myself, what am I doing? Do I want to take care of two children and manage someone else's household? At times, my own priorities were taken over by cooking, laundry, doing dishes, and being a mom. It was not an easy transition for me, and I have to admit, there were days when I felt a bit like Cinderella. And I was not the one invited to the ball. However, this was part of my role here in Italy, to be a caregiver and nanny. This was not a vacation for me. I had to work very hard and was, at times, regarded by others who did not know me with expressions of disrespect and indifference. This realization made me wonder how others serving in this type of role feel on a daily basis. It made me rethink how I felt about their world for sure.

On more than one day, I honestly felt as if I should go back home and admit that it was a crazy idea to do this. However, I eventually just let go of my ego and went with it. I was going to be defined as the nanny at this point in my adventure. Meeting Emma made it all worth it. She always made me feel like I was an important person to her.

Emma was six when I first met her. She had captured my heart within the first few days. She also opened my eyes to what it is like to grow up in Italy as a young person. Emma was bilingual and spoke both English and Italian. In fact, she spoke Italian with the same vivacious accent and passion as an eighty-year-old nonna (grandmother). She had learned all of the nuances of the language and culture within a few months of moving to Italy. In the first weeks of my arriving to San Gusme, Emma also taught me so much about what she needed from me. And gave me a purpose for staying and not retreating back to Minnesota when I had my doubts about staying.

The first day that I started working as the nanny, I trudged up the steps to the third-story apartment where the family lived. I could barely find a place to put my feet because each step had a carton or two of eggs sitting on it, among other things. The entire house was filled with eggs and kids. It was the week before Easter and my friends had planned an Easter egg hunt for the village.

Pam greeted me with a frantic look. "Can you help the kids color the eggs? I have a pot of eggs boiling in the kitchen. We need to boil all of these," she said, pointing to the many cartons of eggs around the house. "And the kids will color them." She then disappeared for what seemed like hours.

There were six kids sitting around a plastic-covered table elbow deep with colors and eggs. They barely even registered that I had entered the room. Italian was the only language being spoken by the kids, and so I felt a bit out of place right from the beginning. However, they quickly made me feel welcome and talked to me even if I could not understand much of what was being said.

I boiled dozens of eggs that day and enjoyed watching how creative kids can be when you just leave them to their own desires. They dipped and combined and swirled colors like I have never experienced. In the end, we had colored around 200 eggs. These would be hidden the next day by the adults of the village with the kids forming teams to compete to see who could find the most eggs. A giant chocolate egg, along with a huge bounty of chocolate candies, was the prize and it was so worth it.

Later that day, I made Emma and her sister, Siena, dinner, and we got to know each other better. Siena was nine years old at that time and already seemed like she was so grown up. She was confident and sure of herself. I could tell already that she was an independent spirit.

Emma climbed right up and made herself comfortable on my lap and gave me a big hug, followed by a quick peek under my T-shirt to make sure I had the right parts to be her second mom. I will never forget how deliberately she checked me out and I let her explore what she needed to in order to trust me. She had the biggest eyes and most expressive face I think I have ever seen. I always knew exactly where I stood with her.

Even though she was only six, she seemed to carry the wisdom of three grown women inside her. She made me wonder who she had been in her past life, because she knew so much for her age. As I got to know her, I understood that she really was a wise old soul stuck inside a six-year-old.

In fact, I would sometimes say to her, "Who are you?" and she would say, "I'm Emma." To which I would respond, "Do I know you from before? I think that we must have known each other in our past lives." She would just look at me with a twinkle in her eye.

Over the next weeks and months, I had a chance to understand what it was like to be a backup mom to Emma and her older sister, Siena. It was eye-opening, frustrating, and fascinating all at the same time.

When I was on nanny duty, I would walk just down the path from where I was living a few hundred feet within the walls of the village to their apartment and sleep overnight. I learned quickly that the morning was a struggle, so I would wake up at least thirty minutes before the girls and get everything prepped for their departure for school. Some days the cat was the first one awake, which meant he would push the door to my bedroom open, meow as loud as he could, and jump up on the bed walking directly on top of me to let me know he wanted attention.

Next, I would wake up Emma and Siena at the same time. Emma was always the first to exit the bed, especially if I had the shower warmed up and ready for her. Her routine was to stand in the warm shower for five to ten minutes to wake up. I could hear her singing or talking as she started her day in the shower. When she was done, she would wrap herself in a giant towel and run out to sit on the couch, eat breakfast, and watch cartoons (which, by the way, were one of my primary sources of learning the Italian language in the early days).

Emma would sit for a while, and eventually her sister would drag out of bed and sit next to her. Siena was never a morning person. At this point, they would do what most sisters do: fight about being in each other's space and who was taking the blanket more. They had terrible names for each other as well. Prune and Pig were two that I remember. I solved some of the conflict by getting them each their own blanket and dividing the couch down the middle by the cushions.

Once they had a bite to eat, they would run and get dressed, grab their backpacks, and race down the stairs to join the rest of the kids from the village as they headed toward the bus stop just outside the walls. There would be last-minute requests for a snack or details about their day as they realized that I was the backup mom, while their parents were guiding tours. I can't even count how many times I needed them to write the "note from mom" in Italian while I would sign it. Most of the time, I had no idea what they wrote.

Like most kids, some days they would miss the bus and I would have to drive them into the next village to get to school. My primary source of travel was an ancient Volvo with a manual shift, that I dubbed the nannymobile. I always prayed that I would not meet someone on the hills or around the narrow curves as we traveled to the next village to their school. I would get back the village parking lot with a sigh of relief that I had made it there and back in one piece.

When the kids were in school, I went back to their apartment, fed the cat, tidied up their beds, started laundry and dishes, and made a pot of coffee for me. This was a full-time job. The laundry was usually stacked high when I would arrive for the week, and it would take me all week to catch up. It did not take me long to figure out why.

Doing laundry in Italy is not at all like doing it in the United States. The washing machine is usually compact and located either in the bathroom or the lower level. Most people do not have a clothes dryer as electricity is just too expensive, about three times what we pay. Most houses also only carry the very lowest level of electricity because of the cost, so this means that you can only use one major appliance at a time. The cycle for the washing machine took up to two hours to complete, which meant that I was stuck with not running the dishwasher or anything else during that time. Everything had to be timed and planned perfectly.

When the clothes were done in the washing machine, I would hang them out on the line with a pulley that was situated between two windows of the house. Only so many clothes would fit on the line, so this also limited the amount of laundry I could do at once, especially if the weather was bad. There was also the option of placing the laundry on the stendino or little stand in the house, but that usually involved rearranging the small space in the living area to make it all fit. The process had to be restarted if the laundry fell from the line onto the square or if a pigeon decided to target an item.

I remember the first time I visited Italy, I thought, how quaint it was to see all of the laundry hanging on the lines between houses. Now I realize that this practice is a necessity of life in Italy that is not romantic at all. All of this experience was vital to me later when I moved to Italy. I did it with my eyes wide open, with the romantic idealization completely out the window now that I understood how challenging some things were in Italy.

After the laundry was started, I would wander out to the main piazza passing by the coffee bar where the locals would gather for coffee in the morning. Sometimes I would stop in for a cappuccino or coffee and say hello to the barista, Irene. Not many in the village spoke English, so it was my opportunity to try out my limited Italian. I also learned how to ask for my coffee or cappuccino "to go" and would take it back to the apartment and sip on it (like an Americana, their name for me). The locals, on the other hand, drank their coffee quickly and downed it within a few seconds while standing. I would later return my cup to Irene all washed up for my next day's cappuccino.

Just after noon most days, the kids would return on the scuolabus, and I would go to meet them near the village parking lot where the bus would drop off all the children in the village. A parent or guardian always had to be there to pick up the kids, or they could not get off the bus. I would wait with all of the other moms and nonni (grandparents) from the village as we anticipated their return.

As soon as Emma and Siena got off the bus, I could immediately sense what kind of day they had. Smiles and excitement or slow-moving disappointment. Emma was so little and her backpack so big and heavy, I would usually offer to carry it for her up the hill into the village and then up the four flights of stairs to their apartment.

Lunch was usually prepped and ready for them as I learned early on they would arrive starving and ready to eat. Pasta was the traditional lunch for everyone, so that is what I prepared most days. I usually had something special for dessert—often from the little market in the village. If it was warm, Emma and I would walk over to the coffee bar and pick out our favorite ice cream and sit and enjoy it together. Afternoons were filled with homework and catching up with their friends in the village.

Being a nanny for Emma and Siena taught me unexpected lessons that I treasure. It reminded me to think outside the norm (all the time), be creative, be silly, and provide unconditional love and support. Emma taught me the traditions and routines of her family, so that when I was there, she could still have some of these very important things around her. She taught me how she loved her bedtime routine, which included a long bath, reading together, chamomile tea with honey, snuggling with her stuffed sock monkey, with an end to each night that involved a well-orchestrated series of kisses as I was tucking her into bed. This started with a kiss on each side of her check, following by one on her forehead, and finally one on her chin. I added my own touch with a little touch on the nose at the end.

I loved being their person when they needed me. I had never been this to anyone before. We had many fun and challenging times together. These included the day when the cat cornered a mouse in the kitchen; being locked out of their apartment for an entire day, followed by a rescue operation that took almost the entire village; traveling to various parts of Italy together on the train; planning to hijack a pumpkin for Halloween; and freeing their pet turtles in a local pond after they outgrew their aquarium.

Cooking for two kids was also interesting. Their apartment had a tiny kitchen that resembled one you might find in a dorm room. I learned how to make their favorite dishes like pasta bianca, which was basically pasta with olive oil and parmesan cheese, pork chops, chicken stir fry, and their favorite dessert, blond brownies or what I called blondies in a small toaster oven in their tiny kitchen space.

I had learned to make blondies from my own mom, and they always reminded me of her love and tender care she gave me every day as a kid. To this day, I still love to make the blondies and think of Emma and Siena as I am eating the butterscotch brownie with melty chocolate chips. This soon became a local favorite for the villagers as I would frequently share them with others. They had never tasted this type of dessert in the little village, and I guess they thought them a bit exotic. I thought that was funny, because to me it was comfort food.

Being nanny to Emma and Siena was one of those unexpected gifts that I will treasure in my heart always. I have had the honor of watching them grow up to be extraordinary young women and can't wait to see what they do as young adults.

BLONDIES

1 cup all-purpose flour
½ tsp. baking powder
½ tsp. baking soda
½ tsp. salt
⅓ cup butter (unsalted)
1 cup dark brown sugar
1 large egg
1 tsp. vanilla
½ cup chopped walnuts
½ cup semisweet chocolate chips

Preheat oven to 350 degrees.

Mix together all of the dry ingredients in a mixing bowl and set aside. In a medium saucepan, melt ⅓ cup of butter. Add 1 cup of brown sugar and stir well. Let cool for 5 minutes.

Next add 1 egg (beaten) to the butter and sugar mixture and stir well. Add 1 tsp. vanilla and ½ cup chopped walnuts.

Variation: For boozy blondies, add an ounce of Nocino Liqueur, which is from the northern region of Italy, Emilia Romagna, made from green walnuts.

Gradually add the flour mixture to the sugar mixture. Stir until well mixed.

Place the mixture into a 9x9 inch pan that has been sprayed with oil spray. Sprinkle 1 cup of semisweet chocolate chips over the top of the dough.

Bake at 350 degrees for 22 minutes.

Let cool and slice into bars and enjoy. These are great with vanilla ice cream.

Recipe note: If you like sea salt, these are delicious with a sprinkle of sea salt (about 1 tsp.) along with the chocolate chips on the top prior to baking.

5

Why Buying a Chicken Takes Time on Market Days

The village grocery store really had everything you might need for daily living, including fresh produce, bread (delivered daily), meat, cheeses, household items, and wine. I loved being able to plan lunch and dinner based on what I found in the shop. And I also got to know the local ladies better this way. I quickly learned the unwritten protocol in the little market as well.

The first person to arrive in the shop had priority and could indicate when and if they were ready to ask for items behind the counter (such as fresh fruit, vegetables, cured meats, cheeses, or sandwiches). Fresh produce was not to be handled by your bare hands, unless you asked if you can pick out items yourself. Otherwise, there were usually disposable gloves that you should use to touch the fruit and vegetable items. It is pretty much off-limits to just pick up, inspect, and touch with your hands at all, which is what we are accustomed to. I made this mistake the first week I was in Italy and felt terrible.

The little grocery in the village is owned by Signora Brogi and her son, Gianni. They wore traditional shop uniforms every day, with her in a white apron and dress and he in white pants, white shirt with a blue apron, and white cotton grocer hat.

When it was my turn, I would simply ask for what I wanted, like this, "I would like four apples, two oranges, and a handful of ripe cherry tomatoes." They would pick out items for me and package them up. There were no grocery baskets in the store; it was too small for this. Most of the ladies had their market bags or carts with them when they arrived.

I got to know both Signora Brogi and Gianni. They were always intrigued by my horrible Italian pronunciation of items and curious questions about everything. I would get interesting looks from Signora Brogi when I made mistakes. If I asked a question about what something was, she would read the ingredients to me very loudly in Italian as if I were hard of hearing.

She always was put together so beautifully for the day, with her silver hair done up perfectly, with elegant earrings, incredible shoes, and a gorgeous dress under her apron. I wondered about her life and how long this little market had been in the family. Later, I would become friends with her and learned that she was born just a stone's throw away from the village, and she and her husband had owned the market for years. He had died a few years back, so now it was her son's responsibility.

Gianni was probably thirty-something at this time. He looked classic Italian, with dark hair, brown eyes, and a nose that instantly struck you as Italian. She and Gianni kept it going strong, but I could tell that running the market was a big burden for them to manage.

Along with fresh produce, the market featured local baked goods, such as crusty Tuscan bread, cantucci (cookies with almonds, chocolate with a nice orange flavor), as well as traditional cakes and sweets. These were different every week—some fruit tarts, some with a lemony custard. The market always had freshly made pesto, meats, fresh mozzarella, and local cheeses and wines. The market was open every day in the morning and again in the afternoon except on Wednesday. I loved to go in just to see what was new. Gianni quickly learned that I had a love of bread and sweets.

"Only fruit and tomatoes today? That's no fun. We have fresh bread and also desserts. Would you like to try a taste?" he would say to me with a devilish smile.

He knew how to get me hooked in and of course I could not help but try a treat. It always tempted me to purchase it then as well as again later when I would see it. He understood the psychology of food shopping and marketing very well.

One of my favorites was the torta della nonna or grandmother's cake. Torta della nonna is made with a shortbread crust with a layer of lemony custard topped with either toasted pine nuts or almonds. Every recipe is a bit different, but I modified this one from two different people as they described how to make it. It is traditionally made with a top and bottom crust, but I like to keep it simple with just a bottom crust.

Torta della Nonna

Pastry Crust

2 cups all-purpose flour

2 large egg yolks

½ cup butter, cut into small pieces

⅔ cup sugar

¼ tsp. salt

1 tsp. lemon zest

1 tablespoon cold water

Preheat oven to 375 degrees.

Mix together all ingredients by hand or use a food processor until the dough comes together to form a ball. If the dough is too dry, add a few drops of cold water. Cover the dough in plastic wrap and place in the refrigerator for 30 minutes.

Place the dough ball between two layers of parchment paper and roll out in a thin circle around ¼ inches thick and 14 inches round. Place the pastry dough in a 9-inch tart pan or pie pan that has been buttered well and coated with a dusting of flour. Use a fork to prick the dough well with little holes. Place the pastry-covered pan in the refrigerator while you make the custard.

Lemon Custard

2 cups whole milk
4 large egg yolks
1 cup sugar
6 tablespoons all-purpose flour
Juice of 1 lemon
2 tsp. lemon zest
1 tsp, vanilla extract

Topping

¼ cup powdered sugar
¼ cup thinly sliced almonds or pine nuts

In a medium bowl, whisk the egg yolks with the sugar until the mixture is pale yellow. Whisk in the flour. Gradually add the milk, whisking constantly. Transfer the mixture to a medium saucepan and cook over low heat, stirring constantly, until the mixture comes to a boil. Reduce the heat and simmer for 1 minute. The mixture will thicken and become creamy. Spoon the custard into a bowl. Stir in the lemon juice, lemon zest, and vanilla extract. Cover the custard with plastic wrap and let cool at room temperature for 15 to 20 minutes.

Pour the lemon custard into the dough-covered pie or tart pan. Sprinkle the top with the sliced almonds or pine nuts. Bake at 375 degrees for 30 to 35 minutes. Place on a wire rack to cool. Dust the top with powdered sugar after it has cooled well. Serve at room temperature. Store any leftovers in refrigerator.

Recipe note: You can also use pre-made pie crust for this recipe if you like. Pine nuts are small, creamy white oval nuts that are from the inside of a pine cone. Pine nuts are used in many traditional Mediterranean dishes. Purchase only in small amounts as they go bad quickly. They can be found near the other nuts or in the bulk goods area of the grocery store.

If I arrived in the shop during a busy time of day when many were shopping, usually around midmorning until noon, it was my responsibility to quickly scan the shop to note who was in there before me, according to protocol. All of the people who are in the shop already had priority over me at this point. So I would patiently wait for my turn.

When Signora Brogi or Gianni would make eye contact with me, I knew that it was go time and I needed to be absolutely ready with all of the items I wanted, and (proper) names of everything so that I did not hold up the others who were waiting after me. It was a lot of pressure at first. After shopping, I would return to the apartment, trudging up the four flights of narrow stairs with bags of food (and bottled water). This was another daily workout for me.

Every Thursday, in the village next door called Castelnuovo Berardenga, a traditional local market sets up in the streets. The name of the village translates to New Castle, which was probably entirely owned by the Berardenga family at one point. This village was also the comune or county seat of the region, and therefore was where all of the local area government offices were located as well as the market and where local events were hosted throughout the year.

Each region had an open-air market that was offered on a different day of the week. Sometimes I would travel to the neighboring villages in Chianti to shop their markets as they were all so different. I loved to see what they had every week if I could. It was like a colorful patchwork quilt that blanketed the street on Thursdays. The market always had fresh local produce, flowers and plants, household items (pots and pans), linens, and clothing. It was one of my absolute favorite outings. Everyone from the little villages nearby traveled in to do their major shopping for the week.

This is a long tradition that has been preserved in spite of the large "one stop shopping" stores that I could see popping up in the larger cities. It made my heart so happy to be able to experience this tradition.

At first, I was noticed as an obvious outsider. I tried to ignore the looks with their curious eyes following me as I walked through the market with my bag. However, my blond hair and blue eyes gave me away immediately, and then when I started to talk, the American accent was hard to hide. I felt a bit anxious each time I went, but it was worth the time and effort to keep going each week as I got to know my favorite fruit and vegetable vendors, as well as the vendor who offered household items and colorful local linens. They eventually accepted me as I learned the language better and understood the market etiquette. Shopping was like a new dance I had to learn.

It had become a tradition for me to stand in line at one of the food stands to purchase a roasted chicken and French fries to bring back to Emma and Siena for lunch. I loved the roasted chicken, but the best part for me was the process of getting it.

I approached the stand around 10:30 a.m. I had learned that this is when the chickens are done roasting, and the best time for me to get one. A few times, I arrived later in the morning and they were frequently out. No matter what, I knew that I would need to spend at least thirty minutes or more for this part of my week.

As I would get in line behind three women, I would think, well, this looks promising today. I thought to myself that it should not take long. But instead, this is how it went.

The first woman in line, a robust woman, asks for her order. "I would like a roast chicken, some French fries and bread."

Sounds simple, right? Just as they were totaling her order, she says, "What is that?" Pointing to the chickpea dish that is also available.

They explain, "That is chickpeas with olive oil and spices."

The woman said, "Yes, I will have some of that as well. And what about this?" Pointing to what looks like a meat sauce.

They explained, "Ragù with tomatoes, garlic, and ground meat."

"I will have two containers of that as well, it looks delicious."

Now her daughter walked up to the front of the line and joins her to see what she is getting. "Mom, thanks for holding my place. I also need to put in my order."

They then had a long conversation about the mother's food choices while everyone waits behind them. The daughter orders additional items. The woman behind the counter did not seem to mind at all, as it was a good day for the business. There were two women behind them and in front of me. One of them was catching up with the local gossip from other women who joined her in line while I was standing there. So now I thought I probably had three people in front of me. While I was standing in line, I noticed that some people just walked right up and picked up their roast chickens, while I waited my turn. I was not sure what to think.

Just when I thought I might be getting closer to getting my items, the mother turns back and says, "Oh yes, I need bread, but only half of a loaf, can you cut it please?" The bread was cut and off they went after about twenty minutes of ordering and questioning.

The others order and pay for their items in a similar way. Finally, after about thirty-five minutes of waiting, I was now at the front of the line and it is my turn.

"Vorrei un pollo arrostito e patatine fritte per favore. I would like a roast chicken and French fries please," I said in my best Italian, and in anticipation of how good it would taste.

Yes, I had done it. The woman looked at me after I had paid for my roasted chicken and fries for lunch and smiles. She seemed to understand my impatience and curiosity.

"Did you know that you can call us the evening before and order a roast chicken? That way, you don't have to wait in line," she said, as if reading my mind.

She then showed me the list of people who had reserved a chicken for the day. That must have been the secret to walking right up and getting the chicken. Although, I have to admit, the way I had always done it, standing in line with the locals was much more fun in the end. I never did call ahead for my roast chicken.

After I finished shopping, I would frequently stop into the local church, light a candle at the altar, sit down, and say a little prayer for myself (to keep exploring and finding my heart) and for the people I loved back home. If I had someone special in mind, I would light a second candle for them and send them my love from afar. I was homesick some days, but this weekly connection helped me spiritually and emotionally in the days I was living in Italy. The church had beautiful stained glass with an altar featuring a painting of a Madonna and child with creamy white travertine floors.

After my time in the church, I would walk into the center of the village and go to the local coffee bar, Bar Centrale, for a coffee and, many times, one scoop of my favorite gelato, pistachio. I would take the little dish of gelato and sit on the bench under the umbrella pines with my market bags and take in everyone around me, watching how the elders would connect with each other every week, with kisses on both checks while exchanging the local gossip. I noticed the moms with their little ones in the strollers, out for a little shopping, being stopped by almost every person, to be greeted along with their children, who seemed to be completely cherished by all.

6

THE HOT DAYS OF SUMMER

The hot days of June arrived, and with school out and the temperature increasing, everyone made plans to go to the seaside. It is common for Italians to leave the larger cities and migrate to the seaside for weeks in the summer. Some families had small houses or campers where they go to enjoy the seaside during the hot summer months. Others travel to the Tuscan countryside where the breezes are cooler than the big cities and the nights are magical with fireflies flirting around in the grass. This is where I was, so for me it was already perfect. A few times, I heard of people leaving for the seaside or beach on day-trips as well. However, I was content to be right where I was at the moment.

I discovered that the village was not far from a natural mineral thermal spring that was famous for what was considered healing waters. The springs were only about twenty-five minutes away, just outside of the village of Rapolano Terme. People would come from all over Italy to "take the waters" for various ailments.

The thermal springs were surrounded by terraced gardens with lavender and broom and lounge chairs to enjoy an easy nap or just to take in the view. I was so happy for this new experience. Pam and the girls had invited me to join them for the day.

As I took off my dress to reveal my one-piece suit that covered most of my flaws, I noticed that nearly everyone else was in little bikinis or even topless soaking in the warmth of the sun and then taking in the warmth and minerals in the water. Not one person seemed to be worried about what their bodies looked like. The ease and comfort that I felt set me free as well.

The pools were designed to fit into the landscape of the area, with curves and different levels of water, each one offering a different degree of warmth. The warmer pool was enclosed and had a lovely waterfall that you could stand under so that the warm water caressed your back muscles. The cooler water pools outside had little perches where you could sit in the water, or even lie in very shallow water that kept your body cool while the sun warmed your face and arms. The only drawback was the smell of the natural sulfur that was in the water, but I eventually became accustomed to the smell and associated it with relaxation and pure joy.

This tradition became one of my favorite outings, packing my swimsuit and a little picnic lunch and spending the day taking in the healing waters of the thermal springs with new friends I was getting to know. It was so relaxing to nap or read a book on the lounge chair among big mounds of lavender looking over the rolling hills of the area. In the distance, I could not help but smile each time as I recognized the familiar slant of the mountainside where San Gusme was located. I was now becoming oriented in this new place. It felt more like home to me each passing day.

The end of June, Pam invited me to attend the local Bruscello with the family. They seemed so excited about this, but I had no idea what this was.

When I asked Pam, she explained, "It's like an ancient form of folk theater, almost like an opera, but done in a more informal way. This form of theater was born in Tuscany within the farm communities. And we have it just down the road. Many of the actors in the play are people we know."

She told me that the actors sang the story in a singsong-like rhythm with long pauses where music is played. I loved music and operas, so I was intrigued. As the evening approached, I met up with Emma, who was also attending, and we planned to bring a little snack, sweaters, blankets, and mosquito spray. She was excited too. As we traveled down the windy road to Castelnuovo Berardenga, I wondered what I should expect. Perhaps I had made it out to be too grand in my mind, so I put the thoughts of what it might be out of my mind and decided it would be good no matter what. This was another new experience for me.

As we settled into our seats, Emma showed me that it was helpful to place the pillow on the hard plastic bench and to be on the side closest to the music—stage left. We could see the musicians warming up with the actors behind the set making preparations. As the opera started, I was instantly mesmerized by what was unfolding in front of me. The music, singing, and costumes were amazing. The Bruscello was taking place on the grounds of an old noble palace called Villa Chigi Sarcini that had designer gardens and statues, all with a musical theme, with the stage located on one of the lower terraces of the palace. This was a protected place and was not open often, only for a few months in the summer and for special occasions.

The words were on cue cards for the actors, so I could see that some had their lines figured out better than others. At first it was difficult for me to understand the words in Italian, but eventually as I got into the rhythm, I started to recognize the words.

All of the actors and musicians were local people. I recognized them from our village or from the days when I would travel to Castelnuovo Berardenga for the market. Even the children were in the production. It was a huge honor to be a part of the production, with weeks and months of preparation, and I felt a sense of honor to be able to experience it. It was a serious story most of the time, but had a sense of humor and tragedy under the surface as was so common in the Tuscan culture.

The night was perfect for experiencing an open-air theater, with a clear sky showing the moon and stars. After intermission, with the music playing and the sparkling of the fireflies around us, it started to get cool, so Emma climbed up on my lap with a blanket and snuggled into my chest. I felt so happy to be experiencing this with her and to have her little heart snuggled next to mine. She slept so deeply later that night. I had to carry her to the car and then up the four flights of stairs to tuck her into her bed. This is when I felt like I really got to experience what it's like to be a mother, and it felt so incredibly good.

7

Figs, Grapes, and Fall Festivities

After a short visit home to Minnesota, I returned to Italy in late August to find San Gusme waiting for me. It felt like it was mine now. Everyone greeted me back with open arms and kisses, just like family, like I belonged to them as well.

I quickly settled back into the work and life that I had started a few months earlier. As the summer months drew to an end, I could feel a shift in the air. It was no longer heavy with dampness and humidity, but instead I felt the warmth of the sun nourishing and caressing the land in order to complete the sweetness of the season. The grapes were soaking in the sunshine as the figs were getting plump and sweet.

One day, as I walked by the fig tree near the village walls, it drew me in with a sweet, fragrant, and exotic smell like I'd never experienced before. I reached out and touched one of the figs that was in my reach near the stone wall. I could see that it was tender and ripe, so I gently pulled it off the tree. As I opened the fig to see what the fruit looked like inside, the green outer covering gave way to a vibrant pink purple inner fruit. I had never eaten a fresh fig in my life. I took a deep breath and put my nose practically inside the fig. Just as

I had my nose in the fig, I looked up to see my friend Gwen smiling at me. She was out for a walk that day too.

Gwen was a young French woman who lived closeby. She and I met earlier in the spring with a group of locals who loved to practice their English conversation. Since that time, we frequently took walks together and went for outings.

"You found the figs," she said. "These are sweet, white figs. My mom makes the best fig marmalade from figs like this." I knew that Gwen's mother was a great cook (like mine) as she frequently talked about what she would cook when we were together.

"I'd love to know how to make jam from these. Can you show me how you make it?" I asked.

"I'll call my mom and get the recipe," she said with a big smile.

"Come over to the apartment on Thursday and we can make a batch of jam together. I'll pick a bunch of figs." I said.

"Make sure you get the really ripe ones. They will be very soft and sticky as you pick them off the tree. Some of these are not ready yet." She reached up and picked a fig that was so ripe it was almost falling off the stem.

It looked too far gone to me, but when she opened it up and showed me the inside, I could see that it was a deeper pink, almost purple color and was so ripe that it already looked like a delicious jam inside. She handed me the other half to taste.

The smell was heavenly, like none I had ever smelled before. I took my first bite and loved it. It tasted like honey and flowers at the same time. For me now, the smell and taste of fresh figs takes me back to that first summer in Italy.

A few days later, Gwen returned to San Gusme for our jam making session together. I showed her my basket of figs that I had picked earlier. She said, "Okay, I talked to my mom and she told me we need to figure out how many we have so we know how much sugar to use. Then we need to wash them with water and make sure that they are good to use."

I had put out a deep stock pot on the stove already and had a colander in the sink. She started looking through the figs and showed me which ones were ripe and good for the jam. She ran them under water and placed them in the colander. I got busy cutting them in half to inspect the inside.

"They should be almost red inside, see look." As she broke one open, she said, "Check to make sure there are no insects."

I got out an old plastic kitchen scale and put a bowl on it and started adding figs. We had around six pounds of figs. She sent a text to her mom letting her know how many figs we had. Her mom provided the recipe based on this. Once we had them all washed and cut into quarters, she poured in a measurement of sugar and I stirred it in with the figs. We let the sugar and figs sit together for a while. After a few minutes, we added a few cups of water, followed by the juice of two lemons. We placed the pot on the stove over a medium heat and they started melting together, with the heat transforming them almost instantly.

The first ten minutes as they bubbled and reduced down, they still looked like figs, but soon after, they eventually became liquid, almost honey-like. The perfume of the jam cooking was heavenly. Another thirty to forty minutes of simmering while we had a coffee together, then she taught me a method from her mom that indicated when the jam was ready by placing a spoon in the jam and showing me that it coated it nicely. I had eight little jars with their lids out on the counter that I had washed and gotten ready by boiling them. We filled the jars and had some left over to taste over bread. It was delicious.

As we chatted, a few of the jars started to pop indicating that they were sealing well. It's a sound that has always made me happy, as I count to make sure all of the jars seal well. Gwen happily parted with half the bounty to enjoy for breakfast each morning. The recipe I include here is based on the one from Gwen's mom, but scaled back to work with three pounds of figs and with a few added ingredients that I love.

Fig Jam

3 pounds fresh figs (white or purple)

2 cups sugar

1 lemon (juiced, about ¼ cup + the zest)

1 cup water

Optional: 4 tablespoons brandy

Optional: ¾ cup chopped roasted almonds

Rinse the figs and cut off the top stem. Cut the figs in half and then quarters and place in a deep saucepan (nonreactive metal). Pour the sugar over the top and stir to coat the figs with the sugar. Let sit for 20 minutes.

Add the lemon juice, lemon zest, and water to the figs and bring to a boil, stirring until the sugar is completely dissolved. Simmer the fig jam over moderate to low heat, stirring occasionally, until the fruit is soft and the liquid coats the side of a spoon, about 30-40 minutes. Add additional water if needed if the figs start to stick to the bottom of the pan.

Take the figs off the heat and stir well.

Optional: Add roasted chopped almonds and brandy at the end of cooking. This is something that I

discovered later after making fig jam with my friend Stefania who said her mom always made it this way. It is a nice addition, so give it a try.

Spoon the jam into three hot, sterilized 1/2-pint jars (to sterilize: place jars and lids in boiling water for 5 minutes), leaving 1/4 inch of space at the top. Seal the jars well and let cool at room temperature. As the jam cools in the hot jars, you should hear a popping sound when the top cover and seal create a vacuum and indicates the seal is good. Store the jam in a cool pantry or the refrigerator for up to 3 months.

Recipe note: When I am in Minnesota, I always find fresh purple figs at Trader Joe's in August. They also carry fresh frozen white figs that will work in this recipe. This jam pairs well with any aged cheese on a cheese plate. This is a fantastic jam to use in the crostata di marmellata as well.

The first weeks in September were the time of the grape festivals and the much-anticipated grape harvest. San Gusme celebrated with a traditional festival for two weeks in early September with the concerts in our little square and traditional dinners with long wooden tables and benches set up in the main square.

The ladies of the village basically open a traditional restaurant each weekend that features local dishes prepared by them in the communal kitchen in the village. Small wooden tables were set up in the smaller intimate square of the village with colorful tablecloths and the traditional ladder chairs. The ladies are the chefs and the men are the waiters for the evening.

I attended one evening with Pam and the girls and was so impressed at how delicious and elegant the meal was. We started with tomato bruschetta and crostini—one with white beans, and the other with liver pâté. Our next course was pasta with wild boar ragù, made in the very old-school way, simmered on the top of the stove for a day or two to marry the flavors of the tomatoes into the tender meat. I can imagine that the recipe is in the head of one of the ladies who is in charge of the dinner each year.

Dessert was a crostata di marmellata or shortbread jam tart. The one I tried featured apricot jam and was simple, tangy, and delicious. Pam and I enjoyed local Chianti wine with our dinner and sipped on vin santo as the evening ended.

CROSTATA DI MARMELLATA

1 cup all-purpose flour
1 cup oat flour (if you can't find oat flour, simply place whole or quick oats in a food processor and blend until a fine flour forms)
¾ cup white sugar
1 stick of butter, or 8 tablespoons (chilled)
1 egg (beaten) plus 1 egg yolk
Zest of one lemon (variation, you can use orange zest or lime zest depending on the jam that you choose for the filling)
2 cups of your favorite fruit jam (warmed)
Optional: ¾ cup of chopped nuts for topping

Preheat oven to 350 degrees.

Mix together the flours and sugar in a large bowl or in the bowl of a food processer. Cut the cold butter into the flour and sugar by pulsing the processor or, if using hands, rub the butter into the flour until you get a crumbly mixture and there are no more visible butter pieces.

Mix in the beaten egg and the yolk along with the lemon zest until the pastry comes together into a smooth, elastic ball. Cover the dough with plastic wrap and place in the refrigerator at least 30 minutes, or overnight.

Take the dough out of the refrigerator and divide into two balls. I only use one crust on the bottom, but if you prefer, you can roll out both and place one on the bottom and one over the top. If you only want one crust, place the other in the freezer for the next crostata.

Roll out the dough between two pieces of parchment paper or plastic wrap to the measurement of your pie or tart pan, plus 2 inches. Place the dough into a 9- to 10-inch pie or tart pan that has been buttered or sprayed with oil. If you are lazy like I am sometimes, simply press the dough into the bottom of the pie pan.

Next, top the crust with 2 cups of your favorite jam that you have warmed in a saucepan for a few minutes. This will give you a very jammy tart. I sometimes like to add a little booze to my jam as I am warming it. If you are feeling extra spunky, you can add 2 tablespoons of brandy, Grand Marnier, or other liqueur to go with your jam.

Because I only use one crust on the bottom, I also like to top the crostata with chopped nuts to add another element of taste and crunch. Use about 3/4 cup of chopped nuts, such as almonds, walnuts, or hazelnuts.

Bake at 350 degrees for about 25 minutes. The jam will be bubbly and the nuts will be roasted and crunchy on the top. Let cool, cut into small triangles and serve alone or with whipped cream or ice cream.

The entire village participated in the preparation for the celebration and all of the work involved. Every evening on the weekend featured a special event, with comedians and concerts in the main piazza, and artisans with little stands selling their handcrafted items. Everyone was included, from the little kids to the elders of the village.

The men of the village prided themselves in organizing the traditional food stand, which included grilled meats of every kind, side dishes of white beans with rosemary, bruschetta with tomatoes as well as bean soup. The kids would set the tables, bring bottles of local wine and water and later clear the tables.

The festival in San Gusme celebrated a man called Luca Cava who was honored with a terra-cotta statue in one of the gardens at the entrance to the village. Luca looked like a clever old farmer who was taking a pee, carefully disguising it with his hat covering his private parts. Everyone thought that Luca was a fictional character; however, the statue was loosely based on an old farmer and paid homage to the fact that San Gusme represented a village of farmers and caretakers of the land around it. The statue also conveyed the sense of humor that most Tuscan people loved to enjoy.

The festival was attended by people from around the region, with hundreds joining the locals for the traditional food and wine with music and dancing later into the early morning hours. To an outsider, it seemed so rowdy and loud, but I realized that this was a very Italian way to celebrate, with everyone talking at once while the music and dancing seemed to turn up the volume even more.

The village hosted works of art from locals that were hung on the inside stone walls throughout the week with all of the area wine makers setting up little stands to offer people a taste of their wines. The second weekend featured the tradition of an old barrel race that was one of the only in the area. Teams of two men dressed in traditional costumes would race by pushing wine barrels through the streets and down country roads for a chance to be the winners.

The last evening of the festival was always reserved for the headliner concert. This year it was Fausto Leali, a famous singer from the 1960s, and he was worth it. With his rough voice filled with passion and drama, he had the entire audience singing and dancing to his songs for three hours. I danced my heart happy, with friends that I had gotten to know—Giulia, Gwen and Sara as well as Emma, who loved the music. I will never forget when he sang the Italian version of "Stand by Me" and "Ora che ho bisogno di te," which translates to "Now, I need you." I thought to myself, I do need you, I need this place. This village and the people.

In late September, the grapes were ready for the harvest. On my walks, I could see large purple clumps of grapes hanging heavy on the vine. Along with the red grapes (mostly Sangiovese), some of the rows contained white grapes (Malvesia). These were my favorite grapes to sneak a taste of on my walks every day. They are crisp and sweet and have a melon-like taste.

Other kinds of grapes that I tried were the red variety called Uva Fragola or strawberry grapes. These were the sweetest red grapes I had ever tasted, similar to a concord grape in the Midwest. Remo's farmer friend Claudio used to bring me these every week for about a month (Remo was the cantina owner from the village). I think that these were the grapes that are used for the sweet treats that I tried from the local market. It was a sweet, crusty bread with grapes soaked in red wine and walnuts. In the area, the bread was called pan co' Santi or bread of the saints.

The ingredients of nuts and grapes (or raisins) along with the wine were traditional. It was also tradition to serve this during the period of the new wine—October or November or along with a little glass of vin santo—or wine of the saints. This bread was also a big part of celebrating All Saint's Day on November 1.

Pan Co' Santi

¾ cup red raisins

½ cup golden raisins

1 cup of red wine (Chianti)

¼ cup sambuca liqueur

1 packet of instant yeast, about 2 ¼ tsp. (quick rise)

1 cup warm water (not hot)

1 cup chopped walnuts

3 cups bread flour

6 tablespoons sugar (use 1 tablespoon to bloom the yeast)

½ tsp. ground black pepper

½ tsp. sea salt

½ tsp. cinnamon

1 tablespoon honey

5 tablespoons olive oil

1 large egg (reserve to brush top of bread with prior to baking)

Start by soaking the red raisins in the red wine. Place the wine and raisins in a small saucepan and warm it over low heat for 1 to 2 minutes. Take it off heat and let sit for at least 30 minutes to plump up the raisins. The longer the raisins sit in the wine, the more taste they will have. Place the golden raisins in the sambuca liquor in a small saucepan and also warm it just slightly. Let sit for 30 minutes as well.

Mix together the warm water, yeast, and 1 tablespoon of the sugar in a small bowl to let the yeast bloom (it will start to bubble). Set aside for about 10 minutes. Even though for instant quick rise yeast, this step is not needed, I still like to do it to make sure my yeast is good.

In a small sauté pan, warm the chopped walnuts over medium to low heat until they are slightly browned and fragrant (about 2 minutes). Take off heat and let cool for 5 minutes.

Drain the wine and sambuca from the raisins and add them to the pan with the walnuts.

Next, in a large mixing bowl, mix together all of the remaining dry ingredients—the flour, sugar, salt, pepper, and cinnamon. Add the yeast and water mixture to the middle of the bowl along with the olive oil and honey and start to stir from the middle outward, incorporating more flour as you stir. Add in the walnuts and raisins and continue to stir until the dough becomes a ball. You may need to add in more flour or water depending on the consistency. The dough should be slightly sticky, not dry and smooth.

Cover the dough with plastic wrap over the bowl and place in a warm area to rise for 2 hours. You can use your oven as a proofing space for this. Turn on your oven to 350 degrees for 1 minute, then turn it off. The warmth will be perfect for raising the dough.

After 2 hours, take the dough and cut into two equal parts. Put flour on your hands to handle the dough. Create two smaller, round dough balls and place on a sheet pan covered with parchment paper. I like to make mine a bit round and flatten it out just a bit. Cut the top of the dough with a knife in a cross pattern. Place the dough in a warm area and let the dough rise again until it is about doubled in size (this takes about an hour).

Preheat oven to 400 degrees. Place a medium roasting pan on the bottom rack of the oven filled half full with water to create steam for the bread.

Brush the top of the bread with the egg wash to add the brown color when baking.

Bake the bread in the middle rack at 400 degrees for 25-30 minutes, until it is golden and brown on the top. The egg wash creates a deep brown shiny color as the bread bakes. Place on a wire rack to cool.

This bread is even better a day or two after baking.

Recipe note: Bread flour can be found near all-purpose flour in the grocery store. Bread flour has a higher protein level and will create a chewy texture to the bread. Sambuca liquor has an anise or liquorice flavor and is a nice combination with the other raisins and walnuts in this bread. If you don't have sambuca, it's okay to skip this part.

On my walks, I watched the families from Casaccia on the hills above the village going about the vendemmia by harvesting their grapes the traditional way. The family members and helpers had hats and baskets, gloves on their hands and a knife or cutter quickly taking the clumps of grapes off the vines and dropping them into the basket. Once their basket was full, they dumped it into a small truck with a bed in the back for all of the grapes. This truck bed is lined with plastic so that none of the grapes could fall out.

An older man was sitting on a wooden chair with his dog close by. He seemed to be surveying the work that was being done, and probably wished he could be out there picking with the rest of them. I am sure that this is the nonno (grandfather) of the family out supervising the work, just to make sure that all was going well. This is his family legacy, so he continued to be a part of it. I knew that this was tradition. Families took care of the grape harvest together.

A more modern grape harvest was happening in the fields surrounding San Gusme owned by Tenuta Arceno, one of my favorite Chianti and Super Tuscan wine makers. This vineyard was owned by an American family, the Jacksons, the same family that owns Kendall Jackson winery in California. They owned a large amount of land around San Gusme and did their grape harvest with machines. It looked a lot like the machine that my dad uses to pick corn. The machinery had a way of moving along the neatly trimmed rows of vines and plucking the grapes, separating many of the leaves and stems along the way. This was done very quickly with the grapes disappearing from the fields in one to two days. Large wagons took the grapes away to get started on the wine-making process nearby.

One day during the period of the grape harvest, Pam said, "Let's go and have lunch with the guys harvesting the grapes at Remo's vineyard."

We packed a lunch of bread, cheese, sausage, and wine. I had made my mom's version of blond brownies that morning, so I took these along as a sweet treat for them to try.

We laughed together as we considered our surprise lunch. "What will they think when we arrive unannounced to join them for lunch?" I asked.

Pam responded with a wink, "They will love it. Two beautiful women bringing them lunch."

We walked about a mile out of San Gusme and came to the main house on the property. We walked around the back of the house and in through the gate, to a small workshop attached to the back of the house. A small table with a collection of buckets and mostly broken chairs were around the work table. Soon the men started to arrive from the fields with their lunch tins and sacks of sandwiches and goodies for lunch. They looked pleased that we were joining them.

"Who is this here? What did you bring us?" they asked with curious looks.

They recognized Pam as she had lived in the area for years now. The men looked very happy, suntanned, and a bit dirty from being out in the fields. This lunch experience felt comfortable to me as it reminded me of growing up on the farm and taking lunch out to the fields with my mom every year when my dad and others were planting or harvesting for days on end and did not have time to return to the house for a proper lunch.

I met Claudio and Guido and a few others who were helping Remo harvest his grapes. They were all over sixty years old, yet seemed to have the energy of much younger men.

I asked, "How is the harvest going?"

Claudio responded, "This year's vintage is going to be excellent. We had early spring rains and a dry, hot summer. The wine will be so sweet and dry."

Their lunches included panini, cold pasta with sauce, and some salads. I could see one of my favorites, panzanella, made with tomatoes, bread, cheese, cucumbers, and onions. Out came the Chianti wine and it was enjoyed as well. Guido looked like he could belong to my family of Norwegians, with bright blue eyes and gray hair and a wonderful smile. I enjoyed listening to them banter back and forth telling jokes and stories. Something about a priest and a goat. The rest I have no idea, and perhaps that is a good thing.

After a bit of food and wine, out comes an unmarked bottle with some sort of homemade clear liquor in it.

Claudio said, "Here, try it. This will help you digest your lunch."

I was curious, and at the same time unsure if I should try it.

I looked at Pam and she said, "Go for it."

So I said, "Why not?" Everyone seemed to be enjoying it.

He took a little shot glass and filled it, with a sparkle in his eye and a little smile. I took a sip and as it slowly warmed my throat, I could see why everyone loved it. I instantly could taste vanilla and anise. Then I realized that it was a homemade sambuca. It was traditional to make your own liqueurs; many had secret family recipes for limoncello, cherry, citron, and walnut liqueurs.

What a fun lunch together. However, I started to wonder if I would be able to walk home. I felt more like I need to just lie down and take a nap. We tried three different wines, vin santo, and then another liqueur.

I had almost forgotten about what we brought them, the blondies I made.

I asked them, "Do you want to try the brownies I brought you?"

They all took one and I could see that they liked them very much. Soon they took another and then another and at one point, they were all trying to get the last one out of the pan, and it fell on the floor, upside down.

They laughed. “Hey, not a problem, these are so good that they will taste good even off the floor.”

They all agreed that I could come back anytime, especially if I brought the blondies again. After lunch, a couple of the guys wandered off to a grassy area and plopped down for a little catnap. The others kept on talking, and eventually someone appeared from the house with a big pot of coffee for the group. This was just what I needed to keep me awake for the long walk home.

As we left, we could see them heading back into the fields, happy to get back to work. The same group of farmers and neighbors participate in the harvest every year together in the long-standing tradition of helping each other. They would not even think of using a modern machine to do the harvest. The men all have to be registered to work in the vineyards by Remo in Siena in order to help with the harvest.

PANZANELLA

4-5 slices of stale bread (any kind is fine)
3-4 medium tomatoes
Optional (½ small red onion, 1 cucumber sliced)
½ cup white balsamic vinegar (I love fig-infused white balsamic for this recipe)
¾ cup olive oil (extra virgin)
½ tsp. sea salt (or more to taste)
¼ tsp. black pepper
10-12 fresh mozzarella balls (small pearl type, called Ciliegine)
5-6 leaves fresh basil

Cut the stale bread into small cubes (like croutons). Place the bread into a medium-sized sauté pan, drizzle with olive oil and heat over medium heat until the bread is browned and toasted. You can also toast the bread cubes in the oven on a baking sheet. Place in the oven at 350 degrees for 8-10 minutes. Set the bread aside and let cool.

Dice the tomatoes, onions, and cucumbers and place into a medium bowl. Add the salt, black pepper, olive oil, and balsamic vinegar and stir well. Cut or tear the basil into small pieces and add to the tomatoes. Place bowl in refrigerator until ready to serve.

Just prior to serving, add the bread cubes to the tomatoes and mix well. Cut the fresh mozzarella into halves or fourths and sprinkle over the top of the salad. Feel free to add more olive oil or balsamic vinegar if the mixture seems dry. The bread will soak up the liquid quickly. Spoon into small bowls and enjoy.

Recipe note: The fig-infused balsamic vinegar I like for this is made by Alessi. It can be found near the other vinegars in the grocery store. Experiment with other vinegar flavors if you like. The mozzarella balls (ciliegine) are usually found in the specialty cheese section packaged with water in a plastic container or shrink-wrapped to keep them fresh. If you can't find these, simply cut 4 ounces of fresh mozzarella into small bite-sized cubes.

8

How Chocolate Cake Makes Sweet Dreams Come True

As the weeks in October went by, I started to mourn the fact that I had to leave what I felt was a little slice of heaven. Even though I had felt like a stranger so many times during the months in Italy, I also felt as if I had found a true friend in Italy. People accepted me for who I was, plain and simple. The people of the village had become my friends and family while I was there. Now, every time I saw someone, I thought, is this the last time I will see this person in my life?

One of the most genuine people I met during this time was a local woman, Giulia, who lived on a farm near the village. She spoke English very well and had a heart of gold. I had no idea how important meeting Giulia would be until later. The friends I had made while I was in the village organized going-away dinners for the last few weeks and days while I was there.

A group of three women, Giulia, Gwen, and Sara, always gathered once a week for English conversation during the time I spent in Italy. Most of the time, they would come to San Gusme to meet as they knew I could not get away easily. We would meet at the local coffee bar or sit out on one of the benches and chat. This experience was grounding for me. I was learning Italian from Tuscan people, which was my base of understanding from those days forward. I loved how they had unique expressions that were only recognized in the area, and how they never pronounce the c in anything, instead it had an h sound. Sara's boyfriend was named Luca, but it sounded like Luha when she said it.

They all loved learning from me and I loved learning from them and having friends with which to speak my mother tongue. We had pizza parties, pub gatherings, trips to Florence for lunch and shopping, and a private dinner that Giulia hosted at her farm with all of the traditional foods I loved.

Dinner at Giulia's house, from left, Gwen, Sheryl, Sara, Giulia.

In late October, we were celebrating a birthday for Pam's husband, Sam, which was hosted at the local restaurant situated in the heart of the village. I had eaten there many times during the weeks and months I was in the village, so it was now a familiar place to me. I was feeling so sad about the fact that I had to leave Italy to return to Minnesota in a few weeks. How I had grown to love the village, the land, and the people of this place.

As I was enjoying my meal that day, I remember wondering about the person, the chef, who had created such incredible food. The love and care that he had taken in preparing the food was obvious from the artistic way it was presented, and the looks of satisfaction and pure happiness as everyone was enjoying the dishes. That day, we had the hot chocolate cake for dessert. Over the months and weeks that I had lived in the village, I had eaten the cake many times.

As I was taking my last bite, I said under my breath, "I could eat this every day."

I did not think anyone had heard me, but Marco, the maître d' and one of the partners of the restaurant, had heard me and replied softly in my ear, "We are here, every day." He knew that I loved the cake and seemed to be tempting me.

That is when I looked at him and said, "I am leaving in a few weeks, could I at least have the recipe?"

Marco said, "Sure, let's go talk to the chef, Vincenzo."

I responded in disbelief. "I can go and meet the chef? We could never do that back home."

That very afternoon, I followed Marco back to the kitchen, and I met Vincenzo for the first time. He looked up as he was stirring a huge pot of soup and greeted me without saying a word. He had these giant oval eyes and a wide smile that took up most of his face. He wore rimless glasses and had on his traditional white coat and checkered chef pants. He was not tall and not short, about 5 feet 7 or so. I instantly felt like he was welcoming me into his kitchen. I could smell traces of the meal we had just enjoyed and was curious about the soup he was stirring.

"What are you making?" I asked in my broken Italian.

"Ribollita for tomorrow," he replied.

Next, I asked in English, "I love your hot chocolate cake. I'd like to have the recipe if possible."

Both Marco and Aldo, the sommelier of the restaurant spoke English quite well and so I naturally thought that Vincenzo would as well.

He smiled and said, "No speak English."

Marco just smiled at me and said, "Well, you will figure it out," and left us together in the kitchen to finish his work.

My Italian was not the best, even after six months, so I wondered how I would really communicate with him to get a complicated recipe.

Emma had followed me into the kitchen and instantly ran up and gave Vincenzo a big smile and a hug. As he reached down to bring her into his arms, she whispered in his ear in Italian, "I can help you with the recipe." Emma knew Vincenzo well, as she frequently would watch him cooking in the kitchen from the main square of the village. She too loved his chocolate cake.

It was a perfect idea. Emma would help me get the recipe. This is where the story of our life together—Vincenzo's and mine—began. All because I asked for a recipe for chocolate cake.

Later that week, I went back to the restaurant with Emma, who was now seven years old, and she translated the recipe for the chocolate cake (now called the chocolate "love" cake) as told to her by Vincenzo for me. I still have the little piece of paper where I recorded the recipe. It is written on a pad of sunflower paper from a notebook that I used to keep all of my favorite memories written down during my time.

♡ October 29
Tortino di Cioccolato
150 grams dark chocolate
150 grams butter
3 eggs
120 grams sugar
120 grams flour
1 o pan levito
1/2 tsp. salt
-Melt butter + choc.
in water bath.
-Beat eggs + sugar
Add dry ingredients
Bake 350°

My handwritten recipe for Tortino di Cioccolato.

Tortino di Cioccolato (Hot Chocolate "Love" Cake)

6 ounces dark chocolate, chopped (use 60-70 percent chocolate)
10 tablespoons unsalted butter
3 large eggs
½ cup sugar
½ cup all-purpose flour
1 tablespoon cocoa powder
1 tsp. baking powder
½ tsp. salt

Preheat oven to 375 degrees.

Melt together the butter and chocolate in bowl over a water bath. You can create a water bath by placing a glass or metal bowl above a medium saucepan filled with water (half full). Warm the water over medium heat. The water should not be touching the bottom of the bowl. Set aside the melted chocolate to cool slightly. You can also use the microwave on 50 percent power for 1 to 2 minutes to melt the chocolate and butter together in a glass bowl.

Beat the eggs and sugar together well with a hand or stand

mixer on medium until the mixture is creamy and light yellow—around 3 to 4 minutes. Slowly add the melted chocolate mixture (a little at a time) to the egg/sugar mixture.

Next add the dry ingredients: flour, cocoa powder, baking powder, and salt. Mix by hand with a whisk for 1 to 2 minutes until the mixture is smooth.

Spray ten individual ramekins (4-6 oz. size) with spray oil or coat the inside well with butter. Pour the chocolate mixture into the ramekins, filling about ¾ full.

Bake cakes at 375 degrees for 10 to 12 minutes (it's better to undercook than overcook these, the middle should remain a bit melted). Turn the ramekins upside down on a small plate to turn out each individual cake. Serve warm with vanilla ice cream and berries.

Makes 8-10 cakes.

I will never forget how Vincenzo greeted Emma, by sweeping her up in his arms and giving her a big hug while she rubbed his bald head and told him how much she loved how it felt without hair. He told her that it was easier to shave it than to wear the silly chef's hat that drove him crazy. There were lots of kisses and words of adoration between the two of them.

That day, I felt a connection to Vincenzo that I could not explain. Some might call it fate, but I had no idea what to think. What I did know was that I felt like he was speaking directly to my heart, because I could not stop thinking about him. That day was the very moment in time that marked the beginning of our love story—and a new beginning for me.

Later that week, while I was out in the main piazza watching the kids play, Vincenzo must have spotted me from his kitchen door. He stepped out from the kitchen and into the square and approached me very shyly. We greeted each other with the traditional kisses on each cheek, as we now knew each other well enough to do this. I noticed a nice tender pause as he kissed each check and thought perhaps he lingered a bit, which I also enjoyed. I thought he was just coming out for a little fresh air and to say hello. But then I thought, perhaps no, maybe he really wanted to see me.

I was so surprised when he asked me, "Would you like to go for a coffee with me? Tomorrow is my day off."

Before I could even register this in my head, I could hear myself saying, "Yes, I would love to," without even thinking.

We agreed on a time he would pick me up from the parking lot of the village. I had no idea how we would communicate, but I figured it was just a coffee, a simple outing. Later on, I panicked and thought I should just cancel this, but I had no idea how to get in touch with him either. I was so nervous and worried about how I would talk to him. I kept thinking to myself, What am I doing? Why did I say yes? What had I just done?

A few days later, I was so nervous as I waited for him to arrive outside of the village walls. I watched him arrive, and without missing a beat, he walked up the stairs to greet me, confidently kissed me on both checks again and looked directly in my eyes as if he had known me for years.

As we walked together to his car, my stomach was doing cartwheels. For two days, I had been practicing a few questions I could ask him during our first date. Or was this a date? I really had no idea.

We arrived at the neighboring village, Castelnuovo Berardenga, and he offered me his arm as we walked together to the coffee bar, Bar Centrale. As we walked into the bar, I could see that the place was deserted, no one but us for that moment.

The owner, Silvia, greeted us with a smile and a twinkle in her eye. We found a table in the back of the coffee bar and had our afternoon macchiato and each other. Somehow we found ourselves immersed in a conversation that we both understood, with a few words of Italian from me (that I had practiced) as well as the language of our hearts. We laughed at each other as we sat down because we both had our dictionaries with us for the conversation.

Little did I realize at this point that speaking with few words and focusing on the emotions we felt and the body language we could see would be one of our main forms of communication from the very beginning of our relationship as a couple.

My questions started with, "Why did you become a chef?"

He responded, "I grew up near a famous cooking school. I learned to cook early in my life from my grandmother. I loved to eat, and so I spent a lot of time with my grandmother in the kitchen. It was either become a chef or be a mechanic like my father."

I also learned that he was born in France, because his parents lived and worked there for the first eight years of their marriage. However, his family was from a little village in the southern part of Italy, in the region of Abruzzo. This is where he spent his summers as a little boy with his grandparents and eventually lived from the time he was eight years old.

Intrigued, I asked, "What is your favorite dish to make?"

He said, "For me I love to make simple, traditional dishes. I love to make fresh pasta especially. And I really love to keep the dishes from Italy pure as they have been for so many years."

I continued with my questions, "How did you decide to come to San Gusme?"

"I was working in Siena with my two friends that are now my partners in the restaurant, Marco and Aldo. We all wanted to have our own place, and we found the restaurant in San Gusme a couple of years ago and bought it together." He went on to explain that he had worked as a chef all over Italy and eventually settled in the area of Siena working for a restaurant in a five-star hotel (Grand Hotel Continental) for a few years prior.

He said, "I love the traditional, simple dishes in Tuscany. I feel at home here."

I also learned that he was eight years younger than I. This was a bit of a disappointment to me. I thought perhaps we were closer in age. The time we had together that day was so much better than I ever expected. We agreed to meet again in a few days for a little drive in the countryside.

As he dropped me back in the village, I walked back to my little apartment and thought I understood every word he said. I also got the feeling that he was a kind, talented, very complex, and interesting man. He had just turned my world upside down completely. My heart was doing flip-flops. My emotions took me totally by surprise.

A few days later, Vincenzo picked me up and took me for a drive to see the Tuscan countryside as the leaves were turning in the hills, and I could see that some of the grapevines were bright red. We stopped and took a walk together through a tree-lined country road that seemed to offer us the privacy we needed at that very moment. At one point he turned to me and kissed me.

He whispered in my ear as he brushed my cheek, "Ti amo."

I knew what that meant: I love you. All I could say was, "Why?"

I went on to say, "You can't know that you love me after only meeting me a couple of times."

He just kept smiling and insisting, "Well, I think I do."

Then I protested (and panicked) more and said in a jumble of Italian and English, "I'm a bit of a broken person and have had too many failed relationships. I'm not ready for this. I am afraid to start a new relationship. I am not sure if I can give my heart to someone again."

Reacting to the intimacy of the moment and the words he was saying was too much for me. All I could hear was my past whispering in my ear saying, be careful. Don't make another big mistake.

I protested and questioned him again, "But how can you know that you love me already?"

He simply stated, "I feel like I've found an angel on earth and have never felt an instant connection like this with anyone before."

He, too, had been in previous relationships that had failed or just were not the right fit for him. He told me that it had been really hard to be in a relationship with someone else. He was never home and always in the kitchen, even for holidays. Most women gave up on him and could not take the lifestyle. I started to wonder if perhaps Vincenzo was the reason that I had such a strong feeling about Italy for so many years and had always wanted to return. Perhaps he had been there waiting for me all along.

We spent a few treasured moments together during the last days I had remaining. I thought that it was such a gift that I had met this kind and gentle man at the very end of my time in Italy. We had intimate moments and shared each other's story. I was not afraid to ask him all of the questions I wanted to ask. Especially because I had no idea if I would ever see him again. Meeting Vincenzo was not at all part of the plan. I really had no idea what I was going to do about these feelings.

The last night I had in Italy, he stayed with me all night. As we were talking into the night, he kissed me again, and this time, I felt like my inner spirit was taking over my body. It was almost like watching the two of us from a dream state, I really did not know if it was real or not, but it felt like the exact time and place it was supposed to be.

I let go of all of my anxieties and worries about who I was and melted into his arms. He kissed me and made love to me in a way that I had never experienced, so gentle and loving, like we were floating for hours. As he caressed me with the warmest hands I had ever felt, it seemed like he was erasing all of the negative thoughts I had about myself and my ability to be loved by someone. He discovered and traced the scars on my stomach from previous surgeries that kept me from having children and kissed them with love and tenderness. In the end, I cried and he just held me and wiped away the tears as they flowed out of me.

We fell asleep together like we had been connected for years. He knew just how I fit next to him, cuddled up in the warmth of his skin with my toes gently caressing his legs.

The next morning, I knew that I had to return home to Minnesota, to my work and my family. I could tell that he did not want me to leave either.

He kept telling me, "Please stay. Don't go away now."

I had been packing some items and not everything was going to fit in my bag. So, I thought, why not give Vincenzo a few of my personal things to keep. Maybe this would be one way to stay connected. And another reason to come back to Italy.

As I struggled to tell him in Italian, "Listen, I have some things I want you to keep for me. I hope that someday I will be back for them, and to see you."

All he said was, "I will keep them forever and wait for you as long as it takes."

As we were saying goodbye, he turned to me and took off a gold bracelet from around his wrist that had been his grandmother's. As he placed it around my wrist, he said, "I want you to keep this, from me. It was my grandmother's and now it belongs to you. I will never forget you."

It was heartbreaking for me to leave that morning, but I did. I cried all the way to Rome, and on the flight to Minnesota, I was in a state of mourning. I kept those memories of our few moments together alive in my heart for another year.

9

Love Letters and Sunflowers

In the six months that I spent on sabbatical with my friends in Chianti, I had focused on being with their children, taking care of their home, and studying for an exam I needed to take for my career. I had also published my thesis from my graduate studies. I accomplished what I set out to do. I felt so fortunate to have had the chance to be immersed in life in San Gusme for those six months. I knew that my experience was supposed to be temporary. But I dreamed of more. Especially after meeting Vincenzo.

However, I returned to my work and life in Minnesota.

After a few months had passed, I connected with Vincenzo with a simple text one day after I had been thinking about him and wondered how he was. I had no idea if he would respond.

He responded within seconds, "How are you, my love? I have been waiting for the day when you would be back."

I was sure that we had something that was so special and so strong. I had to reconnect with him. I sent a handwritten letter to him in Italian that took almost a week to write. He wrote back with lovely words that I will always treasure. His words conveyed the message that he had never felt this way about anyone before and that he had never missed a day when he did not think of me.

We kept in touch with each other during the months that followed with letters, in a time when emails and text messages were the primary way to communicate. Instead, we were sending handwritten letters. He still has all of the letters that I wrote to him during this time. The letters went back and forth for months, and I had hope and happiness in my heart.

Deep inside, I understood that I had to return to Italy, and so I made a plan to do just that. I returned to Italy for a two-week vacation in March of the next year (2009). It had been over a year since I had been in Italy. I rented an apartment in San Gusme and could not wait to go back to the place that had a large piece of my heart. Also my instincts were telling me to take a chance on love with Vincenzo. I had returned to Minnesota after meeting Vincenzo over the chocolate cake recipe, and we had only a few days to get to know each other. Our first "date" was over coffee with only a few words spoken. Now I was ready for more. Vincenzo was planning to be in Rome to pick me up from the airport. I was so nervous. All I could think was that I hoped this was all as real as it felt.

When I arrived in Rome, I nervously walked out of the baggage claim area with high hopes. We saw each other immediately. I dropped my bags and ran into his arms. I finally felt free to really share who I was with him and also reveal my heart's desire. We traveled in silence and comfort back up to Tuscany and San Gusme. All I could do was hold his hand and look into his eyes during the ride north. At one point, I feel asleep, and when I woke, I looked out the window and could see the landscape of Chianti. My heart was so happy to be back.

We spent every minute that we could together for ten days, with trips to Siena and intimate dinners in the little apartment that I had rented. He continued to show me the beauty of his world and slowly revealed who he was to me. We found a connection that was very strong. I could not believe that I might be falling in love with this man, but I was, and I did.

During this visit, my friend Pam invited me to their house for dinner. I had the chance to see how Emma and Siena had grown over the past year. As we talked, she asked how it was to be back and to see Vincenzo again. I could not help but show my happiness. However, I was struggling to understand how the relationship could ever work if I was in Minnesota and Vincenzo was in Italy.

Pam offered me a solution. "Our travel business is growing like crazy and we could use your help. I think you should come and live here and work full-time with us."

She went on to explain that I could work as a travel planner helping them to organize aspects of their private tours. They again needed a part-time nanny for Emma and Siena, especially during their busy touring season. I knew exactly what this included. I had learned much of what was needed the previous year. Inside, I was secretly excited that I could reconnect with my inner mom as well.

"I'll go home and give it some very serious thought," I said.

Inside I was bursting. This was epic. This kind of decision was more permanent and even more risky than the one to be in Italy for a defined period of only six months. This could be a forever decision. Once again, I struggled with making the decision. I had a great job with a group that I loved. However, I knew that this time, it was not just about my work, it was about my heart and finding love as well. Inside, I knew that this was a chance I had to take, despite my hesitation and worry about what it would mean for me professionally.

A few months later, I bravely wrote my letter of resignation and sent it to my administrator. Once again, people were shocked that I would take such a big risk. I understood their perspective, but once again, I was sure that if I did not listen to my heart, I would regret it for the rest of my life. I was able to negotiate to keep my connection with my work as a nurse as they offered me a position with the same team as a supplemental writer and educator. This gave me a bit of security. If it did not work out, I could always return to a full-time position later.

With that, I took a chance that returning to Italy was the right decision. I had one foot still connected to my professional life, and one foot daring to take a chance on love with Vincenzo and a life in Italy.

Once again back in Italy, it was early in the summer of 2009. This time, the move was more permanent—a leap of faith that I would learn a new way of living and working. Most of all, I wanted to discover more of who I was inside. I was eager to reconnect with the things in life that filled my senses and made my spirit happy. It was a defining point in my life.

In my first month, I got settled into my new little apartment, which was situated right in the main square of the village. Just next door was the old church with the traditional tall bell tower that rang out every hour during the day. The walls of my apartment would actually vibrate when the bells rang. I soon got used to the regular sound, and it helped me register the passage of time throughout the day. Instead of meeting notices and calendar invites popping up on my email, instead I had the sound of ancient bells ringing out.

At noon and at sunset each day, the bells had a special song that was meant to call everyone together for lunch and dinner. On Sunday, the bells rang out regularly to call everyone to Mass. Even as I would go out walking during the day, I could always hear the bells from San Gusme calling me home.

Vincenzo had helped me find the apartment. As an outsider, I could have never found the apartment, or perhaps even be trusted to rent it. As soon as I walked in, I felt that it was the perfect place for me. It had a small bedroom, bathroom in the back and kitchen with a little space for a table in the front room. The main part of the apartment was mainly the kitchen and was the heart of my new home. The floors were terra-cotta with old rustic beams and bricks on the ceiling.

The apartment had two windows in the back that looked out on the Tuscan hills where I could see olive trees and the grapevines in the distance. Another favorite part of the apartment were the front windows and the main door that opened up to a lovely terrace that overlooked the square and looked directly to the door of Vincenzo's restaurant. I think he loved it so much more because I was just across the square. He could stop over on his afternoon break, and I could stop in anytime during the day to say hello to him as well.

I remember feeling a bit strange during this time. I was so excited to be in this place that I loved, but I once again had to redefine who I was. I was no longer manager of a busy department at a major hospital, I was not working in my traditional role every day, so who was I? I made many new discoveries about myself. I had the chance to examine the real me, inside and out. This was my opportunity to dig deep and discover who I was for the first time in my life. I felt a deep connection to the spirit of the country that had drawn me back, but also to my past and my country-girl roots.

Every day, I would retrace my favorite hikes down ancient noble roads and soak in the new beauty that was around me. My feet automatically knew the way. One of my favorite things was the day I discovered the little fields of sunflowers that are sometimes planted in the wheat fields that are resting for a year. These bright yellow patches were nestled in between the hills of olive trees and vines. I usually would pick one or two little ones from the edge of the field along with any other wildflowers that were growing along the path and brought them back to my apartment for a summer bouquet.

Each day I learned more about the people of the village and carefully started to see how I would fit into their lives on a more permanent basis. The village was like a friend to me now, one that had welcomed me back and wrapped its arms around me. I wanted to connect even deeper with the customs, traditions, and routines of this place that I now called my home. I noticed everything that I loved from my past experiences in these first few days and weeks. The birdsongs that greeted me in the morning, the sound of a Vespa arriving at 7:00 a.m.—it was Gianni who owned the little grocery store. He always opened his store in time for the children of the village to stop on their way to the school bus for their daily panino for a snack. I knew the ladies from the village will be there later, picking out their groceries for lunch and dinner.

Later, I could hear a few people out in the square saying their hellos. Some of the ladies of the village were sweeping their stoops while others hung laundry from the lines between their windows, the squeak from their pulleys were my indication that it was a sunny day and also time for me to do laundry. The smell of the fresh-baked brioche and the swooshing sound of the espresso maker in the restaurant were common to me now in the morning. I also heard the sounds of doors opening and closing with children's voices talking and laughing as they headed off to school for the day.

I was thankful every day for the opportunity to soak in every sight, sound, and experience. My eyes, mind, and heart were wide open to everything, like I was a child. This new sense of mindfulness created an appreciation of life that I carry with me even today. Each day was a new experience, with my heart slowly healing and my sense of self growing within me. I further immersed myself in the language, foods, and traditions of the village. Every night, I would fall asleep amazed and content like I had never ever experienced in my life. I honestly never knew that I could feel so happy and peaceful.

During this time, I worked with Pam's travel business again planning their group tours and some private tours. I also reconnected with my inner mom and continued to be part-time nanny to their two girls, Emma and Siena, while my friends traveled for work. This was also an unexpected gift for me to have them in my life, which gave me the opportunity to enjoy the blessings and struggles that all moms have with children.

My focus with them was homework (even in Italian), cooking, and cleaning. I loved making cookies and cupcakes with Emma, even played the tooth fairy when she lost her first couple of teeth, brushed and braided hair, did laundry, and rushed them to the bus in the morning—once in my pajamas—made after-school snacks, and snuggled them when they needed love. I treasured this time together.

Even their two cats recognized me as the mom at times seeking me out in the village when they were hungry. Meowing to me from a bench across the square as I was out doing my laundry at my apartment to get my attention. Even today, I have a very special relationship with both girls and love the fact that I was mom number two for them for these years. I still love connecting with Emma to bake on a regular basis, especially for special occasions and Christmas.

10

Whatever Will Be, Will Be

It was only a matter of a few weeks before I asked Vincenzo if he wanted to move in with me. He was there with me during his free time most days anyway, and I had a very good feeling about the ease in which we could coexist in the same space. My apartment was so cozy and it was near to the restaurant, I felt like it was just the perfect way for us to also get to know how we might live together and perhaps take our relationship to the next level.

We easily fell into a daily routine where we would start our day with coffee and breakfast together. He would go off to the restaurant, and I would start working with the travel planning, writing, or my nanny duties. At the moment, I had three jobs keeping me busy. Around 3:00 p.m., he would usually get a break and come home to take a little nap together. This was our time to really connect. We talked, we touched, we made love, and we slept like angels. This was probably the first time in twenty years that I slept soundly and felt so content with my life and the person I was sharing it with. I had no idea what this feeling was like until it happened to me and I was amazed.

In July, summer set in and the weather got warmer. It can be very warm and humid in Tuscany. With no air conditioning,

I learned how to use a fan again and put up the traditional hanging beads across the doorway so that I could keep the door open during the day to let the breeze in and keep the bugs and flies out. The up side was that the laundry on the little stendino dried in less than a day out on the terrace.

It was getting close to the middle of July and my birthday when my Pam and I planned an outing to see an open-air opera at San Galgano, a ancient stone abbey that was in ruin, but still absolutely stunning. The abbey is set out in the countryside, even though it was missing the roof, it still had the walls surrounding it. It was an incredible experience to be in such an intimate place listening to the sounds of music playing and bouncing off the stone walls. We attended the opera on the eve of my birthday.

I arrived home around 11:30 p.m. that evening to find Vincenzo waiting for me with a bottle of prosecco. He finished up talking with his mom rather abruptly as I walked in the door. I knew that this was his habit, as it was with many Italians, a call to mamma was obligatory at least once a day. I instantly wondered what was up, as he rarely drank prosecco.

As he planted a kiss on me and the biggest hug I have ever received, he said, "I was waiting for you. Welcome home. Go take a shower and put on your pajamas to relax."

"Is something wrong?" I asked. I got the sense that he was nervous or worried about something under the obvious excitement that I could see, but I could not put my finger on it. While I was in the shower, he was planning his big birthday surprise for me.

As I stepped out of the shower, he held out the towel for me with a big smile and a twinkle in his eyes. It was now after midnight, and I was really exhausted from the day's fun outing. As I headed toward the bedroom, all I could think of was the sweet feel of the soft pillow for my head. I pulled back the covers and discovered a present with a gold bow on it.

"Buon compleanno amore mio," Vincenzo exclaimed.

"Oh, Vincenzo, what have you done? My birthday is tomorrow."

"It's after midnight, so it's already your birthday, let's celebrate," he said with a sparkle in his eyes.

I was so excited that he had thought of me on my birthday. He had waited until midnight to give me my gift as it is bad luck in Italy to celebrate birthdays before the actual day. As I untied the bow and started opening the box, I could tell that he was getting even more nervous. I had no idea what was making him so jumpy. Then I realized that inside the box was a smaller box that looked like it would hold jewelry. I thought, this is wonderful, he bought me earrings or a necklace.

Inside the small box was the sweetest engagement ring—a white gold ring with a band of diamonds and a second band next to it with two hearts intertwined. I looked at the ring and at him with a look of surprise.

"What does this mean?" I asked.

I really had no idea, but as soon as he saw my eyes look at his, he said this: "Well, I know that it is really early in our relationship, but I am so sure that I want to be with you for the rest of my life. I want you to be more than my girlfriend. I want you to be my wife."

I was speechless. This incredible human being, Vincenzo, was pouring his heart out by letting me know that he wanted me, forever.

I let this register for a second or two, and said, "Yes, I will and I am sure about you too."

He put the ring on my finger in the early hours of my forty-third birthday. We toasted with a late-night glass of prosecco and dropped into bed together. This ring has not left my hand since. It is a perfect symbol of our two hearts that found each other in such a serendipitous way.

Later the next day, we Skyped my parents to tell them the news. I could tell that they were surprised and unsure. We both reassured them that we would wait to be married for another year to get to know each other and also so that he could meet my family and I could meet his.

Vincenzo also had planned another surprise for later that day. He made one of his decadent celebration cakes for me and invited friends to come to our apartment for cake and prosecco together. His celebration cake is still a family tradition for special occasions. He makes it with layers of puff pastry that are baked crispy with sugar on top. Between these layers of puff pastry he assembles with a layer of chocolate mousse followed by a top layer of pastry crème dotted with fresh berries such as strawberries, blueberries, and blackberries. The top is decorated with fresh berries and even flowers to make it look just spectacular. The cake is called millefoglie cake, which means many-layer cake.

What a birthday surprise, we would soon be family, and how symbolic was the cake with our many layers of love to celebrate.

Many Layers Celebration Cake

Note: This cake requires a time investment, but in the end it is totally worth it. It helps to make all of the ingredients one day and assemble it the next. This cake is worthy of any celebration. Vincenzo would make a version of this cake for birthdays, baptisms, and weddings celebrated at the restaurant.

2 packages puff pastry (4 sheets) thawed
½ cup sugar
1-2 pints of fresh berries, such as strawberries, raspberries, blackberries, and blueberries
2 pints heavy whipping cream (reserve for top and sides of cake)

Chocolate Mousse

17 ounces dark chocolate (use 70-80 percent)
8 large eggs (separate to 6 yolks and 8 whites)
1 pint heavy whipping cream

Chantilly Cream

1 ½ cups whole milk
½ cup sugar
¼ cup all-purpose flour
4 large egg yolks
1 tsp. vanilla extract
Zest of one lemon
Zest of one orange
½ pint whipping cream

Preheat oven to 350 degrees.

Defrost the puff pastry for 30 minutes. Place the puff pastry sheets on a baking sheet covered with parchment paper. Poke the pastry well with a fork. Sprinkle each pastry sheet with ¼ cup of sugar.

Bake at 350 degrees for 15 minutes or until golden brown. Set the pastry sheets aside to cool.

To make the chocolate mousse: Melt the chocolate in a glass or metal bowl over a water bath. You can create a water bath by placing a glass or metal bowl above a medium saucepan filled with water (half full). Warm the water over medium heat. The water should not be touching the bottom of the bowl. Set aside the melted chocolate to cool slightly.

Once the chocolate is melted, add the egg yolks one at a time. Stir well after each one until all yolks have been incorporated.

Place the 8 egg whites in a mixing bowl and whip on high speed until stiff peaks form. Slowly spoon the egg whites into the chocolate mixture a little at a time and fold in with a spatula, lightly mixing so that the air of the egg whites stays in the mixture.

Next, place the heavy whipping cream in a mixing bowl on medium speed, once it starts to thicken, whip on high speed until thick with stiff peaks. Gently fold the whipped cream into the chocolate mixture with a spatula. Place the chocolate mousse in the refrigerator until ready to assemble the cake.

To make the Chantilly cream: Warm the milk with the vanilla, lemon and orange zests in a medium saucepan until you start to see wisps of steam. It should not be boiling.

In a medium bowl, whisk together the sugar and egg yolks. Add the flour a little at a time, mixing well after each addition. This will form a thick paste.

Next, pour a little of the hot milk into the egg mixture and whisk to combine. Continue pouring the milk slowly, whisking continuously. When all the milk has been added to the egg mixture, pour everything back into the saucepan.

Set the saucepan back over medium heat. Whisk constantly while heating. It will start to thicken after a few minutes. When it has thickened to a pudding-like consistency, pause whisking every few seconds to see if the cream has come to a boil. If you see large bubbles popping on the surface, whisk for a few more seconds and then remove the pan from heat.

Pour the cream into a glass bowl and cover with a piece of plastic wrap pressed directly on the surface of the cream and chill completely.

Once the Chantilly cream is chilled and just before you are ready to assemble the cake, whip the heavy cream until it forms stiff peaks and gently fold the whipped cream into the pastry cream.

Now, you are ready to assemble the celebration cake. Start by taking three of the puff pastry sheets and cutting them to the size of the cake that you would like. Most sheets will make a cake that is 8 by 10 inches. Place a sheet of puff pastry on a baking sheet covered with parchment paper.

The first layer should be a layer of chocolate mousse. Spread a thick layer of the chocolate mousse on top of the baked puff pastry. Depending on how thick you would like the layers, you may have extra mousse and cream.

Next, place a second layer of puff pastry over the top of the chocolate mousse and press down.

Spread a thick layer of Chantilly cream over the top of the second puff pastry sheet. Add 1-2 cups of fresh cut berries to the top of this layer. Press the berries into the cream as you place them.

Next, place a third sheet of puff pastry over the top of the cream and berries, press down lightly.

Whip the remaining 2 pints of heavy whipping cream until it forms stiff peaks. If you prefer, you can add a couple of tablespoons of sugar or honey to sweeten the cream.

Spread the whipped cream over the top and sides of the cake. Decorate the top and sides of the cake with remaining berries, fresh flowers, or other decorations. Be creative with the sides. They can be covered well with crushed bits of remaining puff pastry, chopped nuts, or toasted coconut.

Store cake in refrigerator until ready to serve. Remove any flowers prior to serving. Serve by cutting the cake into 3x3-inch squares. This will serve around 16 to 18 people.

Recipe note: Puff pastry can be found in the frozen section near other frozen breads, pie crust, or dough. One box usually has two sheets in it, so you will need to purchase two boxes for this recipe. Take out the box of pastry, remove the sheets, cover with a tea towel, and let it sit on the counter at least one hour prior to baking them so that they are soft and easy to work with.

Vincenzo in the restaurant decorating a cake for an event.

A week later, our friend Giulia invited us to a dinner party at her farm to celebrate our engagement. She was a big part of my experience with friends in Italy, and I cherished her as someone with a beautiful and generous spirit. The farm was just a few miles outside of the village, near an ancient battle site called Montaperti.

We arrived for the dinner party in the early evening. As the sun set in the distance, I was drawn to the edge of the grass to see the horizon. From her farm, I could see golden hills of summer wheat, dotted with olive groves and grapevines. Just near the house was a field of sunflowers with their faces pointed toward the sun.

At that moment, I recognized the view and horizon, and it hit me. I realized that on my very first visit to this area two years previous, I had stayed in a villa just next door. I could see it in the distance. I remember sitting among the lavender outside on a warm July day along with my friend Cathy thinking the feeling of this place was special. I distinctly remember the warmth of the sun and slight breeze touching my face and knowing that there was a message swirling around me saying, you are home, you are here, this is where you belong. I had no idea that Giulia lived just across the field and that my future self would be celebrating love in that very spot a few years later.

That night, we had a traditional Tuscan-style dinner party al-fresco. She had invited friends and neighbors. We sat at a long wooden table outside under the umbrella pines outside of the main house. There was salami, prosciutto, and cheese to start out with a glass of prosecco. This was followed by pasta with pesto, and rounded out with steak and sausages grilled over a wood fire.

We sipped on Chianti and warmed each other with our summer sweaters once the sun went down. She brought out a special bottle of vin santo made from her own vines, and we enjoyed with the biscotti that I had made for the evening. With the jazz music playing on the stereo into the night air, Vincenzo and I shared a spontaneous slow dance as the sunflowers faded and dropped their heads for the night as the sun set. This felt like it was a perfect ending to a life-changing week.

As I settled in to village life, I made our little apartment into a place of comfort and a part of me. It was only partially furnished, so we purchased a couple of items in the first few months. I went to the market to pick out linens and kitchen items. I loved being able to personalize this space for the first time in my life with the things that I wanted. I found linens decorated with lemons and olives and one with lavender flowers.

I naturally gravitated to anything with a sunflower on it too. The hand-decorated pottery was all so interesting and unique. I loved the painted poppies, sunflowers, and traditional Italian designs. For the bed, I found an old-fashioned chenille-type bedspread that was woven with colors of cream, blue, and purple.

For the main living room and kitchen area, I purchased the smallest red couch for two that I could find and a little desk and chair for me to work. I placed this near the fireplace as I knew in the winter it would be cold and damp in the house. The kitchen originally had a plastic table and two chairs in it, but for me this was one of the most important items to update. I found a square cherry table that expanded to twice its size with six chairs. I was already anticipating dinner parties in this space. The bedroom was spacious and even had a nice built-in closet.

The windows opened up to the back of the village with views of the Tuscan countryside that took me by surprise every day. We had no air conditioning, so the windows would frequently be open in the evening and through the night with a cool breeze coming in.

In the early morning, I would wake up to the songs of mourning doves, pigeons, and other birds. I even got used to the neighbor's cat who would sneak out from their back door and run up the rooftop past our apartment to check out what was happening. She would always peek into our apartment to check on us with her curious looks.

We could also hear the neighbors, Giancarlo and Vilma, next door out in their garden early in the morning, usually scolding the chickens for trying to escape or eating what they weren't supposed to. On the other side of us was a very elderly woman who would put out her laundry and sweep her back steps each morning.

The front of our apartment had a covered terrace with brick and stone arches overlooking the main square. It was like having box seats in a theater for any of the concerts or shows that were held throughout the year in the main square. And what a lovely way to take in the daily happenings of the village around me in these early days of settling in. I had planted red and pink geraniums in terra-cotta pots so that the terrace would be even more picturesque. Just off the terrace was a tiny room that held our washing machine. Only one person could be in the space at any time as it was that small. I learned that the laundry was, once again, one of my primary jobs. We did not have a clothes dryer, so each week was carefully planned out according to which laundry needed to be done and hung out to dry, rotating between Vincenzo's white chef uniforms and our regular clothes and towels. I would start each day with a pot of coffee and a load of laundry.

As I would go to hang out the laundry, I could hear the village ladies catching up and people passing by in the square. Our neighbor Nara would usually be out on her little terrace doing her laundry or tending her flowers as well. She would wave and say hello, although she could not say my name yet, so every day it came out different. Sometimes it was Sharon, Cheri, cielo (sky), or simply cara, which meant dear.

One day I thought I heard someone trying to get my attention. As I looked across the square, I saw Siri in her pink bathrobe through her open window off the second floor apartment. She was waving and trying to get my attention.

"The pigeons are taking your geranium blossoms," she yelled. "I just saw one try to take the whole plant away. Keep your eye out for them."

I waved and thanked her for the warning. She was a sweet older woman who could not really leave her apartment much, so most of her day was spent looking out her window and taking in the activity of the village from above.

In the summer months, when English or American tourists would pass through the village, I could hear them say, "What a beautiful terrace, I want a picture. And look at the flowers. Oh and a local woman is doing her laundry, isn't that quaint."

Little did they know that I could understand every word. I wonder how many photos I am a part of from other people's vacations to Italy. Me on the terrace hanging out the laundry surrounded by my geraniums.

The upstairs neighbors were an older couple that only came to San Gusme in the summer. They were probably around eighty years old and very sweet. They kept to themselves for the most part, but living below them, I did get to know a little about them by what I heard and witnessed. They would go out for their morning shopping and return about the same time I was hanging out my laundry for the day. I could see that he would help her up with the bags and make sure she could navigate the two flights of stairs. Their car was an old Fiat Panda and could get around the hills of Chianti and wind through the narrow roads as well as the entrance to San Gusme.

In the afternoon, they would take a nap for about an hour, as I could hear their shoes heading into the bedroom and then the noise of the old springs creaking on their bed as they settled in for a nap. This was usually the time I would be working and writing on my computer—the quiet of the afternoon was perfect for this. Sometimes I would be working on making a few jewelry creations as that had become another creative outlet for me.

They would wake around 4:00 p.m., and she would start preparing their evening meal. From my apartment below, I could smell the herbs and tomatoes from the sauces and other fantastic aromas coming from the upper level.

Many days, he would get out his accordion and play a few songs. I could hear them as if he were in the same room with me. I just loved this. I distinctly remember him playing and singing "che sará, sará" one afternoon.

I could not help but sing along in my apartment. "Whatever will be, will be. The future's not ours to see, che sará, sará."

I had forgotten about this song for so long, but as he played it, I remember that this was one of my grandmother's favorites. I remember her playing the same song, featuring Doris Day, on her record player when I was little. Another random connection coming full circle from the past to my present. And I thought it was the perfect perspective to have at that moment. Whatever will be, will be. I was enjoying actively watching my dream for my life unfold.

11

Vincenzo's Restaurant: A Tuscan Treasure

In our lives, the restaurant was central. It was where we first met and where we later spent many hours together. Nestled in this tiny, medieval village in the heart of Chianti, a restaurant waits for locals and travelers to find her. Once you step inside, the brick and stone architecture, terra-cotta floors, and a large wooden door from centuries ago welcomes and instantly warms you.

You are greeted by Aldo or Marco, who will smile and say, "Buongiorno or buonasera," and offer you a table surrounded by vintage Chianti wine bottles, handcrafted baskets, and antique furniture.

Once at your table, the traditional Tuscan bread basket arrives and a pour of prosecco is offered. This is followed by a plate of warm fried stuffed olives for you to enjoy as you sip your prosecco and take a look at the menu. The experience is like being welcomed home to your mother's house and instantly warms your soul.

In the meantime, a tiny bell alerts the kitchen staff that someone has arrived, and everyone is on alert, wondering, what will be ordered. A local dish of Tuscan meat and cheese to start? A bowl of ribollita? Risotto? Deep fried rabbit, or a hearty dish of pasta hand made in the local tradition? Vincenzo waits in the kitchen, ready and determined to make an impact on each and every person who eats at the restaurant. He knows every aspect of the kitchen like it is his own house. Every item is placed in a strategic way to make preparation go smoothly when things get busy in the kitchen.

Vincenzo is formally trained from the traditional Italian culinary institute in Villa Santa Maria. This culinary school is in the mountainous region of Abruzzo where he is originally from. His inspiration to become a chef was his grandmother, who taught him at an early age how to make gnocchi and pasta at home in Abruzzo. Vincenzo has talents from his years of experience working as a chef in restaurants in five-star hotels all over Italy, including Rome, Venice, and Florence.

Now, he has found his home and has his own restaurant in Tuscany, where he and his two friends opened the restaurant La Porta del Chianti, which translates to "the door of Chianti." This is also meaningful as San Gusme sits on the border and entrance to the small region in Italy where Chianti wine is made.

Vincenzo takes care of people with his food like an ancient healer cares for others knowing they need sustenance to make them stronger, happier, and whole again. His recipes are very traditional, with deep roots in the region of Tuscany, specific to Chianti. He knows that the people here (primarily farmers) have been eating like this for centuries—traditional Tuscan fare. He developed a few of the recipes based on traditions from this village specifically, getting the idea for the fried rabbit from Vezio, the tailor. The ribollita soup recipe is from the local ladies. With local flavor is the tender wild boar in a tomato-wine sauce over grilled polenta, or the lasagna with handmade pasta that would make anyone's cold winter day brighter and better.

Giancarlo, one of our neighbors, brings in fresh rosemary and sage from his garden behind the village for the restaurant every day. In return, he has breakfast with the three as they prepare for the day. As they work, they catch up on the local gossip and talk about who won yesterday's soccer match and prepare the lunch tables for their noontime guests.

Those who are lucky enough to find the restaurant will have a unique experience that they will never forget. This tiny village where the restaurant is located sits just north of Siena along one of the most picturesque roads in the Chianti wine region. It is a fortified village with some of the original walls from the fourteenth century. One of the walls still shows the damage from WWII when the Allied forces tanks came through to liberate the village. The villagers left it damaged to remind them of what they and the country went through in the war. Originally, the village was an important outpost for Siena during the medieval times when Florence and Siena were fighting for power in the region. Just down the road ten minutes is the famous Ricasoli Castle Brolio where Baron Ricasoli developed the perfect formulation of grapes for Chianti Classico wine in the late 1800s.

Most people traveling through might look up from the road and see the village nestled on the hilltop and be curious enough to take a turn off the road looking for an adventure. No cars are allowed inside the village, so you have to park in the parking lot outside the walls and walk up and in through one of the old doors of the village. Immediately, you may get the feeling that you are someplace special, perhaps back in time, but yet somehow still in the present.

The locals greet visitors with a smile and a look of pride in their home. They might give you the shortened Tuscan greeting "Giorno" or "Sera," if it is after noon. They know exactly who belongs to the place and those who are traveling through.

As a visitor, you might get the sense from the locals that they know what a treasure they have, and it is a feeling of protection and preservation as the circular design and walls of the village welcome and surround you like you are being cared for by a good friend who has known you forever. This is a place where children can play outside until midnight during the summer, and the locals all sit out on their benches catching up with each other throughout the day, but especially in the cool breezes of the evening before dinner.

Around the corner of the main square, the restaurant greets visitors with an intimate space with outside tables, surrounded by old wine barrels and covered with umbrellas in the summer and warm inviting lights from the inside and the incredible perfume of artisan food wafting through the air.

The inside of the restaurant is surrounded by history. The setting for the restaurant is the lower floor of the original palace building. It was originally the stables and later a workshop and still has the original well from around the 1300s. The brick and stone walls form arched ceilings that are an architectural feat like none other. The tables are covered with antique yellow cloths and little vases with sunflowers peeking out of them. Marco or Aldo will greet visitors and invite them to sit for lunch or dinner, or perhaps a glass of wine and aperitivo to take in the activities of the village.

At this point, most will agree that they have found a treasure and decide to stay to enjoy the food. The wine choices are spectacular with Aldo's expertise as a trained sommelier, pairing the food selections with just the right wine from the region. The wine service is elegant and traditional. He carefully opens the wine, smells the cork, and takes the first taste before pouring a taste for the appointed person at table. Once approved, the wine is poured into each glass only after coating them with a thin layer of the wine—so that nothing will interfere with the taste of the wine from your glass to your lips.

After a long look at the menu, it's hard to decide what to eat. Everything is so delicious and unique. Now it's time for Vincenzo to do his work. He carefully prepares each dish as if it were for his family. His love for rustic, traditional recipes is evident from the menu. For him, it's very important to respect the long-standing version of recipes from long ago. He also loves to re-create "cucina povera" or "poor man's dishes" as these are what peasants and farmers in the region have been eating for years. Wild boar ragù with polenta, gnocchi with tomato sauce, pici with cheese and pepper sauce, pumpkin ravioli, and the list is endless.

Local ingredients, fresh and bright, only the best pasta—always handmade, vegetables in season, local pecorino cheeses, olive oil, and Tuscan meats. When the dish arrives to the table, you cannot help but stop and take a minute just to admire the beauty of it before eating. It's like a work of art in front of you. As you eat each bite, you can't believe that food can taste this good. Simple, yet so delicious, in taste combinations that are perfect.

As the plates return to the kitchen, Vincenzo will check to make sure that they are empty, which is a signal to him that all is fine. If the plate is not empty, he usually wants to know why. He might even come out of the kitchen to greet you if you are a friend or local.

Dessert is a must, with creations such as hot chocolate cake (you know, the one I fell in love with), cream brûlée with star anise, lemon cream, melon mousse with lemon cake, and on and on. Each one is a creative combination from Vincenzo's culinary experience and his understanding of what people enjoy most. Each year in the early spring, the restaurant hosts a tasting event that gets much local and regional attention. Every year, the dessert is the star of the show, with people asking for the dish for years to come. Once a meal is over, careful respect is shown not to rush people off too soon. People are encouraged to stay as long as they like, to enjoy the music of the people around, the last few tastes of the flavors from dessert still fresh on the taste buds.

Coffee and grappa may be an option as well, as this is the traditional way to help digest the food just enjoyed. It is true that the bill will arrive, but only after asking more than once—usually three times. This is also very traditional. Vincenzo will peek out from the kitchen and give a big, warm smile and greeting as visitors leave.

If you are a local, he may give a quick kiss on both checks. Otherwise, a wave and kiss in the air to send you on your way. You float out of the restaurant, thinking to yourself, "Was that for real?" and then you realize that it was and that you had one of the best food experiences of your life.

I wanted to share a few of my favorite recipes from Vincenzo's restaurant. These are very traditional and served only in the region of Tuscany.

Soffiato di Pecorino con Pere al Vino Rosso (Pecorino Cheese Soufflé with Pears in a Red Wine Sauce)

14 tablespoons unsalted butter

½ cup all-purpose flour

12.5 ounces aged pecorino cheese, grated

8 large eggs

Salt and pepper to taste

Panko bread crumbs

For topping:

½ cup pecorino cheese grated

¼ cup olive oil

Preheat oven to 350 degrees.

Make a water bath (place a medium-sized metal or glass bowl over a medium saucepan, half filled with water). Place the pan over medium heat and melt the butter in a saucepan. Add the flour to the butter and mix together until smooth. Next, mix in the grated pecorino cheese a little at a time. When all of the cheese is mixed in, let stand for 10 minutes, until a bit cool.

Now, add the eggs, one at a time, mixing well after each one. Combine all ingredients well. Grease 10 individual aluminum or ceramic ramekins with butter and coat the inside with panko bread crumbs. Pour the pecorino cheese mixture into the ramekins, filling almost to the top of the tin.

Bake for 10 minutes in a 350 degree oven.

WINE SAUCE:

30 ounces of red wine (Chianti)

½ cup sugar

Four large pears (cut into small cubes)

Combine the wine, sugar, and pears in a saucepan. Cook until the wine reduces well (about 20-25 minutes). Pour over the individual soufflés and serve with freshly grated pecorino cheese and a drizzle of olive oil.

Serves 10 people.

Recipe note: Pecorino cheese is an aged sheep milk cheese traditionally found in Tuscany. This cheese can be found in the specialty cheese section of most grocery stores.

MALFATTI ALLA FIORENTINA (SPINACH AND RICOTTA CHEESE DUMPLINGS WITH BUTTER AND SAGE SAUCE)

18 ounces spinach (cooked and chopped, remove all water from the spinach; if frozen, thaw and squeeze out extra liquid)
18 ounces ricotta cheese (drain off extra liquid)
4 tablespoons all-purpose flour
5 large egg yolks
4 ounces parmesan cheese, grated
Salt and pepper to taste
1 cup salted butter melted
6-8 fresh sage leaves
4 ounces parmesan cheese, grated (for the top of the dumplings)
Coarse salt for the water.

Preheat oven to 350 degrees.

Mix the chopped, drained spinach, ricotta cheese, flour and egg yolks together in a bowl. Shape the Malfatti dumplings packing them tight using two large tablespoons (it will look like an oval dumpling). Place each dumpling on a sheet pan covered with parchment paper.

Bring a large pot of water to boil. Once the water is boiling, salt the water with about 2 tablespoons coarse salt. Place the Malfatti dumplings carefully into the boiling water for 5 minutes (4 to 6 at a time). The dumplings will float on the top when they are cooked well.

Take out of water with a slotted spoon and place on a baking sheet covered with parchment paper or sprayed with oil spray. Melt one cup of butter with sprigs of fresh sage for taste. Pour half of the sage butter over Malfatti and top with grated parmesan cheese.

Bake for 8-10 minutes at 350 degrees.

Serve with the remaining sage butter and grated parmesan cheese.

Serves 8-10 people.

Ragù Finto (Tomato and Vegetable Herb Sauce)

4 tablespoons olive oil
1 garlic clove
1 medium onion
3 carrots
4 celery stalks
2 sprigs of fresh or dried rosemary
2 tablespoons chopped fresh or dried parsley
½ cup dry white wine
2 tablespoons tomato paste
½ cup of water
Salt (to taste)
Fresh basil (5-6 leaves, chopped)
Parmesan cheese
Olive oil for serving

Place the vegetables together into a food processor and chop until fine. In a medium saucepan, add 4 tablespoons of olive oil to pan and warm over medium heat. Next add the vegetable mixture and sauté for 5 minutes, then add the white wine and the chopped rosemary. When the wine has evaporated, add the tomato paste and simmer for 15-20 minutes.

Add the basil and parsley just before serving. Serve with gnocchi with grated parmesan cheese over the top and add a drizzle of extra virgin olive oil.

The name of this sauce translates to mean "fake ragù" and is a poor man's dish that substitutes vegetables instead of meat.

LEMON CREAM

3 fresh lemons (medium size)
30 ounces heavy cream (just less than 2 pints)
¾ cup sugar

(Note: A food thermometer is needed for this recipe. Temperatures are measured in degrees F.)
Place the heavy cream and sugar in a medium saucepan and slowly warm over low to medium heat until the cream reaches a temperature of 167 degrees. Take off the heat and let cool slightly until the mixture reaches a temperature of 149 degrees.

While the mixture is cooling, zest the lemons and squeeze the juice into a small bowl. When zesting the lemon, take off all of the outer yellow peel, down to the white pith.

Once the cream reaches 149 degrees, stir in the lemon juice and lemon zest.

Pour the lemon cream into individual glass parfait dishes (the cream should fit in about 8-10 parfait dishes that are at least 4 ounces each). Let cool slightly (20 minutes). Place parfait glasses covered in plastic wrap in refrigerator.

The cream will set up and be ready to eat in 4-6 hours. This is best prepared the day before you plan to serve it. It can be stored in the refrigerator for 4-5 days.

Recipe note: The lemon cream pairs well with fresh berries or the lemon biscotti recipe that follows.

Lemon Almond and Pistachio Biscotti

½ cup unsalted butter (room temperature)

¾ cup sugar

1 large egg

1 tsp. vanilla extract

1 tsp. lemon extract

1 lemon (zested)

¾ tsp. baking powder

¾ tsp. sea salt

1 ¾ cups all-purpose flour

½ cup roasted almonds (whole)

½ cup roasted pistachios (whole)

Preheat oven to 375 degrees.

Cream together the butter and sugar. The mixture should be light yellow and smooth. Add the egg and beat well. Next add the vanilla and lemon extract, baking powder and salt. Mix well.

Zest the lemon and add to the dough. Add in the almonds and pistachios, mix well.

Add the flour 1 cup at a time, mixing well. You may need more or less flour depending on the humidity. The dough should not be too sticky. You should be able to handle it with your hands without sticking.

Separate the dough into three equal parts and form three logs of dough that are about 1½ inches wide and 10-12 inches long. Place on baking sheet that is covered with parchment paper.

Bake at 375 degrees for 10-12 minutes. The cookies should be light golden brown.

Let cool for about 5-10 minutes.

Reduce oven heat to 350 degrees.

Place the cookie logs on a cutting board and cut into individual slices about ½ inch wide (like slicing bread, except don't use a sawing motion when cutting, use a sharp knife and cut in one motion down through the cookies). Place the cookies back on the baking sheet with one side down. Bake again for 8-10 minutes until they are just slightly brown.

Recipe note: These biscotti (cookies) are a variation of the traditional almond biscotti called cantucci made in Italy. They are not as hard, but are still great to dip in coffee or tea or serve with the lemon cream.

12

Grandma's Gnocchi

At the end of the summer, I had plans to return to Minnesota to spend time with my family and work for a few weeks back at my job again. Vincenzo and I decided that we should first take time to travel to Abruzzo to meet his family. He said that they were all eager to meet me, his fiancée.

On our way to Abruzzo, which was about a six-hour drive from where we lived in Tuscany, we stopped in Rome to pick up Vincenzo's younger brother, Gian-Piero, or as I sometimes call him, JP. JP is like a giant version of Vincenzo, but with night and day differences in their personalities. Vincenzo is steady, reliable, predictable, and mostly traditional. JP is everything else. He is unpredictable, loves to joke around, is a bit of a procrastinator, and breaks every rule in the book, especially according to his mother. However, everyone can't help but fall in love with JP as well. JP is over six feet tall with a warm smile and a quirky sense of humor.

We pulled up to meet him on a busy street on the outskirts of Rome just outside his apartment. I knew it was him because he looked just like Vincenzo.

He walked up to me and gave me a big bear hug and said to me, "Ciao bella." Followed by these exact words: "Anyone who has agreed to marry my brother has to be a good woman—and very patient. Are you sure you know what you're getting into?" he added with a little smile.

After finding JP, I hopped in the backseat with the luggage, and we headed east from Rome across Italy toward the Adriatic Sea. On the way, I saw rugged and steep mountain views and what seemed like hundreds of tunnels traveling directly through the mountains. As we got closer to his home, it became dark and so I had no idea what the landscape was like.

Vincenzo and his brother talked continuously in the front of the car to each other. It was obvious from the way the two brothers were connecting that they were close. Vincenzo's voice was full of happiness. It had been many months since they last saw each other. They were a close family as it was just the two of them and their parents.

Every so often Vincenzo would check on me in the rearview mirror and send me a wink and a smile. I thought it was strange that I could barely understand what they were saying to each other. They were speaking Italian, but most words were a mystery to me. Vincenzo had mentioned that the region he was from spoke a dialect of Italian that was not quite the same as the true Italian I had learned while living in Tuscany. I did not think it would be that much different, but it was. I was in trouble. They were speaking Abruzzese.

As we got closer to his home, the car seemed to just know the way. Vincenzo and his brother were so busy talking that they were oblivious to the fact that the road climbing the mountain to his house was full of hairpin turns and potholes. I was in the back, just hoping for the best and praying that I would not be sick. To them, this was the road home, nothing special or unusual.

When we arrived at his parents' house, all I could see was an old cement home that seemed like it was on the very top of a mountain. It was dark, but I could make out lights down below in the distance. I had no idea how far up the mountain we had traveled, but I could sense the height, even in the darkness. And the place smelled different to me, deep humidity, more farm-like, with noises of the night birds and the scurry of what must have been a cat in the distance. I would have to wait until morning to let the horizon reveal itself.

I became a bit nervous now. Soon I was going to meet my future husband's parents for the first time. I was terribly worried what they would think of me. An American woman who could barely speak Italian, not to mention speak or understand the dialect that they spoke.

We walked into the house together, and I immediately smelled something divine coming from the kitchen. As we entered, this is what I saw: a kitchen that had not been updated in about forty years, with a stainless steel countertop, a few cupboards, a sink and small gas stove. In the corner near the stove was a tiny built-in refrigerator. In the middle of the room, a small wooden table was set with dishes for five, decorated with a traditional blue-and-white checked tablecloth that is typical from the region. Two loaves of crusty bread were resting on a cloth on the table with a knife next to it, and a little aluminum olive oil decanter with a long spout had been placed next to the bread.

His parents were busy getting dinner ready. His father was tending to a fire in the fireplace next to the table, and his mother was stirring a pot on the stove, checking to see if the sauce was just right. They both turned to greet me with warm smiles and each gave me kisses on both checks as Vincenzo introduced me. Vincenzo's grandfather—also named Vincenzo—lived with them too; however, as was his habit, he had already eaten early and gone up to sleep for the night. I would meet him tomorrow.

His father, Angiolino, had the same warm brown eyes as Vincenzo and so this made me feel at home. He greeted me by saying, "I have a beautiful future daughter-in-law. We've been looking forward to meeting you."

His mother, Anna Concetta, was more focused on her two boys. She had many questions for them as they arrived, not so many for me yet, but that time would come. She seemed to have nervous energy all around her, as most mothers might when seeing their two sons in person after a long period.

"How was the trip over from Rome? Did you stop to eat anything? Are you tired?" she wanted to know. All without stopping for anyone to actually answer. Perhaps she knew they would not actually give an answer.

Next, without really pausing, she said, "What do you think of the menu for the evening?"

She went on to list all of the things she had planned for the evening, primarily directing this at Vincenzo and JP for approval.

"I've made pasta with my canned tomatoes, roasted rabbit with potatoes. I just put them in the coals of the fire. Oh, and I got the cheese from the neighbor that you love, cured sausages and a salad of greens and fennel." She stopped for expressions.

Vincenzo and JP just looked at each other and said, "Oh boy, here we go."

"What do you think, it's enough? Or maybe I should make another pasta dish?" Hearing from everyone that it was more than enough, she smiled looking back at the stove, regarding all of the items she had prepared in process and returned to stirring and checking the sauce. "Okay, I guess we have enough for tonight."

Next she turned to me and spoke in true Italian, not dialect. "It's so nice to meet you. Please call me Concetta. My real name is Anna Concetta, but here are so many women named Anna in this area, I go by Concetta. How was the trip for you?" she asked.

"I'm so happy to be here, but I'm a little car sick from all of the curves in the road," I replied. In my mind I was already thinking about how I was going to eat everything that she had mentioned.

To which, she turned to Vincenzo and scolded him: "What did you do? Don't you know that not everyone is used to our crazy roads here? You need to be more careful."

He looked at me and her and said, "Yes, JP and I got to talking and I was probably driving too fast." He came over and kissed my head.

We sat around the table and started eating our first meal together. Vincenzo's father cut the bread, which was passed around to each person where we set a piece or two to the side of our plates for the meal. As he cut the bread, I noticed how large his hands were. His father was a mechanic for years and had developed giant muscles in his fingers and hands from all of the work he had done. He was also very tall, around six feet with dark hair, full lips, a traditional Italian nose and glasses. His mother was very short, less than five feet, matronly in shape, with short, red hair and eyes that never seemed to stop looking as if she was getting ready for the next question. Now I understood the big differences in height between Vincenzo and his taller brother.

As we started the meal, I could see that I was the main attraction for the evening. Vincenzo's parents were very kind and so gentle on this first meeting. I caught the little glances my way as I was eating. I loved the pasta the most. It was rigatoni with a tomato sauce that was fresh and delicious. My favorite part was the fact that the sauce and cheese would hide inside the tubes of pasta as well as around it. This was Concetta's signature tomato sauce. We all ate it with a ton of parmesan cheese over it, and I used my bread to clean my plate.

His mother frequently checked with me. "Do you like the food? How about a little more?"

Vincenzo insisted each time, "She does not eat as much as we do. She is not used to this." Finally he just said, "Mom, leave her alone."

I could tell that this was going to be an interesting visit from a foodie perspective. I carefully paid attention to the traditions around the table and tried to make mental notes to help me in the next days. I did my best to eat as much as possible that evening. It was all so delicious. I knew that this was an important show of respect. They laughed when I was too shy to use my hands to eat the roasted rabbit off the bones.

His mother looked at me and said, "Look, the meat next to the bone is the best tasting, pick it up with your hands and eat it," as she bit into the tender roasted rabbit with all the gusto of a farmer who had not eaten for hours.

Concetta's Mother Tomato Sauce

2 tablespoons olive oil
2 stalks of celery, chopped small (add a few of the celery leaves chopped as well)
¼ small onion, chopped small
1 small zucchini (diced into small pieces)
1 clove garlic (leave whole)
¼ green or red pepper (diced into small pieces)
1 large can (28 ounces) of whole tomatoes (Note: I really like the taste of Muir Glen tomatoes. San Marzano tomatoes are also a great choice.)
10 ounces strained tomato sauce (Note: I love to use Pomi brand in the box.)
Salt to taste
Parmesan cheese (grated over the top when serving with pasta)

In a medium sauce pan, drizzle 2 tablespoons olive oil. Add the chopped celery, onions, zucchini, and peppers. Sauté for 2-3 minutes over medium heat. Add the can of whole tomatoes, squeezing them with your hands to break them apart as you add each one. Next, add the strained tomato sauce and stir well. Add the whole garlic clove at the end. Cover and let simmer on low heat for 60-90 minutes. Take it off the heat and let it sit until you are ready to serve.

You can start this sauce in the morning and let it sit on the stove until you need it later. The longer it sits, the better it tastes. The vegetables are cut so small that in the end, they just melt into the sauce. You don't actually get pieces of them in your mouth.

Just prior to serving, retrieve the garlic clove from the sauce and add salt to taste. This is enough sauce for 6-8 people.

This is a versatile sauce that you can use over any pasta. I love it with rigatoni as I first tasted it. Serve it with freshly grated parmesan cheese and a drizzle of olive oil.

It has taken me a few years to get this recipe written down. Concetta always started to tell me a few of the ingredients and then would get distracted by something. One day I watched her make it as she was busy talking and wrote down everything she put in.

As the conversation ebbed and flowed that evening, I did not understand much. They would drift in and out of true Italian and the Abruzzo dialect with each other naturally. I did my best and would frequently ask Vincenzo to translate in Italian to me what had just been said. Both of his parents have a great sense of humor, but it took me years to appreciate it.

After our meal, we sat by the fire. I must have looked like I was ready to drop into bed to sleep. At midnight, we said our goodbyes until the next day. Vincenzo and I had arranged to stay in a house that belonged to his cousin and was a few minutes away.

As we said goodnight, his parents mentioned how much they had looked forward to meeting me. I told them, in my broken Italian, "I also look forward to getting to know you both better."

At the end, I added, "Thank you for creating such a kind and gentle man who I will spend the rest of my life with."

They both looked at me, and then each other and that was it. I had won their hearts. Vincenzo kissed me on the cheek and helped me out to the car.

The next day, I woke up early and peeked out the window of the house where we were staying. I will never forget the first time I experienced the view of the steep mountains on one side of the house, and a view in the far distance on the other side out to the Adriatic Sea. Vincenzo's home village is steeped in rustic beauty with a landscape I had yet to experience during my time in Italy. The village is set on a ridge within the smaller mountains of Abruzzo—and in the distance, the snowcapped central Apennine Mountains.

The village where Vincenzo is from, Roccascalegna, is medieval with an old castle built on a stone ridge from the 800s. It had a very different mountaintop feeling than those

in Tuscany. The countryside was dotted with steep hills covered with olive groves and farms. The houses were made mostly of stucco and the surroundings much more rustic and farm-like than in Chianti where we lived.

As we were traveling to meet Vincenzo's extended family, I made him drive slowly so I could take it all in. The steep mountains in the distance had little villages perched on the top of them. It was hard for me to imagine how someone might get there, or live there. He kept looking at me like it was nothing that special.

At one point, we encountered an older woman dressed very traditionally—a dark blue dress with an apron over it and a dark scarf covering her head. She was carrying a basket from one house to another on one of her shoulders. I noticed that some of the older women here wore black each day as a symbol of mourning if they were widows. This was a long-standing tradition in southern Italy. As I looked around, I could see little stalls with cattle and, in the distance, fields of golden wheat near the flatter land that sloped toward the Adriatic.

As we were driving, Vincenzo told me that this area is famous for the production of pasta and is home to the famous De Cecco pasta. In fact, this is Vincenzo's favorite dry pasta to work with in his restaurant, so now I understood why. He also notes that De Cecco pasta is the best pasta to hold up well in a dish and stay al dente. Many of the people from this area work in the De Cecco pasta factory or other factories producing goods such as textiles and cars. With the proximity to the Adriatic, it is a busy industrial port.

We headed back up the narrow mountain roads again making our way to his parents' home, this time in the daylight. Around every curve, I could see more and more of the big mountain in the distance that looked like it was a giant volcano with a flat crater at the top. I wondered how long ago this mountain was created. In the near distance, little hilltop villages looked like they were from a fairytale, with the houses all perched up on the steep hill, seeming to cling to each other to stay in place. In the middle and usually at the highest spot was a church with a bell tower piercing the sky above it.

We climbed higher and higher, and just as we were taking the hairpin turn that made me so sick the night before,

Vincenzo told me that the land around this curve is owned by his family. This is where they have the olive trees for olive oil production each year.

As I looked, I could see a collection of old rugged olive trees against the blue sky with puffy white clouds. We have since named that curve "Sheryl's curve" because I usually have to remind him to go slowly around the curve for me or I will lose my appetite for whatever is waiting for me at his mother's table.

As we approached his house, I started to get nervous again. I was worried. I told him, "Another day of trying to figure out what everyone is saying. And your mom always has so many questions and is worried about if I am eating enough. It's exhausting."

"Don't worry, just be yourself and everyone will love you," Vincenzo said as he looked at me with his warm, reassuring smile. He knew exactly how I was feeling. We joined a couple of close friends who were visiting for a midmorning coffee. This was just the start of getting to know all of Vincenzo's cousins, aunties, and uncles, some of whom are not actually related at all, but he calls them his aunt, uncle, or cousin. During this first gathering, I was bombarded with curious looks and questions.

One of his friends, Simona, said, "Wow, she is American. How did you meet? Does she speak Italian? Does she understand our dialect?"

Simona's sister, Enza, asked, "Is her hair really blond [even touching it]? Look at those blue eyes. So exotic."

"Oh, she is a nurse. When are you getting married?" asked Simona. They were all talking at once.

Finally, we got to the heart of what was most important here on a daily basis. They both asked, "What is your mom making for lunch?" This is followed by a list of their favorite dishes that Concetta makes. Roast lamb, chicken in tomato sauce, cheese balls with sauce, and on and on.

As we were discussing the lunch menu, Concetta added some commentary. "Everyone always says how lucky I am to have a chef for a son. But instead I'm always cooking for him."

He looked at me and agreed. "It's true, no one can cook like my mom. Not even me."

Finally, as they were leaving, they asked, "Do you have plans for dinner tomorrow evening? You must come over to our house for dinner while you are here." It was all too much for me to track.

Later that morning, we walked to greet Zia Elisa and Zio Pietro and family who lived in a neighboring house. The family was three generations living together. This was family on Vincenzo's father's side. I could see that Zia Elisa and her daughter-in-law Tiziana were starting to prepare their noon meal of pasta in the large side kitchen. They too had curious looks and many questions. Coffee and homemade sweets were offered and accepted.

Over the next few days, I met at least a hundred new people, all whom seemed to be relatives of Vincenzo in some way or another. I also met a few of his childhood friends and began to understand a few of the words from the dialect they were speaking.

I also started to notice a pattern of foods. At around 1:00 p.m., we always had a traditional lunch, which included a beautiful ceramic dish of pasta covered in homemade tomato sauce and pecorino cheese, eaten with crusty bread. In the evening, meals usually included hearty meat dishes with roast chicken, rabbit, and lamb. Most people still roasted the meat in their fireplaces with a little metal basket holding the meat over the coals of the fire.

The rhythm of eating goes like this, from start to finish of the day: morning cappuccino with something sweet, followed by lunch at 1:00 p.m. including pasta (a must), sauce, cheeses, cured meats, bread, olive oil, fruit, and coffee. This was followed by an afternoon nap for an hour, followed by another cup of coffee with a sweet treat about 4:00 p.m.

At 7:00 p.m., a small snack is offered, which may include a little sandwich or something salty. Dinner was served around 8:30 or 9:00 p.m. which is typically a roasted meat dish with a side of vegetables, salad, and potatoes. Fruit and dessert may be offered. At the end of the day, planning for the next day's meal started, with plans to go to the market and pick up fresh ingredients for the day just after breakfast.

During my visit, I also met Vincenzo's grandfather, Vincenzo. It's tradition to name the first son after the father's father. I could see that his grandfather was a bit different than the rest of the family. He seemed to have sharp edges to him, not very warm and friendly and quite withdrawn. His grandfather had a tracheostomy from cancer and so did not have a voice. He also walked with a cane and seemed a bit frail.

Nonno Vincenzo mostly lived in his own world. When I went over to his chair to say hello, he looked up directly into my eyes and gave me a smile of approval.

Each night, as we dropped into bed, I had a million questions about the experiences from the day. One night in the darkness with our heads sleepy on our pillows, I could not help but ask what it was like to grow up in this area.

Vincenzo told me stories from when he was little. He said, "My brother and I lived here in this family house with three generations of family members. With my great-grandfather, my grandparents on my father's side, and my parents. It was crowded at times, and always something was going on."

"Where did you sleep?" I asked.

"Well, the house had two kitchens, one living room, three bedrooms back then, and for many years, the bath and shower were located outside in the storage shed. I slept in a little bed in the same room as my grandparents. In the winter it was so cold upstairs that I had to wear a hat and gloves to bed," he said with an expression of gratitude that he did not have to do that anymore.

He went on to say, "In the cold winters, when I would go out to the bathroom or to take a shower, I had to put on my coat, hat, and boots."

He went on to explain that before everyone had indoor plumbing, the village also had communal water sources where the ladies would bring their baskets of laundry to wash. Most farmers made their own baskets for harvesting olives, aging cheeses, and other uses. We have a collection of antique woven baskets that his grandfather Camillo (who is no longer living) and his brother on his mother's side, also Angiolino, made by hand in a very traditional way. At age eighty-four, Angiolino still worked in his little workshop every day weaving baskets or carving wooden utensils. On that first visit, he gave me a wooden spoon from his collection that I treasure each time I use it.

Zio Angiolino making a basket by hand.

His grandmother Ida (his father's mother) was a fantastic cook and usually made the primary meals for the entire family. This is the grandmother who originally taught Vincenzo how to cook. Cooking for such a large family was a full-time job. She made gnocchi, fresh pasta, sauces, roasted meats, bruschetta, and salads. Everything was made from local food or produce, either from their garden or sourced from the farmers who they lived among.

The pasta was made early in the morning so that they would have it for lunch. In the evening, grilled meats would sit on the open fireplace in the communal kitchen. Fresh cheese was made just next door at a neighbor's who had cows. Meats came from local sources as well. Many were from their own farm. Each year, they canned enough tomatoes for the entire year.

Each farm also had olive trees and produced their own oil. The olive oil from Abruzzo was absolutely stunning. Bright green in color with a buttery, fruity taste that was so mellow in the mouth. The oil was stored in large terra-cotta or steel vats with generous helpings of oil infused into each traditional dish. In each small village, you would find a community mill to grind and press the olives each year with the farmers lined up to take turns with their wagon loads of olives during la raccolta.

Many families still practiced the traditional way of harvesting olives, by hand. The trees are surrounded by nets placed on the ground around them and each person harvesting also wore a handwoven basket cinched around their waist to collect the olives as they stood on ladders and used a small hand rake to coax the ripe olives from the trees.

Grandma's Gnocchi

2 pounds medium russet potatoes, cleaned

1½ cups all-purpose flour

1 large egg

1 tsp. salt

In a large pot, boil the potatoes in salted water until tender to the fork (40-60 minutes).

When the potatoes are tender, take them off the heat and drain. When cool, peel the skins off the potatoes. Rice the potatoes with a hand potato ricer or potato mill and place into a large bowl. If you don't have either of these, you can use a hand potato masher.

Add 1½ cups of flour, 1 tsp. of salt, and mix together with the egg.

Use your hands to mix together until it forms a dough ball (dough should be moist but not sticky).

Cut around 8 sections of the dough off and roll each section of the dough by hand (use flour if needed to keep from sticking) to make a long log that is no higher than about ½ inch (should be like the thickness of your thumb).

Cut ½-inch sections of the log with a knife to form small gnocchi dumplings. There are many other techniques for this, such as rolling the dumplings off a fork or a wooden tool that has ridges in it, but this was the simple way that Vincenzo's grandmother always made them. They look like little square pillows.

Bring a large pot of water to a boil, add 2 tablespoons salt, then boil the gnocchi (around twenty dumplings at a time) for 4–5 minutes (when they float easily to the top of the pot, they are ready). Remove from the water with a slotted spoon and add to the pan with your sauce already warm.

Continue cooking until you have all of the batches of gnocchi boiled. If using pesto, add the pesto to your dish first and then add the gnocchi on top and gently stir.

Serve with your favorite tomato or pesto sauce.

Serves 6–8 people.

Vincenzo's grandmother Ida was the one who taught him to make fresh gnocchi with potatoes, eggs, and flour—starting at age nine. He told me that as she was teaching him, she told him to "treat the gnocchi as if you are caressing a woman's skin, as delicate as possible."

He told me that he started hanging out with his grandmother as a child because he was usually hungry and was curious when the food would be ready. She just put him to work when he would join her.

Some of these dishes are old-school recipes he used in his restaurant. The traditional foods from rural Abruzzo are poor man's dishes (vegetables used instead of meat), much like those in Tuscany, using every possible option to feed the entire extended family. Many of these traditions are still followed today. Most family homes are still multigenerational with communal kitchens where handmade pasta and breads are still made.

His mother makes a cheese ball, or as they are called in the local dialect, Pallotte Cace e Ove, that were traditionally used in red sauce as a substitute when meat was not available. One day, she was making them in the morning when we arrived. The house smelled delicious. I could see that she was frying them and placing them on paper towels. I thought maybe they were some sort of donut.

As I approached to say hello, she looked at my expression and realized I wanted a sample, so she said, "Go ahead and try one."

As I popped one in my mouth, I must have had the best expression on my face. "Wow, these are incredible. What in the world is in here?" was what came out of my mouth.

"Cheese, egg, and bread," she said. Later, lunch included the cheese balls that had been placed in her tomato sauce where they bubbled around and became almost puffy with the sauce. Inside, they were tender, melted, and the yummiest exotic thing I had tasted so far. I loved cheese, so these were a big hit with me.

Concetta's Pallotte Cace e Ove (Fried Cheese Balls)

2.5 pounds white cheddar cheese curds (Cheese curds are the closest type of cow's milk cheese I can find in the States to make this recipe taste like it did in Italy.)

4 large eggs

1 clove garlic (minced)

1/8 cup parsley (chopped)

1/2 cup bread crumbs (use stale bread or Panko)

Olive oil for frying (you will need about 35 ounces or 1 liter). Use light olive oil for this.

Place the cheese curds into a food processor and chop until the cheese is broken down into very small pieces. Place in a medium mixing bowl. Next add the eggs, minced garlic, parsley, and bread crumbs and mix well.

Using your hands, form the cheese mixture into 1-inch round balls, pack them as tight as possible. Place them on a sheet pan until you have used all of the cheese mixture.

Next, place a very heavy frying pan with deep sides (cast iron is perfect, but others will work as well) on the stove. Add the olive oil and start to heat over medium-high heat.

You will need a large platter or baking sheet covered with paper towels and a slotted spoon or small wire spider to retrieve the balls when they are done frying as well.

After 2 minutes, test the oil by placing one of the smaller cheese balls in to see if the oil is ready for frying. It should immediately start to bubble and fry. If it doesn't, wait another minute and try again,

Place 6-8 of the cheese balls in the oil at a time and fry until a deep, golden brown. Turn the cheese balls every few seconds to make sure all sides are fried well. This may take 4-5 minutes.

Once the cheese balls are golden brown in color, remove from oil and place on paper towels to cool.

Serve the cheese balls alongside a tomato sauce for dipping, or eat the traditional way, by placing the cheese balls into Concetta's tomato sauce and let them bubble around in the sauce for 5-6 minutes. The sauce and cheese balls can be served with or without pasta as well.

I always enjoy eating these just as I did the first time I had them. Like a little cheese donut when they are fresh from the fryer, and in Concetta's tomato sauce, with no pasta added—just the cheese balls and the sauce.

Serves 4–6 people.

Recipe note: This recipe can be doubled. That is how Concetta makes it. The cheese balls store well in the freezer as well. Cool them well after frying and place 8–10 in a freezer bag. Thaw well prior to using and place into tomato sauce for 8–10 minutes to warm prior to serving.

Later during this same visit, Vincenzo recounted a story about Nonno Camillo who had a donkey that he used every day to get out to the field. He would get on the donkey and click his tongue, and the beast would know by the number of clicks where he needed to go. Nonno did not have a driver's license, and with the donkey, he could get anywhere he needed to. Vincenzo remembers his grandfather would frequently fall asleep on the donkey on the way home. Once the donkey reached home, he would signal that he was home by braying a hee haw, which would wake up his grandfather.

Vincenzo told me that they did not need to travel far in those days to have everything they needed. The house was within walking distance to a little shop where they could buy pantry items as well as close to the church and cemetery. Everyone helped each other out to get by, trading meats, cheeses, vegetables, and pasta with each other.

His father eventually opened a mechanic shop and fixed cars just across the road from their house. He was known in the village as the car doctor because he could diagnose a problem with the car just by listening to it run—if it did run, that is.

Many from the older generation did not speak true Italian as we know it. They spoke in a dialect that is known only to people from the small surrounding area. This is one of the reasons I had so much trouble communicating among the older family members. Vincenzo told me that even from village to village there were differences in the language.

Vincenzo recounted the stories of when he started to go to culinary school, which was only about thirty minutes from where he grew up. He would ride his motor scooter down the hill to the town at the bottom of the mountain where the train station was. If he missed his train, he would hitchhike his way to school. Those were the days when it was still safe to do this, and it was frequently how he would get from place to place.

Villa Santa Maria culinary school was famous for training in traditional Italian cuisine. I think he felt fortunate to live so close to the school that could provide him with the training he needed to do what he loved so much—even today after working as a chef for over twenty years.

Once he finished the first three years of training, he was sent around the country as an apprentice chef to learn the dishes of each region during the summer months. This was real hands-on training. He worked restaurant kitchens in Venice, Milan, Northern Italy, Rome, and Florence. Many times, the restaurants were located in famous hotels with four- or five-star ratings. In each different location where he cooked, he learned the traditional foods of the region. This is why his skills and knowledge have such depth. He knows the history and traditions that are behind each specialty. Each region has its own unique pastas and sauces as well. It is fascinating to understand how diverse the food traditions are from all of Italy.

In the north, the dishes are hearty with cheese, cream, and meats and influenced by the surrounding countries such as Germany, France, and Switzerland. In the south, dishes are smattered with local influences from Greece and Turkey, with spices, tomatoes, olives, and fish.

After five years, at age twenty-one, he finished cooking school and served one year of military training, which was mandatory at that time. When they discovered he was a chef, they moved him from munitions to the kitchen where he improved the quality of food for everyone eating at the mess hall. He told me that this is where he learned how to cook for 2,000 people.

All areas of Italy use what is local first and foremost. Italy only imports certain items to the country as they are very proud of the foods they produce on their own. The wines and cheeses from each area are also diverse. Italians in this area are primarily farmers at the heart of everything they do. This is what I loved the most about the traditions of Abruzzo. My Minnesota family is deeply rooted in the traditions of farming and farm living so this farm-to-fork cycle made me feel comfortably at home.

One morning as we stopped at his mother's house, she was busy making pizzelle, a sweet waffle in a rectangle or heart shape. The batter was made with eggs, flour, and milk with a little aroma of vanilla or brandy added. The waffle iron was traditional, warmed over a gas burner or directly over the flames of the fire as it had been done for centuries. As he saw the pizzelle, Vincenzo's eyes got as wide as his smile.

All he could say to his mom was, "Where is the Nutella?"

She pointed to the table where she had the jar of Nutella out for him already. Nutella is a creamy, chocolate hazelnut spread that is used in Italy like we use peanut butter in the States. It goes on bread and sweets, in pies, over gelato and can be eaten directly out of the jar with a spoon as well. Vincenzo once admitted to me that he had eaten an entire jar over a period of just two days. Now, that's my kind of man. We sat at the table and spread Nutella on the warm pizzelle and ate them to our hearts' desire. This was my first taste of a treat that I know well now. These are part of every celebration that occurs in this region.

PIZZELLE

6 large eggs (separated)
6 tablespoons sugar
½ cup olive oil
6 tablespoons all-purpose flour (you may need more or less depending on how large the eggs are)
1 tsp. baking powder
1 tsp. vanilla extract
2 tsp. grated lemon or orange zest (optional)

In a large mixing bowl or using a stand mixer, beat the egg whites until they start to form soft peaks. Add in the egg yolks one at a time, mixing well after each one. Next add in the sugar, olive oil, vanilla, and orange zest. Mix well. Add the flour and baking powder at the very end. Mix until the batter is smooth and looks similar to pancake or waffle batter.

Depending on the thickness of the batter, you may need to add 1-2 tablespoons more or less flour. When I tried to get exact measurements for this one, it was really hard. Concetta kept saying, "Just enough. I usually put in a large spoon of flour for every egg, but if the egg is really big, you might need extra."

In Abruzzo, the pizzelle waffles are traditionally made with a rectangle-shaped iron that has a diamond pattern to it. The iron is placed over the gas flame on top of the stove or in the fireplace. Each one is made by heating the iron with a little olive oil added for the first one to keep them from sticking. The iron is turned immediately after adding the batter and continued to cook for about 10-15 seconds. The waffles should look golden brown and come out of the iron easily.

Cool the pizzelle on paper towels and store in a plastic container in a cool dry place for up to a week. These are delicious served with ice cream or made into a sandwich with a layer of Nutella.

Note: In Minnesota, we have an electric pizzelle iron that makes five little heart waffles each time. Thank goodness, Nutella is available everywhere in the United States now.

Later during the week, we met up with Vincenzo's best friend Antonio and his family. Antonio and his wife had a little boy, Michele, who was celebrating his first birthday in a few days. Vincenzo is Michele's godfather. This is a very important role in Italy, so he takes it quite seriously. The family had been planning the birthday celebration for weeks. Vincenzo had planned to make one of his celebration cakes for the occasion.

As we talked and caught up together, I could see that Antonio and his family also lived with multiple generations in the same house. This house was much grander in nature, with marble floors and a modern kitchen. As the planning continued, Vincenzo and I eventually went down to the basement area where the household had its ovens and pasta-making area. The oven was a beauty, still fired by wood and aged with years of patina.

Antonio's mother was baking bread along with a version of a rustic flat bread infused with olive oil that is called pizza scima. Another first for me and it was delicious, with a smoky flavor from the fire outside and inside was soft and flaky from the heavy dose of olive oil and salt.

Pizza Scima

3 ½ cups all-purpose flour

1 cup extra virgin olive oil

1 cup water

1 tsp. salt

Preheat oven to 425 degrees.

Mix together all ingredients in a large bowl. Once the dough starts to come together, take it out and knead it slightly on a floured surface until the dough forms a smooth ball. Place the dough ball on a piece of parchment paper and roll the dough into a 9-inch round circle that is about ½ inch in thickness.

Transfer the parchment paper with the dough to a cooking sheet. Score the top of the dough with knife making a deep crisscross diamond pattern. Place on the middle rack of the oven and bake at 425 degrees for 30-35 minutes. Let cool for 30 minutes. Break off pieces, eat, and enjoy. Cover any remaining bread with a tea towel.

We planned to make the Vincenzo's version of his celebration cake the next day. It was to serve over a hundred people, so it was a major undertaking. In the morning, we gathered the ingredients we needed including puff pastry, sugar, eggs, cream, chocolate, berries, and flowers. It was a long day together, but I was excited to help him make the cake for his godchild and get to know the family of his best friend.

We started in the morning after a heavy dose of coffee, and our car was loaded down with all of the ingredients. As we arrived at the house, Antonio's mother said that the ovens were ready for the pastry to bake. Because it was the end of July, we were already sweating from the heat and humidity of the morning.

As the day went on, Vincenzo carefully created the chocolate mousse with me sampling it at every chance I had. This was followed by the making of the Chantilly cream. There were huge bowls of both layers ready to assemble the cake. We realized that it was too hot to make the cake down in the lower kitchen, so we took everything up to the modern kitchen where they even had air conditioning.

The large dining table was covered with a plastic tablecloth, where he assembled the work of art for the party the next day. Everyone watched as he carefully cut the pastry to the size and shape he wanted and then started to layer the chocolate mousse, followed by more pastry, then the cream layer gets started.

I had been washing and cutting berries the entire time. The cream layer was dotted with fresh strawberries, blackberries, and blueberries and was then topped with another layer of puff pastry. Fresh whipped cream was placed over the top of this. Finally, Vincenzo carefully decorated the top with a few decorations, flowers, and a long cookie that looked like a ribbon where he wrote, "Buon Compleanno Michele."

The next day, we arrived at Antonio's family house to help with the birthday preparations. A gathering of ladies were carefully cutting all kinds of fresh fruit into tiny little pieces for a macedonia, the Italian version of a fruit cocktail. The fresh breads and pizzas were everywhere. A large roasted pork called porchetta was visible on a long wooden board, and the men were all in the lower kitchen cutting prosciutto and sausages that had been cured directly by the family.

As the afternoon went on, people started to arrive with presents and bottles of wine and other goodies. The celebration started around 6:00 p.m. with prosecco for the adults and sodas for the kids. We ate and celebrated into the night. The celebration cake was a huge hit, with people taking pieces and carefully enjoying each bite. The party ended around 1:00 a.m., when everyone pitched in to help in the cleanup.

I remember saying to Vincenzo, "I have never seen a birthday party like that."

To which he responded, "That's nothing, you should see what happens when a couple gets married."

I looked at him with weary eyes and said, "We are in for it, aren't we?" He just smiled and rubbed my tired feet and tucked me into bed. The next day, I had to pack my bags as I was flying back to Minnesota soon. It had been quite an experience meeting everyone from his family as well as his friends. I remember sitting in the plane on the way home for a visit to Minnesota wondering what my future would be like and thinking to myself, I hope I'm ready for this.

13

What Would Our First Christmas Be without Lasagna?

I returned to Italy in the late fall and settled back into life with Vincenzo. The fall and winter season can be mild in Tuscany until around January. Our collection of geraniums was still blooming in December as we decorated our little terrace with Christmas lights. We decided to use a small potted rosemary bush as our little Christmas tree in our apartment as we had no room for a bigger tree. I loved the fragrance of the rosemary in the house and frequently snipped branches from it as I used it to top focaccia bread that I made on a regular basis.

Nativity scenes were a must in Italy during Christmas. One day we stopped into an antique shop in Siena and bought a ceramic angel with her wings outstretched and inside was the nativity of Mary, Joseph, and baby Jesus. It is traditional to wait until Christmas Eve to place the baby in the manger, so I carefully put baby Jesus away until that time.

I wanted to bring my family traditions to our home as we celebrated our first Christmas together, so I organized a Christmas cookie baking day at our apartment. I invited Emma to help me as she loved baking with me. The day of the baking arrived and we started early in the morning making traditional cut-out cookies with shortbread and almond frosting.

We made my mom's sugar cookie cut-outs and decorated angels, stars, bells, and Christmas trees. I had made different colors of frosting and had every kind of sprinkle and decoration I could find. We made some of the most colorful and creative cookies I had ever seen. I might even say they were works of art.

Later we made thumbprint cookies with homemade raspberry jam as well as my recipe of Christmas biscotti with pistachios and dried cranberries with white chocolate. When Vincenzo arrived home later that day, we just smiled at each other as the house was taken over by cookies, frosting, and sprinkles. We had so much fun baking and listening to Christmas music. For weeks after, I found sprinkles on our tile floor.

Our little village was also preparing for Christmas. As with everything here, this was a community effort. The men put up a large, live pine tree in the middle of the square and decorated it with little white lights. This was just outside of our apartment, so I felt as if we had our own private Christmas tree to look at every day.

The children of the village thought that the tree was too plain and so they all made handmade Christmas decorations and placed them on the tree in the days just before Christmas. I noticed that they were out decorating the tree, so I brought out a big plate of the Christmas cookies we had made. The kids loved them, and so did their parents.

This became an annual tradition for us each year in the village—decorating together and enjoying Christmas treats from my house. Slowly, I was being accepted as part of the village family as I revealed who I was to them. I wanted to show how much I appreciated the culture and traditions, and also add my touch of how I loved to care for others, with generosity and great food. It felt comfortable and good.

THUMBPRINT COOKIES

1 cup walnuts (reserve ½ cup for coating the cookies)
½ cup unsalted butter
1 egg
¼ cup sugar
1 tsp. vanilla extract
1 cup oat flour or all-purpose flour
½ tsp salt
½ cup of your favorite jam (I love to use both raspberry and apricot jam for a variety.)

Preheat the oven to 350 degrees.

Spread the walnuts on a cookie sheet and toast in the oven for about 6-8 minutes. Cool and set aside. When cool, place the nuts in a food processor and pulse the nuts until they are finely chopped. Variation: you can also use vibrant chopped green pistachios for this recipe instead of walnuts. The green color along with the red raspberry jam are perfect for Christmas time.

Cream the butter and sugar with a hand mixer until light and fluffy. Add the egg and vanilla extract, mix well. Next add in ½ cup of the chopped walnuts, the flour and salt and stir until the dough is well combined.

Wrap the dough in plastic wrap and place in the refrigerator for 30 minutes to an hour.

Take the dough out of the refrigerator and roll into small balls (about ½ inch round). Roll each ball with the remaining chopped walnuts. Place the cookies on a parchment-lined cookie sheet and use your thumb to make an indentation in the cookie. Carefully spoon a small amount of jam into the indentation. It may help to warm the jam a bit to make it easy to work with.

Bake the cookies for 10 minutes or until golden brown. These cookies are best eaten within a few days. That never seemed to be a problem for me.

MOM'S CHRISTMAS COOKIES

1 cup unsalted butter (room temperature)

1 cup sugar

1 large egg

1 tsp. vanilla extract

1 tsp. almond extract

2 tsp. baking powder

½ tsp salt

3 cups all-purpose flour

Preheat oven to 400 degrees.

In a large bowl, cream the butter and sugar together with an electric mixer until light and creamy. Next add the egg, vanilla, and almond extract and beat well. Add the baking powder, salt and flour, one cup at a time, mixing after each addition. The dough will be very stiff. You may need to mix the last cup by hand. Place the dough (covered) in the refrigerator for 30 to 60 minutes.

Divide the dough into 2 balls. On a floured surface, flatten each ball into a circle about 12 inches in diameter and 1/8 inch thick. Use a rolling pin covered well with flour, add more as you roll out.

Use your favorite shaped cookie cutters to cut out cookies. Transfer the cookies with a floured metal spatula to a cookie sheet covered in parchment paper.

Bake cookies for 6-8 minutes or until lightly browned. Baking time may depend on the size of the cookies.

Repeat steps for additional cookies.

Frosting

1 cup confectioners (powdered) sugar
3-4 tsp. milk
½ tsp. vanilla
½ tsp. almond extract
2-3 drops of food coloring (optional)
Sprinkles

Mix all frosting ingredients together until smooth and creamy.

Once the cut-out cookies are cool, frost them with the icing using a small spoon or knife. Add sprinkles and decorate as you like.

Vincenzo and I made plans to visit Abruzzo for Christmas that year. The restaurant was closed the week of Christmas, so it gave us a chance to be together and travel to see his family for a change. We purchased a few presents for his parents and brother as well as for his little god child, Michele. I had packed a few plates of the cookies I had made along with some goodies and treasures from Tuscany to enjoy with family and friends while we were there. These special items included pecorino cheese, Chianti wine, fresh pici pasta, lardo from Colonnata, and a couple of bottles of Tuscan olive oil from our neighbor Remo.

One night I asked Vincenzo what to expect with the traditions of his family and that region, and his response was, "Just be ready to eat. A lot. My mom always makes a feast for Christmas."

This thought brought me excitement and trepidation at the same time. The foodie lover in me was happy to have the opportunity to experience the foods of a traditional Italian Christmas feast; however, I knew what his mother was like. Everything would be over the top for sure.

A few days before Christmas, we packed the car and made the six-hour trip south and east to Roccascalegna. It was only my second time visiting the area, and I was looking forward to enjoying the beauty of the landscape along the way. I remembered how I had loved to see the mountain roads with perched villages that looked as if they were teetering on the top.

We arrived at his parents' home later in the afternoon, and immediately the talk was about dinner later. His mother had prepared one of Vincenzo's favorite dishes, roast chicken and potatoes. I had to admit, I was hungry after the long trip, so this idea sounded fantastic to me too. We unpacked all of our goodies into the room adjacent to the kitchen, which was already stocked with cookies, cheeses, fresh fruits, and vegetables and bags of dried pasta to get us through the holiday. We had decided that instead of a big present, we would give them a little money to help with the holiday festivities.

As Vincenzo discreetly handed his mother the money, he said, "Mamma, this is from Sheryl and me for the Christmas celebration. Put it somewhere safe."

She quickly took it, as if she was afraid someone might snatch it directly from her hands, folded the money, and reached inside her shirt and tucked it inside her bra between her breasts. I could not help but give out a little giggle when I saw this.

Vincenzo turned to me and said, "That's the safest bank in Italy. People here still worry about being robbed during the holidays especially. It happens." Later he said that it was a common place for women to hide their money. I had to admit, it was not such a bad idea.

Celebrating Christmas in Abruzzo was wonderful. I was starting to learn a few of the words in the Abruzzo dialect as well. Every chance we could, we traveled to see friends and relatives that Vincenzo had not seen for many years. He wanted everyone to meet his future wife. Each day, we ate special lunches of fresh pasta and gnocchi, and in the evening we had roast meats. His mother was an incredible cook, and so I could see why it was natural for Vincenzo to be a chef.

She whispered to me one day, "Do you want to learn how to make my lasagna tomorrow?"

I responded, "Yes, I would love to." I felt like this was her way of inviting me into the family and showing me the traditions that she had to give us.

I told Vincenzo later that this was our plan, and he just smiled and said, "Well, tomorrow you will be busy all day."

The next day, I could see that Vincenzo's mom had already started to prepare for the lasagna making. She was checking on a big pot of meat sauce that was already bubbling on the stove. Vincenzo took the wooden spoon to his mouth for a taste. From the expression on his face, I could tell that he approved. She gave him a scolding look, as if he were still nine years old and getting into her sauce without permission.

She started to give us the errands that we needed to complete before lunch so that we could start making the lasagna right afterward.

"Okay, I called the store and they will have the fresh pasta ready for you to pick up by ten," she informed us. "Then, you need to stop and pick up mozzarella. I already have the parmesan cheese here and will grate it with the machine."

"Do you want to also put in prosciutto?" Vincenzo asked with a hopeful look.

"Oh yes, I almost forgot about that," she said. "Stop at the butcher and get the really good prosciutto. And don't forget to stop and get bread for the holiday. We can't be without."

Prosciutto (which is a kind of ham) in the lasagna? Okay, sounded pretty good to me.

After coffee together, Vincenzo and I headed out with the car to pick up the fresh ingredients.

When I asked about the fresh pasta, he said, "No dried pasta in our lasagna here." That would be almost unthinkable. The local store at the bottom of the mountain specializes in making fresh pasta and it's the best in the area. Mom does not always have time to make her own, so we always get it from them."

We made the rounds and picked up the ingredients. The pasta was carefully placed in a little paper tray and covered so that it did not dry out. When we picked up the cheese, I was surprised as it did not look like fresh mozzarella to me.

"This is a little aged, probably a week or two," Vincenzo said, holding up the cheese that is tied and looks like a little cat sitting up, with a bigger round shape to the bottom, tied in the middle with a smaller round for the head and two little thin triangles of the cheese pulled up to look like ears. The outside of the cheese had dried a bit in the aging process.

We arrived home with all the goodies. Lunch was a quick dish of pasta, and the table was cleared for the lasagna-making process. Vincenzo settled in the chair near the fire to relax and take it all in. I asked for an apron and a coffee for energy.

The water was already boiling on the stove to cook the pasta. Each sheet was boiled for just a few minutes as it was fresh pasta. The sheets were laid out with damp towels between the layers. Concetta asked me to start cutting the mozzarella into tiny little pieces. I did as I was told, and when I was done, she showed me the ham and said to do the same with that. When I was finished, I had two giant bowls of mozzarella pieces and ham pieces. Next to this, Concetta placed a bowl of finely grated parmesan cheese. I could see that she had also placed two eggs into a bowl and was beating them.

"Okay, now we have everything we need," she said as she set the eggs next to the cheese. She then told Vincenzo, "Bring me one of the lasagna pans from the pantry."

He went into the pantry to find it. She followed him as she already knew he would have trouble finding it. She knew right where it was, but was too short to reach it.

They returned with two lasagna pans, and she sprayed them with oil spray.

"Let's get started," she said.

She brought over the large pot of meat and tomato sauce and placed it near the cheese. She then took a ladle and placed a thin layer of sauce on the bottom of one of the pans, followed by the other.

"You always start with sauce," she said. "Otherwise, the pasta will stick to the bottom of the pan. Next, we'll put a layer of pasta." She took one of the sheets and carefully placed it over the sauce. "On top, brush with the egg wash and then sprinkle parmesan cheese. Next is meat sauce and then a layer of mozzarella and ham."

This is the base recipe. We continued this process until we had five layers of pasta total. As I was working with his mom, I asked Vincenzo, "How does she make the meat sauce?"

"It's like a Bolognese sauce, with ground beef, ground veal, and ground pork and pancetta. You simmer the meat with salt, pepper, onions, and garlic, add red wine, bay leaves, and canned tomatoes, plus a bottle of tomato sauce. She also adds the rind of the cheese to melt into the sauce. This is how I make it too," he said.

It took about three hours to completely prepare ingredients and make the lasagna. His mother was meticulous with each layer, making sure that there was enough pasta to completely cover the sauce and enough egg wash on each section to keep the cheese in place. I could see that her attention to detail was incredible. And I was completely exhausted, but so excited to eat the dish later that evening.

Christmas Eve arrived, and we gathered around his parents' little table. Along with the lasagna, Concetta had also prepared her traditional recipe of brodo, which was a chicken broth, filled with incredible tastes of little tortellini, egg noodles, big pieces of roast chicken and cubes of pizza rustica, which is like a frittata with parsley.

Next came the lasagna, which was the best lasagna I had ever tasted in my life. This was followed by a golden delicious roast leg of lamb and potatoes. For dessert, we had a traditional Pandoro cake in the shape of a star with fresh berries and cream.

Vincenzo was right; his mom had created an amazing feast. We started eating around 9:00 p.m. and went until just before midnight. Christmas Eve was traditionally celebrated in much of Italy with the Feast of Seven Fishes. Some families in the area of Abruzzo also follow this tradition with an all-fish menu on Christmas Eve.

I had mentioned that I wanted to go to midnight Mass to see the ornate nativity scene that Vincenzo told me would be there and to experience his local church during the holiday. We put on our coats and ventured out to attend Mass together, just the two of us. It was cold in the mountains, so we both had on our wool sweaters and heavy jackets.

As we greeted his friends and extended family after Mass, the conversation was focused on one thing: what we had eaten for dinner and what we were having for Christmas day lunch. Food was front and center to each conversation, with everyone trying to top each other with the long list of delicious food that was being served in their homes. Roasted fish, leg of lamb, lasagna, tortellini, brodo, roast rabbit in tomato sauce, and on and on.

After midnight Mass, we traveled back to the house where we were staying. Somehow, he had arranged to have a beautiful bouquet of roses waiting for me in our bedroom. He kissed me and told me how lucky he was to have me in his life. I told him that this was one of the most special Christmases I had ever celebrated.

We put on our warmest pajamas and crawled under the wool blankets to snuggle in for the night. The houses were cold here, with only a fire or a small radiator to heat a large room. I quickly learned how to dress for this when we would visit.

Christmas day meant traveling to his aunt's home for another feast. I could see that Zia Cristina had been cooking and baking for days. Cristina is the sister of Vincenzo's grandfather and one of the youngest in the family of five children. It was obvious that she was a great cook and enjoyed it very much. Lunch included her homemade crepes filled with meat and cheese, fried fish and roast potatoes and rabbit, followed by a large plate of her pizzelle and cookies from a local bakery.

There were ten of us around the table looking at each other with anticipation and pure joy at each new dish that was presented out of her little apartment kitchen. I did not think I could fit one more morsel in me. To get to Zia's house, we had traveled over an hour across a steep mountain pass deep into the higher altitudes of Abruzzo. As Vincenzo drove us home, we all feel asleep in the car like babies.

The next few days were filled with visits to friends and nights out for pizza or invitations to eat together with friends. At one point, we went with Concetta to get a few groceries at the local market, and it turned into a spontaneous bridal shower for me. I was admiring a set of dinnerware with handpainted sunflowers. Soon, I saw that Concetta was motioning to the owner that she wanted them for us, so these were brought out and put in our collection of items.

Next, I asked, "Where could we find a larger ceramic bowl for serving pasta at our house?"

The owner put out her hand and said, "Wait here, I have the perfect bowl." And she searched the back storeroom and presented us with a beautiful creamy white oval bowl with a giant red poppy painted on it.

"I love this, it's just like the one you have, Concetta." As I looked over at his mom, she was smiling from ear to ear.

We tucked away all these treasures for our new home together in Tuscany. We had a wonderful time, but we were exhausted from all of the traveling, catching up, and eating. Vincenzo's mom had carefully packed boxes of her canned tomatoes for us as well as a good supply of olive oil for us to bring back to San Gusme for the season. Angiolino snuck in a few packages of handmade sausages that he knew Vincenzo loved.

As we packed the car to travel back to Tuscany, we both looked at each other with a sense of relief. We were both thinking: let's go home.

MAMMA'S RAGÙ SAUCE

2 tablespoons olive oil
1-2 stalks of celery (chopped)
1-2 carrots (chopped)
1 small onion (chopped)
1 clove garlic (minced)
1 pound ground veal
1 pound ground beef
4 oz. pancetta (similar to bacon, cube into small pieces)
1 cup of red wine
1 tablespoon all-purpose flour
2 tablespoons tomato paste
1 (28 oz.) can San Marzano tomatoes
(crushed with your hands)
1 bouillon cube (vegetable)
2 bay leaves
1-2 rinds of parmesan cheese
Salt and pepper to taste

Sauté the celery, carrot, onion, and garlic with the olive oil until tender (5-8 min). Add the veal, beef, and pancetta to the pan, breaking up the ground meat into small pieces with a wooden spoon as it browns. Cook together until all of the meat is cooked well and browned. Add red wine to the meat and when it has evaporated, add the flour, tomato paste, tomatoes, bay leaves, bouillon, and parmesan cheese rinds, salt and pepper. If needed, add one small tsp. of sugar to sweeten.

Simmer on low heat for 2 hours (stir every 15 minutes). Retrieve the remains of the cheese rinds and bay leaves prior to serving. This sauce is better the day after making. Serve this sauce with cheese-filled ravioli or a short pasta like penne or rigatoni. It's also delicious as the meat sauce in a lasagna as I describe in the story.

Recipe note: Pancetta is like bacon and can be found in the specialty meat area of the grocery store or at the butcher shop. You may find it already cut into little cubes or it may be sliced thin like a round bacon. Parmesan rinds are the hard ends of the parmesan cheese that you might normally throw away. I always store these in a ziplock bag in the freezer until I need to use them. They add a nice flavor to any sauce or soup.

14

Quiet Winter in Chianti—Oh, and a Wedding Date

After the holidays, it was time for Vincenzo to have a little adventure. The restaurant was closed for the month of January, so we decided he needed to travel to Minnesota to meet my family. This was a big step for him, as he had never been on a plane and had no idea what to expect in America.

We flew from Rome to Minneapolis and took a little shuttle into Rochester where my parents were waiting to pick us up. I could see that Vincenzo was taking it all in. I kept telling him that Minnesota is lush, warm, and green in the summer, but the winters seemed more like a flat, frozen tundra.

We arrived at my home in Minnesota during one of the coldest periods of the year. I had prepared Vincenzo for the below-zero temperatures we have, so he was ready with layers of wool and a long winter parka. The weather did not disappoint. It was frigid. Still, we took time together to see my home and the area where I grew up.

We stayed with my parents as I had moved a few of my items into one of their bedrooms so that I could have a place to land when I was back for visits. My parents had arranged a Sunday afternoon gathering a few days later with all of my relatives complete with traditional Minnesota hot dishes and desserts. He loved every minute. And they immediately fell in love with him too.

My sister-in-law, Lara, had planned a family cruise for all of us to take so that we could all be together and everyone could meet Vincenzo. After two weeks in the cold, we packed our bags again and traveled by plane to Florida to get on our six-day cruise. It was like a family party every day. With my parents, my two brothers, and their families, we were fourteen total. We dined together, went to shows on the cruise ship, and headed out on adventures at each port we traveled to. Our favorite stop was the island of Tortola in the British Virgin Islands.

Enjoying some time relaxing on the creamy, white sand beach with the intense blue water was a welcome experience after being in the below-zero temperatures of Minnesota for two weeks. This trip was really the perfect way for my family to get to know and love Vincenzo, immersion style.

After our visit to Minnesota, we traveled home together and continued to settle into life in our little village experiencing the quiet winter months in Tuscany. It was cool and rainy for weeks, with not much activity in the area. The village seemed almost deserted at times, with the short moody days of winter limiting any light that might break through the cloudy, rainy weeks. During this time of year in the village, most days absolutely nothing happened. I continued to go out for daily walks when I could, but tended to spend more time inside focused on writing and work.

Our routine at home became comfortable as a couple as well. Vincenzo always had to be up a bit earlier than I, so he would carefully prepare my breakfast for me so that when I woke up, a prepped pot of coffee (Moka) ready to heat on the stove and my favorite muffin would be out waiting for me. I loved traveling into Siena to do some shopping or have a cup of tea or hot chocolate on these days. Siena in the winter months was quiet and peaceful, with only the locals going about their daily lives. Not crowded and noisy with tourists. This was a lovely time.

Chocolate treats and drinking hot chocolate were especially reserved for the winter months. I loved seeing the creative chocolate displays in the cases of the coffee bars and bakeries. As the days grew near to March, the winter wheat fields became as green as Ireland, and I could feel the land and people waking up again.

Vincenzo and I explored the local area on his day off, which was usually a Sunday. We traveled to Orvieto, Volterra, Siena, Collodi (the home of Pinocchio), and other picturesque villages within the region. I taught him the art of getting lost on purpose as my dad had frequently done with our family when I was a kid. Without the seasonal tourists filling the streets, I got to see what the local life was like, quiet and tranquil. Sometimes we would just stay home, cozy and warm together as we slept late. I loved to make him risotto on Sundays, followed by a long afternoon nap together, usually catching up with each other on news from my parents in Minnesota and his updates on what was happening at the restaurant.

We also made a habit of having a pizza date almost every Sunday night. We would go to his favorite pizzeria near Siena—La Capannina—and have some of the best pizza I ever tasted. They made their own dough fresh each day, and with a wood-fired pizza oven in the middle of the restaurant, we could watch as our pizza was made and placed far into the oven for a few minutes, turned and watched carefully so that it was taken out just at the perfect time. I loved how the crust was chewy and crisp, with charred edges and bubbles from the heat of the oven.

The sauce was simple, just crushed tomatoes, covered with fresh mozzarella and torn basil for me. Vincenzo always had a pizza bianca or white pizza covered with cheese, arugula, prosciutto, and fresh cherry tomatoes. Eventually, they got to know us so well that we did not need to tell them what kind of pizza we wanted.

In the winter season, the activity in the restaurant was slow. There were days when Vincenzo would come home and tell me that they had only a handful of customers for the day. Because it was a slow season, this was a time when many of the restaurants in Italy (as well as neighboring countries) participated in the Girogustando, which is a tasting event celebrated between two restaurants and their chefs.

One restaurant hosts the other invited chef and challenges them to a taste off of sorts. Each chef would choose a tasting menu that showcased their best dishes with the traditions from the region. The event was also a way to engage the locals in a special event to enjoy.

Vincenzo's restaurant was always invited to participate in the event. This year, he was hosting a chef from Budapest. The event brought new life to the quiet winter season as everyone anticipated the celebration and appreciation of both traditional cuisines. In the weeks prior to the event, Vincenzo worked on his ideas for the tasting menu, and I happily joined in sampling each trial dish.

As the days got closer, reservations for tables were called in and a team of judges was assembled for the actual judging. I was so excited to be a part of the evening. I had my assignment of cutting bread, carrying plates out to each table, and washing wine glasses at the end of the evening. Everyone who was working that evening, from the servers, kitchen staff, and dishwasher, sat down at the family table prior to the start of the event and tasted a few of the main dishes.

I especially remember the new tastes of the Hungarian dishes with the white wine from the area. I could tell that Vincenzo was in his element, also enjoying sharing his kitchen with the visiting chef. I could see them both absorbing the skills and ideas from each other as they worked side-by-side in the kitchen. Soon after we had finished our tasting, the work started. It was to be a long night.

A group of four sommeliers arrived to focus on pouring the various wines for each tasting course, additional servers arrived, invited judges were foodies and bloggers from the area as well as our local mayor and a few other dignitaries. A violinist played classical Hungarian music at the beginning of the event as people arrived and the first glasses of prosecco were poured and antipasti were served.

As the night went on, the various dishes were planned like clockwork arriving out of the kitchen to each guest. First Vincenzo's dish, followed by the Hungarian for each course. In all, the tasting menu had eight items and six wines.

Journalists and a cameraman covered the evening, even slipping into the kitchen with close-ups on both chefs cooking, and captured the entire event for TV as well as a special publication that featured the restaurant, photos, and recipes from the evening.

I stayed in the background, taking in every moment and peeking out from my little station to check on Vincenzo in the kitchen every so often. I had regular turns in the salon to deliver the plates from each course. This gave me a chance to eavesdrop on the judges and hear the comments from the people attending the event. The plates were wiped clean with pure happiness from both sides.

Some from our own village had even dressed up for the evening and were in attendance. I hardly recognized a few of them as I had never witnessed them in such formal attire. It was a very formal event, which was uncommon in our little village. The women looked stunning with black dresses, beautiful scarves, and the highest of heels. Men looked handsome in their black or gray suits and evening shadows of their beards.

Even their shoes were spectacular. I felt like perhaps we were in Milan and not in a little village in Tuscany. I was glad that I had put my hair up with some elegant earrings along with my black server uniform for the evening.

I think some people thought I was from the Hungarian team with my blond hair. Most did not realize that my connection was to the chef until the end of the evening as the awards were being given out. Vincenzo invited me to join him with the others and planted a big kiss on my lips in front of the journalists. That was the moment when I felt like Cinderella at the ball and my prince had just placed a glass slipper on my foot.

Winter moved into spring with blossoms on the trees and the grapevines getting greener and coming to life again in the vineyards. I also had a renewed sense of joy with the idea of Easter coming soon. It was one of my favorite holidays in Italy. Once again, the village prepared for the celebration.

In the days prior to the Easter holiday, especially during the days celebrating Carnevale, it was traditional to make frittelle, which are little fried donuts made of rice, sugar, and flour rolled in sugar. I think the ladies of our village made the best ones. I remember waiting for the Sunday when I knew they were making the sweet treats and wandering over to the communal kitchen where they were gathered making the donuts.

The ladies of San Gusme making frittelle.

Frittelle sign, indicates the treats are available for sale.

There was a little sign on the door, "Frittelle," indicating that people could come and purchase the local treats. I could hear the voices of the ladies of the village I had gotten to know in the past few months. They were busy mixing up the dough, frying them, and rolling them in sugar all while talking together at the same time and laughing.

As I peeked in to say hello and purchase my donuts, they all stopped and gave me big smiles, especially Dina who was the tiniest little lady I had ever met.

She said to me, "Wait, I will get you fresh ones that are still nice and warm." She took a large bunch of the donuts and mixed them with sugar in a little white paper bag and handed them to me. At the same time, she gave me a traditional kiss on both cheeks and a little hug. I left with sugar all over my shoulders and cheeks.

The frittelle were absolutely delicious. Every village boasts that they have the best recipe for their frittelle. I had a chance to compare a few during this time and I have to agree, the ladies of San Gusme make the absolute best.

Frittelle

2 pints whole milk

¾ cup short or medium grain rice

½ cup sugar (plus more for coating the donuts)

3 large eggs (separated)

1½ cups all-purpose flour

1 lemon (zested)

1 tsp. vanilla extract

2 tablespoons orange liqueur, such as Grand Marnier (optional)

Oil for frying (use light olive oil or peanut oil)

The night before making the frittelle, mix together the milk and rice in a medium saucepan and cook over low to medium heat until the rice is creamy and tender, about 40 minutes, stir often. Let the rice cool overnight in the refrigerator.

The next day, add the sugar, egg yolks, flour, lemon zest, vanilla, and liqueur to the rice and mix well. Whip the egg whites until they form soft creamy peaks and fold into the rice mixture gently.

Heat the oil over medium heat in a large, heavy, deep fry pan or Dutch oven (cast iron is perfect). Test the oil after 2-3 minutes with a small ball of the dough to see

if the oil is hot enough for frying, but not too hot. The oil should be simmering gently. Place 6-7 small dough balls (1-1 ½ inches round) into the oil at a time. Turn the frittelle so that each side gets golden brown, about 2 ½ minutes.

Place the fried donuts on a sheet pan covered with paper towels to cool slightly. Roll the frittelle in sugar and place on a paper-covered plate. Serve warm. These are best eaten immediately, so plan to share these if you make them.

Recipe note: You may need to use more flour in the recipe depending on how the rice and milk cook down. I use arborio rice for this recipe as it gets very tender and creamy.

As spring moved forward, Vincenzo and I started to consider where and when we would be married later in the year. I really wanted to get married in Tuscany with our friends and family as witnesses in a small, intimate gathering with a courthouse ceremony. The mayor of Castelnuovo Berardenga was a friend of Vincenzo's from the restaurant and so we frequently traveled over to the county courthouse to ask about the process and paperwork needed for us to get married in Italy. It was a complicated affair, as only the Italians could make it.

For us to be married in Italy, I had to officially translate all of my important documents from English to Italian, which included my passport, original birth certificate, divorce decree, and a few other items. It had taken weeks to have all of the documents ready. I had to arrange a visit to the US embassy in Florence to request official paperwork.

On the day of the embassy visit, it was a winter March day in Italy, so very cold and rainy. We were running late to arrive at the embassy, so instead of taking the bus from our parking spot outside of Florence, I thought we should get a taxi instead.

Vincenzo had his doubts. I remember him yelling at me, "You can't just hail a taxi on the street here like in America."

At that very moment, a taxi passed in front of us, and I put up my hand to indicate that I wanted a ride and yelled at the top of my lungs, "TAXI."

It screeched to a halt a few feet in front of us. We hopped in and the taxi raced us to the embassy.

He looked at me with complete surprise and said, "You are determined, aren't you?"

Once we arrived at the embassy, we realized that the appointment was only for me. This was considered US soil, so Vincenzo had to wait outside in the cold rain. I had to fill out paperwork for our wedding application that included the birth dates and full names of his mother and father. I had no idea. I think I filled this out at least six times before I had it correct. Each time, I would run out to the little square outside of the embassy with the paper to check with Vincenzo to see if I had it right.

Consider his parents' names for a minute: Angiolino Giangiordano and Anna Concetta De Laurentiis from Roccascalegna, Chieti, Italia. I knew them as Angelo and Concetta. It would be many months (and years) before I could spell everything correctly. This was just the beginning.

To celebrate getting the paperwork done, we stopped into one of our favorite little trattorias for pasta. The pasta dish we had was a tortellini with pears and asparagus in a delicious cream sauce. With a glass of Chianti, we celebrated getting this milestone completed. To this day, this little hideaway is still one of our favorite places to visit in Florence. I tried to re-create the recipe later at home and it's not bad, but the original dish eaten at Quattro Leoni in Florence is the best.

Little did I know that trip to the embassy was actually the easy part of the paperwork process. After I had permission to marry in Italy, I also had to submit paperwork to the Siena government house. They required that I have letters from people who knew me well in Italy that could attest to my character and that I was free to marry Vincenzo. They also required a background check to make sure that I was not a criminal. I also needed to have at least six of the special francobollo (stamps) that were like paying a tax to be able to have the permission. Every time we inquired, we learned something new. Each time we thought we were done, we discovered that we still needed just one more form—and of course another francobollo.

We finally had everything together and waited in line (with about thirty other people needing to submit one form or another for government permission) outside of the communal office in Siena.

When it was my turn to submit the required documents, the woman helping us said, "And where is your witness that knows you here in Italy?"

"Witness? I had no idea that I was supposed to have someone with me for this." I started to cry, really sob. I couldn't believe that I would need to return yet another day with a witness with me.

When Vincenzo heard this, he very calmly stepped out from the office, saying to me, "Wait here just a minute, I'll take care of this."

He walked out and asked the next person in line—a sweet-looking local woman—if she would come in and be my witness and sign the document for me. It made sense, she had been waiting a long time in line and she also wanted to get in to complete her business, so she said, of course she would help.

This is when I learned how the system works in Italy. The rules are there, but there is always a creative way around them. So we have a new friend in Siena that I had never met before, who signed my witness paper stating that I was of sound mind, a good person, and free to marry Vincenzo. Only in Italy would this happen.

Now that we had all the official paperwork done, we could finally set a date for the wedding. We traveled to the mayor's office in Castelnuovo Berardenga to see when he could perform the ceremony.

He carefully looked at the mountain of paperwork that we had completed and said, "Okay, looks good." He took down a paper calendar from the wall and said, "What date would you like?"

I almost fainted, after all that I had done, it came down to something as simple as a little paper calendar hanging on the mayor's wall.

We had discussed a date in the middle of July, so Vincenzo said, “Can we have July tenth?”

He saw that nothing else was written on the tenth, so he circled it on the calendar and put our names on the date. He told us that we could choose where the wedding would take place, in the tribunal (courthouse) office or inside one of the rooms of Villa Chigi Saracini, which was the historic old palace in the middle of the village that the commune owned. I was so excited to know that we could be married there. I had attended concerts and local theater productions in the park just outside the villa and it was absolutely dreamy beautiful.

Finally, he said, we have just one last formality, he said, “We need to officially post the announcement of your intention to be married on the wall of the tribunal. This way, if anyone wants to object (perhaps a long lost husband or someone who thinks I am unfit), they can.”

I was, once again, surprised with this old tradition. So we posted the announcement, and no one came forward to protest our marriage, thank goodness. We had officially set our wedding date. After ten trips to the local mayor’s office, five translations, one trip to the Florence embassy, eight Italian francobolli, and hundreds of euros for paperwork.

15

Wedding Day Approaches with Almonds, Lingerie, and Hot Springs

Once we had the date for the wedding, I started to think about what kind of celebration we should have together. It had been so painful just getting the permission to get married in Italy, I was ready to really celebrate. I wanted it to be simple and meaningful, with our family and a small circle of friend surrounding us. The date for our marriage ceremony was July, which meant it would be probably be very hot and sunny.

One day, we were having coffee with our friend Giulia and discussing where we would hold the lunch after the ceremony. Giulia had just agreed to be my witness for the wedding. I would have loved to host it in Vincenzo's restaurant, but that would mean that Vincenzo would probably have to work way too much to get ready.

As we were trying to think of a place, Giulia said, "Why not have it on my farm? I have a lot of space, even a little chapel. We could set up tables under the shade of the pine trees for the lunch."

The offer was from her heart and was so generous. We loved this idea and immediately starting planning the event with Giulia. Once again, the connection came full circle to an important friend and to a place that I loved.

I have mentioned how important my friendship with Giulia was during this time, and we continue to be lifelong friends. I was introduced to Giulia when I did the nanny work for my friends and their two girls. Giulia was a local woman who occasionally helped out with Italian homework and cooking. She spoke English very well, and we became instant friends. She was such a significant part of my life in Italy.

Giulia was in her midtwenties when I first met her and had lived in the area for most of her life. She is one of the most naturally beautiful people I have ever known, with big dark brown eyes and a wide, engaging smile. Giulia's story is important to tell because it shows the struggles and challenges that the younger generation may face in Italy.

Giulia was born to an artist mother and a father who was a psychiatrist. Her mother was a fairly famous artist during her day, as Giulia told me that they lived for a period in New York City when her mother was showing her works in galleries on the East Coast. This is one of the reasons why Giulia spoke English so well. However, most of her time growing up was spent living in Florence.

When she was just eighteen and at the university studying in Florence, she received the news that her father had passed away. What she never expected was that she had inherited her father's farm in Tuscany. The farm had been in the family for many generations. Later, at age twenty-one, she had to make a difficult decision: stay in college and finish her degree or return to the countryside and take responsibility for the family farm.

The farm is called Inchiostri. When I asked about the meaning of the name, Giulia told me what she knew about the history of her farm. It was once a convent in the Middle Ages, dating back to around 1100. In Latin, the name convent meant in claustrum, which translates to "in a closed place." The current name for the farm had been derived from this. As she was telling me, I could only imagine the deep responsibility she had for the history that she was preserving and caring for each day.

The farm is still a working farm in the heart of Chianti, with many acres of vines and hills of olive groves. Some of the land is also used to grow either wheat or sunflowers, depending on the year. The farm had a main house with many different rooms and separate apartments for other members of the family and extended family. In the lower level, you could still find what was originally a stable for animals. It had been converted into a living area with a little kitchen and dining room.

She also had many other buildings including a wine cellar and storage and another separate house where the farmhand and his family lived. There was also a quaint little chapel with an incredible altar that the family had once used as their private chapel. Having a private chapel was common for families with a certain amount of wealth and nobility.

In the yard were towering pine trees, and cypress lined the drive and back garden. The back garden had one of the most stunning views over the Tuscan countryside I think I have ever experienced. From there, I could see for miles—the hills and valleys that looked out onto the vast land of the Crete Senesi, with miles of golden wheat fields. In the distance, I could usually see another farmer's herd of sheep grazing on a green hill. In the spring, she would move out the traditional potted lemon trees for the warm summer months. Later in the year, they were moved inside in order to survive the harsh winters that the area has.

The farm also had fruit trees everywhere; cherry, fig, and apricot were just a few that I remember. In the middle of the farm was a little pond that was full of water and frogs in the spring, and later in the hot summer months, it dried up completely. This type of a farm would have supported a large and extended family at one time. However, now there was only Giulia and a couple of her father's cousins who were older and not interested in taking care of the farm. However, they would still come to stay in the summer months when it was tradition to move from the hot city into the cooler countryside.

In all the years I have known Giulia, I have admired her ability to be proud of her heritage and her roots. I know that she struggles so much, both personally and financially to keep the history and purpose of the farm going each year. She takes care of the land, the vines, and the olive trees as well as all of the buildings on the farm. She pays high taxes to keep her land in the family name. With little in return, she cares for the vines and harvests the olive oil each year. She does things very much in keeping with traditions of the past.

In order to keep everything going, she works two or three additional jobs as well as studies to at last complete her degree in psychology. She has one of the best senses of humor I have ever known, constantly laughing, smiling, and trying to make the best of her situation. Under the laughter, I can see that she is worried and struggles. She wants to have her own life, a love, a family. However, it always just seems too far away from her grasp.

I believe in Giulia and what she is doing so much because my family also had the same struggles keeping the family farm alive in Minnesota for years. Her experience paralleled my family's experience with my dad caring for the family farm for years with little money coming in and so much hard work and sacrifice every day.

Now that we had decided on Giulia's farm for our wedding lunch, we needed to decide on a menu and cake. Our fortune in planning our wedding was that Vincenzo was in the restaurant business, so he knew a great catering contact. I had told him that I wanted to serve traditional Tuscan fare with a pastry layer cake like the ones that Vincenzo always made for celebrations. We made one visit to the catering group and told them of our menu. Summer fare, prosciutto with melon, plates of meats and sausages, grilled vegetables, and a real porchetta on a wooden platter, head and all. Other items were focaccia and local cheeses with honey.

They asked me what color I would like for the napkins, and I spotted a dark blue in their collection. I immediately said I wanted blue as that was an American tradition for good luck. It was so easy, one meeting with them and meal planning was done. I had no question that they would make the celebration perfect.

The most fun for me was the search for just the right wedding cake. If Vincenzo could not make the cake, I wanted it to be as close as possible to the kind he always made for celebrations. We visited as many of the bakeries as we could in Siena and requested samples to taste. It was really one of the only things that I really wanted to be very specific. Puff pastry with layers of pastry cream infused with fresh strawberries and chunks of dark chocolate.

We eventually found a pastry shop in Siena called Pasticceria Peccati di Gola, which translates to mean the sins of the throat. This is what I loved about Italians and their culture. There was always a passionate meaning behind everything, even how they name their bakeries. And it was considered one of the best in Siena. They had created a small version of the cake I had requested. I was immediately happy with the way it looked and the taste was perfect. We chose a large round cake with a smaller top layer. Both of our names and the date of our wedding on the top with a small flower decoration. Simple and beautiful.

Now we had our date, the venue, the menu, and the cake organized. I could not believe how quickly everything was coming together.

One day when I was in Castelnuovo Berardenga for market day, I took a chance and stopped into the local flower shop to see if I could talk to the owner about ordering my bridal bouquet and flowers for the celebration. She was a sweet woman whom I had gotten to know during my rounds for shopping. She always had the most interesting and unique flowers and plants.

I was hoping that I could speak to her and that she would understand what I wanted. As we talked, I explained, "I would love sunflowers and lavender in my bouquet and in the flowers for the tables."

She looked at me and said, "That's not very traditional. The lavender might be too strong to go into the arrangement. What about roses?" And smiled as if I should probably change my mind.

"Really, no roses for me. Sunflowers and lavender is exactly what I need, this is not a traditional wedding," I said with a persistent look. I was not giving up on this idea.

She organized a novel idea to combine little white anemones with various sizes of sunflowers and sprigs of lavender. It was a compromise, and I knew it would be perfect. I had her also make similar arrangements for the tables and wedding party. Once again, I was so thankful that I was able to ask for something that truly reflected what was in my heart.

Sunflowers had become a symbol of our love together, each day seeking out rays of sun to keep it alive. Lavender was the calming and aromatic connection to how comfortable we were together. It was a perfect combination.

As we continued planning the wedding, I really wanted my immediate family to be able to attend. They were so excited to have an excuse to come to Italy. I thought it would be a great opportunity for me to show them a piece of Italy. With my travel planning knowledge, I created a wedding tour for them with a few days exploring Tuscany and Chianti just before the wedding day and then time in Rome and Pompeii after the wedding.

My parents had never been to Italy and had always wanted to see Pompeii and Vesuvius, so it was the perfect opportunity to plan a visit. I was so happy that they were coming to share our celebration day together. I couldn't wait to show them our little piece of heaven in Italy, especially our beautiful little village.

We assembled our small list of wedding invitees and got our invitations out to everyone. This also included a few family and friends from both Siena and Roccascalegna. We wanted to keep it small and intimate. In the end, we had around seventy-five.

I learned about the traditions surrounding wedding celebrations as well. Vincenzo reminded me that it was a custom to give little gifts to each family or couple who attend your wedding. It was also traditional to give five confetti almonds that represented health, wealth, happiness, fertility, and longevity arranged in a little bag with the name of the bride and groom and date of the wedding. This was the perfect task to give Vincenzo's mother.

His parents lived not far from Sulmona, which was famous for making the sugar-covered almonds used for celebrations in Italy. We also said that his mother could arrange to bring traditional Abruzzo sweets from the area for the dessert table that day. She was excited to have this task. I had no idea what she had in mind, but this would eventually teach me how exuberant she would be when it comes to food and celebrations.

As our wedding day grew closer, we carefully planned the seating arrangements and table theme. With Giulia's picturesque farm and countryside as a backdrop, I thought it would be perfect to have each table designated with a pot of summer herbs. We had lavender, mint, basil, oregano, sage, rosemary, and thyme in little terra-cotta pots with the names of our guests assigned to each table based on the herb in the center. The wedding table was set to have a pot of lavender, of course.

When I asked Vincenzo if he had a nice suit to wear, he just smiled at me and told me the last time he had a suit on was when he had to wear a uniform in the military. So off we went to find a wedding suit for him. We found a stunning gray suit with a lovely sheen to it that was made of a lightweight material perfect for the summer heat.

We consulted Vezio, the tailor from San Gusme, to hem the pants and asked him what color shirt and tie he should wear, and without hesitation, he said, "Oh yes, I know just what he should wear, a gray pearl shirt and tie is the perfect combination with this suit."

For us it was an honor to have Vezio tailor Vincenzo's wedding suit. He was beaming from ear to ear when we arrived with the news. Everyone was enjoying getting involved in our special day.

As all of this was happening, I started to wonder if my fairy tale was real. I had dreamed of finding love in someone who really understood me and accepted me just as I was. I felt so fortunate at age forty-four to be in love with a man who was sweet and kind and made me his priority. Every day, I sent out gratitude and love to the universe for sending me this gift. Eventually, the week of the wedding arrived, and so did my family for ten days of memory making that I have as a beautiful treasure in my mind.

My family was arriving in Rome, so I had arranged a driver to take me to the airport to meet them. I was so excited to see them all come through the doors from passport control and greet me with hugs and kisses. It had been about eight months since my last visit home. There they were: my two brothers, Darel and his wife, Barb, and Dave and his wife, Lara, and my parents.

My mom had packed my wedding dress in her carry-on bag. Originally, I was only planning to wear the traditional wedding dress for our church wedding back in Minnesota, which was set to be in January of the following year when Vincenzo had a break. However, I never found another casual dress that I loved enough to wear for the Tuscan wedding day, so I asked her to bring it with her. She also had our wedding rings tucked away in her purse, so she was nervous and happy to have arrived with these important items for our wedding.

We all got in the van and our driver whisked us on our way north to Tuscany. This was my family's first time ever visiting Italy, so they were taking it all in at first, with great anticipation. However, after the two-and-a-half-hour drive, I was the only one still awake when we arrived at their little apartments for the week. I had arranged for them to stay at a local villa. It was only about fifteen minutes away from San Gusme with a lovely setting and swimming pool for us to all enjoy on the hot July afternoons.

We got them settled in for a short nap, followed by family dinner together at Vincenzo's restaurant in San Gusme later that evening.

In the summer, San Gusme would come alive when the cool evening air arrived. I will always remember our dinner at his restaurant that evening, chatting together and catching up on the outdoor patio of the restaurant with incredible local dishes created by Vincenzo coming out of the kitchen.

Sheryl's family eating together before the wedding, from left, Jim, Irene, Lara, Darel, Barb, and Sheryl.

We celebrated with prosecco and fried olives to start, followed by Chianti wine and fried rabbit, gnocchi, lamb chops, summer zucchini soufflé and lemon cream and my favorite chocolate cake for dessert. They wanted to try everything on the menu. We started kidding around that evening that Vincenzo's chocolate cake was really a chocolate "love" cake because it had brought us together.

Every few minutes, someone from the village would stop in to greet my family with smiles and hellos. Vincenzo came out and sat with us at the end. I think it was at least midnight by the time we finished and everyone was more than ready for bed and a good night's sleep.

My family had already fallen in love with Vincenzo earlier that year when we were home for a month. I could tell that they were happy for us both and excited to be part of our wedding celebration. The next few days were a whirlwind taking my family around Tuscany and Umbria to my favorite spots. We saw the medieval towers of San Gimignano and tried the famous gelato and walked to see the ancient ruins and alabaster artisans within the walls of Volterra. I loved watching my family wonder as I originally did walking the ancient cobblestones with their eyes constantly looking with pure curiosity at everything they experienced.

We also traveled to Orvieto and explored the caves and stunning views from the top of the rocky perch that the village was built on. Orvieto was a treasured place for me. I had arranged reservations for lunch at one of my favorite restaurants, Le Grotte del Funaro, that is set in a series of underground caves first used by the ancient Etruscans. We were all sitting around an old wooden table inside together and it started storming with a passion, like it can only storm in Italy—wind, rain, hail, and lightning all at once.

A little window opening just behind our table allowed us to see the raging storm. We were safe and protected inside the cave at that moment. I wondered how many times these caves had served as protection for its inhabitants. During all of the wars that this country had faced, people were protected by the caves of Orvieto, including popes and politicians, and regular people like us too. By the time we were done with our lunch, the rain had stopped and the sun was shining. Just like that, the drama was over and life was calm and peaceful again.

Later that day, as we all continued shopping and exploring, my dad did what he usually did in the afternoon—took a nap. I'll never forget finding him asleep next to our purchases on a bench outside one of the stores. Classic dad move.

Two days before the wedding, Vincenzo's parents arrived with their car brimming with items. Vincenzo's mom had planned to bring a few items for the wedding, including the traditional sweets from Abruzzo. As per her usual habit, she exaggerated the amount just a bit. There seemed to be enough for about 500 people. There were bocconotti, which are a shortbread-like cookie in the shape of a little tart filled with dark chocolate and other cream fillings; others that were half-moon–shaped and filled with the traditional, slightly fermented grape jam; little sandwich cookies that looked like peaches and were almost like two tiny sponge cakes with a layer of apricot jam in the middle. Each one was like a work of art.

She also had little boxes of the sweets packaged to give to each couple as a parting gift, as well as the traditional confetti almonds and a little venetian glass bottle opener. Both of his parents looked so happy to be part of the preparation and celebration. It made us so happy too.

One of my favorite memories is when my parents first met Vincenzo's parents. I had taken my family out to experience the local market that is in Castelnuovo Berardenga each week. They tried everything they could taste at the market, including prosciutto, mortadella, porchetta, pecorino cheeses, sausages, and the local bread. It was here that my parents first met Vincenzo's parents. I will always remember my dad sitting on the bench talking to Vincenzo's father. Both speaking a different language, but seeming to understand each other just fine. They were smiling, joking, and having a great time already. Then I remembered that that was the exact bench where Vincenzo and I had one of our first kisses early in our relationship.

Vincenzo's parents, Concetta and Angiolino, and Sheryl's dad sitting on a bench in Castelnuovo Berardenga.

The day before the wedding, I had arranged for a family outing to spend the day at the local thermal springs to enjoy and relax. On the way to the springs, we could see the rocky quarries where they mined the local travertine stone. My father loved this as he, like me, also loved rocks. We had a great time relaxing and creating fun memories. Everyone soaked up the sun and did as the locals were doing, plastering the sulfur that was in the water on their skin to enjoy the healing of the minerals. My parents loved enjoying the warm mineral waters, and my brothers just kept telling me how lucky we were to be so close to such an amazing setting. I had to agree.

That evening, my friend Pam had arranged for a bridal shower for the women in my family, along with my girlfriends from the area. She had mentioned to them that they should bring something to add to my lingerie collection, of which I really had nothing. My best nightgown was a pink night shirt from Victoria's Secret. We had a great night with prosecco and cheeses and pasta.

When I started opening my gifts, I was totally surprised. I had everything from a beautiful silk nightgown and robe to a skimpy pair of men's bikinis with the Italian flag on them. Apparently a few of my friends had no idea what the shower was about, so they bought me the silliest underwear they could find. They understood that they were to bring me underwear, so this was their interpretation of that. Translation is everything. Tuscans are famous for their wedding jokes, so I assumed it was the beginning of a few yet to come.

Toasting together at my bridal shower, from left, Giulia, Sheryl, Sara and Gwen

16

Our Big Hot Tuscan Wedding and the Flying Cake Flop

The day of the wedding finally arrived. I slept in the apartment with my brother Darel and his wife, Barb, the night before so that I would not see Vincenzo prior to the wedding, as is traditional also in Italy. It was a gorgeous day with the sun shining bright and a deep blue sky.

Like most brides in Italy, I got up early and went with my mom to have our hair done. I felt like a princess, getting the attention of the owner of the salon, who had already done a trial run of the updo I wanted for the wedding day. I had found a beautiful pearl comb on a little trip to Scotland and had him place this in a French twist in the back with the comb tucking in my hair. He also did my makeup, and I was ready to go. Mom loved her hairstyle too. She looked so beautiful. We had fun with the primping experience together.

We arrived back at the apartment and I pulled on my dress that Mom had carefully packed. It went on like a glove. I was so relieved. The dress had been in storage in Minnesota for months, so I was not even sure it would still fit the same. I could see in my mom's eyes that it was perfect and that she approved of the strapless cream-colored wedding dress with a beads and lace. Simple, but elegant.

Along with the dress, I had a sheer, cream-colored bolero and a pair of sandals that I had discovered on a recent shopping trip to Rome. I put on a traditional blue garter underneath with a penny tucked in my slip for good luck. I had made my wedding jewelry, which consisted of creamy freshwater pearls and white faceted topaz stones. It was the perfect match for the beaded and lace strapless gown.

The ladies ready for the wedding, from left, Barb, Lara, Sheryl, and Irene. Emma in front.

Shortly after I was dressed, Emma arrived as she was to be my flower girl. She had turned ten that year and was growing up so fast. She looked so excited to be a part of our big day, with the sweetest lace dress and white sparkly ballet shoes. Emma had her own bouquet of sunflowers and lavender as well, which she loved. We had fun posing for pictures with my brothers as we waited for the time to leave for the courthouse and our ceremony.

At one point, my brother Dave peeked his head into the apartment and said, "Hey, sis, I think your car is here."

I looked out and saw the cutest vintage Fiat 600 from 1969 sitting out in the square. I just looked at him and said, "No, that's not for me. Maybe it's someone else's car." I was expecting Vincenzo's friend Marco with his car.

He just said back, "Well this one looks like it's for you. I see a sunflower in the back."

I could not believe it. I had no idea that Vincenzo's friends had arranged this special car and driver to take me and my father to the courthouse. They had even thought of putting a sunflower in the back window of the car. I was beside myself with joy. What fun! I checked to see that I had everything together, and Emma and I squeezed into the backseat of the car along with my sunflower bouquet. Dad got in the front, and we were off to the wedding.

As we arrived at Villa Chigi for the ceremony, I realized that I really had no idea where exactly I was supposed to go. It was a huge villa with many levels and gardens. I had asked the vice mayor about this a while back, and the response I got was, "Don't worry, when you arrive, you will know where to go."

The driver was not from the area, so he had no idea either. I had this fleeting panicky thought that perhaps I would be late to my own wedding ceremony. Eventually, we found a few local friends who were waiting for the wedding

and showed us where to go. Everyone was waiting patiently for us to arrive. I saw our friend Giulia waiting for me there as well; she was to be my witness for the ceremony. As we jumped out of the little Fiat, clapping and cheering started from the guests.

I looked at my dad and said, "Okay, I really have no idea what to do, but I think we need to start walking and they will show us the way."

I took his arm and we started to walk together. As we walked, Giulia and Emma followed, along with others who started joining in walking with us. This included new friends from the area, a handful of Vincenzo's friends, my mom, my brothers, their wives, as well as Vincenzo's family. Soon everyone was following behind us. The wedding processional was such a meaningful and spontaneous moment that will always live in my memory.

Everyone seemed as if they knew exactly what to do. I remember thinking to myself, I planned a simple courthouse ceremony to make our wedding legal in Italy. I had no idea that this day would be so incredibly beautiful and touching. It was much better than anything I could imagine.

Family and friends join in the wedding processional.

As we reached the top of the hill of the historic villa, I could see Vincenzo waiting for me along with his brother and the mayor. As we first made eye contact, I could see his eyes light up and my future unfold. He looked at me and seemed to be a bit shocked that this was all happening as well—like perhaps it was not real. My dad and I walked up to Vincenzo, and Dad presented me officially to my future husband.

With grace and pride, Dad turned to Vincenzo and said, "I know that you're a good man and that you will take good care of her. You have our blessing and love for this marriage."

I took Vincenzo's arm, and we walked into the historic hall where the ceremony was to take place. Vincenzo whispered in my ear, "You look more beautiful than ever. You took my breath away when I saw you today. Like an angel. My angel."

Big tears started in my eyes as we looked at each other, and he gently reached up and quickly wiped them away.

As we approached the front of the chamber, I wanted to take in every detail of each moment so that I would have it stored away in my memory forever. We had asked a friend who was a violist to play music at the beginning and end of the ceremony as well as at the lunch. She was playing softly as we walked in.

The red velvet chairs were arranged in two aisles with our guests finding places to sit. I could see our parents and family in the front, with a large wooden table with four chairs around it. I could also see the mayor, Roberto, smiling at us as we approached the front of the room. He was dressed in his finest today, with a blue suit and his official Italian red, white, and green silk sash indicating his connection to the government of Italy.

Giulia and JP followed behind us and took their places with us at the front. Emma and Alessandro, the eleven-year-old son of one of Vincenzo's partners in the restaurant, who had our rings on a traditional embroidered pillow, were close by. The mayor greeted everyone and invited us all to sit.

The ceremony was not long, but was so very meaningful. I remember concentrating on the mayor's every word so that I made sure that I understood what he was saying in Italian. He talked about the importance of finding love and being connected to each other as husband and wife. He also mentioned that we should respect and honor each other in our daily lives. He made a little joke at the end that he had known Vincenzo for a long time and been eating his food for years, but this time was the first time that he had ever seen him dressed in anything but his chef uniform, so handsome and elegant he was away from the kitchen.

With a little smile, he said, "This life looks good on you."

At the end of the ceremony, he asked if we both agreed to be married, and we both said yes emphatically. Vincenzo leaned in and gave me little kisses during the entire ceremony. I could tell he was so nervous. I just enjoyed the kisses. We exchanged our rings and had our official kiss.

At that moment, everyone in the room clapped and started cheering and celebrating. The music started again, and we signed the official documents along with our witnesses, Giulia and Gian-Piero. JP was hugging Vincenzo so hard, I thought he might break something. At one point, he lifted him up off the floor with his giant arms. I gave Giulia a big hug and kiss and thanked her for everything she had done for us. My emotions were so full of gratitude at that point.

After the ceremony at Villa Chigi, we greeted, hugged, and kissed everyone who had attended. As this was happening, Vincenzo's phone rang—a call from his godmother from France calling to congratulate him in French. He was smiling from ear to ear. Both Emma and Alessandro were by our sides the entire time. All four of us squeezed into the little Fiat 600 and started on our way to Giulia's farm for the wedding lunch. We asked the driver to take us through San Gusme on our way to do a little round in the car of our village.

As we arrived, the ladies were out waiting for the bread van to arrive and the kids spotted us right away. The driver honked and the kids started chasing the car and yelling as they ran. The ladies looked with surprise, and when they realized it was us, they had big smiles and cheered and clapped. As we passed under our little terrace in the main piazza, I could see our apartment had been decorated with a giant white bow and draped with blue ribbons. This was the work of Vincenzo's parents. It was so special to see everyone cheering and waving after us.

From San Gusme, we headed in the direction of Giulia's farm on a winding, narrow road through the vineyards and olive groves. The little farms were dotted with fig and cherry trees and surrounded by golden wheat fields. The contrast between clear blue sky, the summer green, and the golden wheat fields was a stunning backdrop for our day.

As we arrived at Giulia's farm, we could see cars and people gathering to join us. It was one of the hottest days of the summer so far, with temperatures approaching the mid-nineties that day. However, a little breeze reminded us of our fortune for the day.

As we exited the car, everyone had gathered to greet us. Many already had a glass of prosecco in hand and were cheering us on. I was in awe of how lovely our little lunch celebration looked. There were eight round tables, each set for ten people with dark blue tablecloths I had picked out, along with creamy white covered chairs tied with big bows in the back.

Each place setting was elegantly set with real china, silverware, blue napkins, and three wine glasses—one for prosecco, one for white wine, and one for red wine. The centerpieces were the terra-cotta pots of herbs as well as colorful confetti candy for guests to enjoy. The tables were placed under the shade of five ancient umbrella pine trees and provided the perfect protection from the hot sun. The air was heavy with the perfume of pine, fig trees, and the summer breeze. With the hot weather that day, the cicadas were singing their summer song so loud, it sounded like a serenade.

Vincenzo and Sheryl on their wedding day.

We posed for pictures and enjoyed taking in the beauty around us. I really felt such incredible appreciation for the creation of such an idyllic setting for us to celebrate our love together, and for the people who were there to share it with us. As we walked toward the shade of the main stone farmhouse where the appetizers were set up, we were ambushed by a few of Vincenzo's relatives who let off cardboard crackers that showered us with confetti almonds, confetti paper, and pennies. Many of these landed directly down my strapless top and would stay there until I undressed later.

In Giulia's chapel, from left, Angiolino, Sheryl, Vincenzo, and Concetta.

From left, Giulia, Sheryl, Vincenzo, and Gian-Piero.

We gathered a glass of prosecco and cheered, kissed and toasted our union with our family and friends. We ducked into the quaint little chapel on the farm and took a couple of wedding shots to remember this special day. Both of my brothers had professional cameras, so they were capturing every moment of our day.

As we left the chapel around 1:00 p.m., I knew that it was time for lunch together. I could not wait to see how our traditional Tuscan fare looked (and tasted). I could see that the catering crew was busy setting up the long buffet table for us. All around were waiters dressed in formal black pants and vests with white shirts. They were so handsome and seemed to be enjoying having some fun with the crowd.

A few minutes later, everyone started clapping and cheering, chanting, "Mangia, mangia, mangia. Eat, eat, eat."

That was our clue to start out the line and gather our plates for lunch. Once again, as I took in the delicious looking buffet table, I was astonished. Here is what I saw: heaping platters of local meats and sausages, pecorino cheeses and local honey, grilled eggplant and zucchini, orange cantaloupe with prosciutto, Tuscan white beans with rosemary, and the most incredible porchetta I ever saw. This was a whole porchetta, which was a roasted pork loin with layers of rosemary and spices inside, the head still attached. It was tradition and, of course, delicious. The table was decorated with little sunflower and lavender bouquets with sprigs of lavender and lemon leaves from Giulia's farm decorating the cheese plates.

We gathered our food and made our way to the bridal table. We sat and enjoyed the feast along with both our families. Alessandro would not leave Vincenzo's side, so he sat on his lap and they ate together. My family was having a great time soaking up the foods and traditions of the wedding. We had our own waiter who filled our wine glasses and took care of our every need.

Every ten minutes or so, the guests would clang their wine glasses, shouting, "BACIO, BACIO, BACIO, BACIO, BACIO…KISS!" Each time, we would stand up and kiss each other. During one of these kisses, Vincenzo placed his hand on my lower back and dipped me in a classic passionate kiss. I had no idea he had this move in him. It took me totally by surprise. The cheers were so loud, they probably heard us in San Gusme.

As we finished eating, we went around to greet everyone at each table to thank them for coming. This was the traditional way of receiving cards and gifts as well. The cards included money, and gifts were similar to wedding gifts given in the States. We received a few household items, linens, and glassware. Wedding celebrations in Italy tend to be extravagant and costly, so the gifts of money usually help offset these expenses for the couple. I felt like our wedding lunch was extravagant for me, but in relative terms, it was quite low key and not at all expensive.

After lunch, we took a walk and led our friends and family to the back gardens where we had planned to have the cake celebration. Giulia's farm had the classic potted lemon trees that were out on the back terrace to take in the summer sun. The gardens included large fig trees and a pergola covered with grapevines. In the distance, we could see her olive trees and the alternating fields of green and golden wheat. As I took it all in, I don't think I had ever imagined such beauty could be possible. And this was our wedding celebration—ours.

The waiters had set up stations with limoncello, vin santo, and sweet Moscato wine to go with the plates and plates of traditional sweets that Vincenzo's mother had brought with her from Abruzzo. Everyone had gathered around us under the pergola to wait for the arrival of the cake. In Italy, the cake was considered the crowning glory of the celebration, so it was usually kept in secret until it is delivered in a big surprise at the last minute. I had not been allowed to see the cake at all. As we were waiting, I could see that everyone was getting excited and also very hot. At this point it must have been close to 100 degrees and everyone seemed to be literally melting.

Finally, we caught a glimpse of a waiter coming out of the lower level of the farmhouse carrying the cake. I noticed that it had a sunflower on it, which I had not specifically mentioned, but I thought, oh well, I do love sunflowers. People were cheering and clapping in anticipation of the cake. As the waiter started walking toward us, he almost tripped and fell with the cake, but easily recovered. Everyone gave an expression of shock and then cheered again as he stumbled once more but recovered.

I thought to myself, well this was explainable, the ground is uneven here and it could easily happen. As the waiter got even closer to us, almost to the point of placing the cake in front of us, he tripped again, and this time the entire cake flew (for me it seemed like it was in slow motion) over the stone wall just behind us. I was shocked. A collective gasp was expressed by the group, including me and Vincenzo. I just remember giving out a little shout and then covered my mouth, not knowing how to react.

We looked over the stone wall behind us and saw whipped cream everywhere. The day had been so perfect, I just kept thinking that if this is the worst thing that happens, it's okay. We have all of these delicious cookies and sweets that Vincenzo's mother had brought; we don't really need a cake after all.

Just as I was recovering from the shock, one of Vincenzo's cousins ran down to try to recover the cake. As he reached down and picked up the cake, I could see that he was laughing. He picked up the platter still upside down and it held the cake, which was still attached. It was then that we all realized that the cake was actually a fake made of a round Styrofoam base with a bunch of whipped cream on the top with a sunflower attached. Everyone starting laughing and cheering again. I almost fell over with laughter (and relief).

Vincenzo was already trying to figure out who was in on the joke. He immediately suspected his two partners in the restaurant—Marco and Aldo. They had created a very elaborate and effective joke with the waiter, and it was really so perfect. In fact, my brother had captured it all on video thinking that it was the real cake, so we have this entire flying cake flop encounter on video to watch and laugh about forever. It is common for friends of the bride and groom to play a joke on them during their wedding celebration. This one went off without a hitch.

Shortly thereafter, the real cake was delivered very carefully by two waiters with big smiles as they carried it to us under the shade of the grapevines. Vincenzo popped a bottle of prosecco and we toasted each other. We also cut the cake together American style and fed each other a piece of cake. Our friends were cheering and toasting together with us.

I remember that I even heard a few English words come out of the crowd from Giulia: "Happy new year," "Happy birthday," and "Merry Christmas." She was having so much fun from the day's activities and the wine, as were we all.

Vincenzo and Sheryl with the real wedding cake.

Everyone joined in, saying any of the English expressions from different holidays that they knew. This was actually very appropriate, as we would celebrate all of these special holidays together as a couple in the future. The cake was perfect, just as I had planned. It had two layers with two white chocolate hearts on the top with both of our names. It was made with layers of puff pastry, fluffy cream with fresh strawberries, and large chunks of dark chocolate. It was delicious and a fantastic way to end our wedding lunch.

As the afternoon went on, it just kept getting hotter and hotter, that I could tell everyone was getting so uncomfortable. I could see from the corner of my eye that Giulia had a garden hose in the corner of the house that the waiters were using to cool off with. At one point, they started spraying each other. Well, this caught on quickly and soon one of Vincenzo's cousins got in on the act. By now, everyone was getting a little spritz from the hose and having a great time. Giulia even had fun spraying guests with the cool water.

We knew that eventually our day together would come to an end. As each family started to leave, we stopped to take a photo with each one of them and give our kisses and thanks to them for coming to celebrate with us. We gave each family a little box of sweets from Abruzzo along with the traditional keepsake gift—ours was a Murano glass bottle opener along with a sachet of confetti almonds with our names and wedding date on them.

After all of the excitement of the day was over, we stopped at our little apartment and changed from our wedding attire to our honeymoon clothes. As I peeled my wedding dress off my sweaty hot skin, out fell a handful of chocolate almond confetti candies of various colors and three pennies that had gotten stuck in my bra from earlier that day. I kept the pennies for good luck. We both took cool showers and felt refreshed and ready for some relaxation. I put on an embroidered white halter dress that was the perfect match for the hot, steamy afternoon.

I was so happy to have celebrated together with family and friends on a day that we will never forget. As we headed out for the Castello to stay one night for our honeymoon, once again, the ladies of the village wished us their congratulations. As we were walking to the car, the post woman caught up with us and hand delivered a telegram of official congratulations from Vincenzo's godmother in France. I had never even seen a telegram, much less received one before. It was so incredibly special.

The Castello delle Serre was only about twenty-five minutes from San Gusme, so we did not have far to drive. Vincenzo only had one extra day off, but spending our honeymoon somewhere special was really important. My friend Pam had reserved the Tower Room for us as our wedding gift.

As we arrived, the owner, Salvatore, had a bottle of prosecco ready for us. He showed us our room, and I felt like my dream was continuing. The Tower Room was one of the oldest parts of the Castello, with three stories. The bottom level had a little sitting room with restored period furniture. Up one flight of stairs was a spacious and ornately decorated bedroom and bathroom. There was a lovely bouquet of fresh flowers, including roses, sunflowers, and lavender sitting on the side table.

One more level up a spiral staircase was the tower balcony where you could see all of the castle grounds, including the pool and gardens. In the distance, I could see the mountain that is above San Gusme. Even from here, I could still see home. It felt good. It felt so peaceful to be so happy in this place and with Vincenzo. I really wanted to keep this particular memory in my mind forever.

Sometimes I think about the kind of love we have together and think that it differs from any other love I had experienced.

As I had grown older, the type of love I needed in my life had changed. I felt like the love I had found with Vincenzo was about something deeper. His love felt accepting, comfortable, and lasting. I knew that my heart would belong to him forever.

We unpacked quickly and put on our swimming suits and ran out to the pool, just like we were kids again. We could not wait for a moment of relaxation after the excitement and stress of the day. The pool at the Castello is one of the most unique and inviting pools that I have ever seen. The rectangular saltwater pool, made with local cream-colored travertine stone with a dark lining to capture warmth from the sun, sits on the top deck of the main grounds of the Castello.

It had been so hot for so many days that the temperature of the water was perfect. The pool is surrounded by gardens and huge lavender plants. As we cooled off in the pool, we kissed and embraced and had a great time letting go. We took a little nap on the lounge chairs and sipped on prosecco in between.

Salvatore, the owner of the Castello, along with his son, Antonio, had been restoring the castle for a few years now. They were only the third family to ever own it. Salvatore has great stories of the previous owner, a countess, and haggling over the antique crystal chandelier in the great room. In the end, Salvatore won and got it included with the price of the Castello. He talked about the first night he stayed in the Castello. It no longer had electricity and all of the gardens had gone to weeds.

The outside was once dark and dirty from years of exposure to the elements. He had since restored it by power washing to travertine stone to its original creamy white. Along with the outside, he carefully restored each of the rooms and spaces and had created one of the most unique hotels in the area.

Salvatore and Antonio are both chefs and had lived in California most of their lives. They had a restaurant there for many years, but sold it to purchase the castle and live there. They had family in southern Italy, understood the culture well, and spoke fluent Italian. They created a lovely wedding dinner for us that included rosettes of pasta filled with prosciutto and parmesan cheese. Dessert was a lemon panna cotta with berries. We drank in the coolness of the night as we finished our meal under the pergola covered with vines.

We slowly walked back to our room, and I could still smell the scent of lavender heavy in the air. I asked Vincenzo if he would take me up to the top of the tower terrace and dance with me under the stars. We had no music, just our happy hearts. It was the most memorable day of my life so far.

As we shared these quiet moments together, I whispered to him, "Promise me that we will return every year to the Castello to celebrate our anniversary if possible."

"I love that idea," he said. "This is our place now too." We danced and reflected on the storybook wedding day we had shared with family and friends.

17

The Family Honeymoon

My family remained in Italy in the days after we got married. While we were at the Castello for our one-day honeymoon, they explored the area just around San Gusme. They all went to Castello di Brolio, which was close by, to visit the old castle and have a formal wine tasting and learn about the making of traditional Chianti Classico. They enjoyed lunch under the pine trees at the Castello's osteria and then took a scenic drive up and around the rolling hills and mountains in the area.

Upon our return, we met up with my family and close friends at our favorite pizza place and had fun catching up on their day's activities. That evening was filled with laundry and packing as I was traveling to Rome the next day with my family as their guide. I had planned a trip to Vesuvius and Pompeii from Rome, so we had a few more days to spend together. This had been on my dad's list of places that he really wanted to see when he was in Italy. I had never been to the area, so I was looking forward to seeing this as well.

I was so sad that Vincenzo could not join us, but the restaurant was open again the next day and that was his priority. It was in the middle of the most busy summer season, and there was no way that he could take extended time away and close the restaurant. It was a bit heartbreaking to leave him there and not be able to share the rest of the week together.

My family and I traveled by car to Rome and settled into one of my favorite hotels in the middle of Rome, Albergo Santa Chiara. As a travel planner, I had gotten to know some of the best places to stay all over Italy. This was a nice bonus. The hotel is situated in the square just adjacent to the Pantheon, so it was close to all of the sites we wanted to experience in the eternal city. I loved that we could walk across the square and take in the magnificent cathedral of Santa Maria de Minerva with the obelisk and elephant tower just outside.

We walked together to the famous Piazza Navona and admired the three fountains: the Fountain of the Four Rivers by Bernini and Fountains of the Moor and one of Neptune, each one unique and dazzling to see. We all enjoyed the freshness of the cool evening air as we dodged the pigeons, people watched, and ate dinner at one of the restaurants skirting the piazza.

The next day, we took a private tour with a guide to see as much of Rome as we could fit in. We traveled to see the Roman ruins of the Forum and Colosseum and visited the Campo dei Fiori, an open-air market first thing in the morning to take in the bustling activities of the place. Here you can find fresh fruit and vegetables of the season, handpainted ceramics, flowers, household items, and many other treasures. While it may not be like it was twenty years ago, it remains one of the last local outdoor markets still available in Rome. This is exactly where I was thrilled to find a traditional crepe pan to bring home to our apartment in San Gusme.

While there, we snacked on pizza and focaccia from a local favorite bakery called Forno Campo de' Fiori. My parents' mobility was a concern for me, so we also arranged a private driver for the two days so that they could rest inside the car with air conditioning, if needed, as we navigated around Rome.

My brothers and their wives hit the ground running that day. At every stop, they took in as much as they could—even walking over to see the Vatican and square. I had advised them on the best gelato places and other major sites as well. I spent my time with my parents as I had visited Rome a few times and had a chance to see most of the major tourist sites. I enjoyed the local places that I had gotten to know.

I showed them one of the best coffee bars, Tazza D'Oro, which was not far from the hotel, and my mom and I stopped into my favorite local leather shop, Mancini Leather, to purchase a few treasures.

The second evening, we ate at one of my favorite local restaurants close to the hotel, Ristorante Grano, near Piazza Rondanini, which offered a quiet dinner of fresh pasta and fish dishes with a glass of crisp local white wine from the region of Rome called Pecorino. Yes, you're not mistaken, this is the name of a variety of grape and a cheese in Italy.

It was so fun to show them the places I had grown to love in the area. Even though I was not a local, it felt comfortable to me. I had always loved Rome since the first visit I had a few years before on my own.

After two days in Rome, we traveled south to see Mount Vesuvius and Pompeii. As we arrived near Vesuvius, I was mesmerized by the lush greenery that surrounded the mountain. It was lost in green tropical plants. We traveled higher and higher and eventually arrived at a place where we could only go farther on foot.

We left our parents at the little café to sit and rest, while my brothers, their wives and I explored the top of Mount Vesuvius together. It was hot and difficult walking, but what a sight we had when we arrived at the top. The cone was incredible to see as the famous volcano was still steaming in some areas. It is scary to think that this volcano had done such devastating damage to the area so many years ago.

After our hike up the volcano, I had arranged for a private lunch at a local vineyard located on the terraced hills around Vesuvius called Cantina del Vesuvio where they treated us to handmade pasta, dessert, and their own delicious wines, called Lacryma Christi del Vesuvio, or tears of Christ. The wines from the area get their distinct taste from the volcanic minerals in the soil and are unique and delicious. My brothers and I tried their grappa and decided it was the best we had tasted so far, with gentle flavors of apricot fruit.

Next on our adventure for the day was the visit to Pompeii with a local guide. This site was breathtaking to see. My dad was in awe of the place and asked as many questions as he could to understand everything that we were seeing. We all had a fantastic day in the area. Later that evening, we headed back to Rome for our last evening together. The next day, my family flew back to Minnesota, and I traveled by train back to our little village and my new husband.

18

Being the Chef's Wife

One of the most fascinating aspects of being immersed in village life was the daily realization that the people living in the village were still practicing centuries-old traditions. These traditions were steeped in the many cultures that had come and gone from this country and deeply rooted in religion.

One of the very first things I noticed was that family life was highly matriarchal. This is anchored by the religious reverence of the Madonna, or Mary. Mothers are treasured; grandmothers, aunties, and women in general are held in high regard and respect. Vincenzo was always respectful of his mother, calling her each day to check in. Even at the restaurant, it was traditional to serve the women first, starting with the oldest to the youngest. As I got to know the strong women in the village, I realized that there was a sense of hierarchy and respect, and it was there for a reason.

Nara and Lina were two elder women who were held in high regard because of their leadership and connection with the church. They were key decision-makers for the village along with the priest. They decided what community and church activities would take place and organized action around them. They also knew how to motivate and organize the men of the village to help them, usually with the promise of food and wine. They knew the songs to sing at Mass, understood the traditions organized around celebrating the harvest of the grapes and the olives, and, most importantly, had the recipes for the traditional foods that represented each celebration. They were also the elders and had carried forward many of the traditions so that future generations would understand them.

Women were somewhat defined by their family life as well. At the beginning, I got to know most of the women as the "grandmother of" someone or the "mother of" someone. This connection was important. The men in the village, especially the elders, were also held in high regard. However, I found that behind every one of these men was an even stronger woman.

I did not expect true acceptance into the world of these strong women as I was an outsider. So I was surprised and thrilled when the women in the village started to call me "the chef's wife," as my primary connection to the man whom I was supporting in life. I was no longer the "Americana" to them. This paid reverence to him and gave me a purpose within the village culture. I was being woven into the tapestry of the village with this true honor and, along with that, the feeling of acceptance.

Men were defined in a more traditional way—around their work. Most of the time, the connection to their children was not as noticeable. However, I always understood what the role of each man was. Vezio the tailor, Giancarlo the former postmaster and protector of sorts, Remo the farmer, Lorenzo the businessman, Mauro the banker, and Don Luigi the priest.

The men supported the women and did what was needed to carry out the work of the village. They organized the harvest, carried the wooden cross in the processionals, set up the wooden tables for the harvest feast, and cooked and served the traditional wine and dishes during the festivals.

Men were not at all afraid to show their respect for the women in their lives. There was not much discord about who was in charge, at least publicly. They also enjoyed the freedom of being men—frequently out having a coffee, grappa, or ice cream together, catching up on the local news and gossip. In the evening, it was common to see mostly men at the local Circolo playing cards or watching the soccer match together. The women were also out together, keeping an eye on the children and grandchildren, walking together, or sitting on the bench also gossiping and sharing recipes or plans for the next day's meal.

The restaurant was like family for Vincenzo and me, as it was such a big part of our daily life. As the chef's wife, I had responsibilities to support my husband and his work as much as possible. The restaurant was open six days a week from breakfast until dinner. This meant that Vincenzo worked long hours for six days a week, especially during the busy tourist season. I wanted to spend time with Vincenzo, so I would frequently finish my work and go over to the restaurant in the evening to help out.

Everyone who was working for the evening would meet around 6:30 p.m. at the family table and eat together before the restaurant opened for the evening. Vincenzo and his sous chefs prepped and cooked this meal as well. I enjoyed being a part of the restaurant family in this way. My favorite nights were when he made steak and fries. He always told me in advance when this was going to be the feature for the family table.

On a busy night, especially during the high season, the people working included Vincenzo and two to three prep cooks and a sous chef in the kitchen, three or four waiters, another of the wives, and me. As we sat around the large round table closest to the kitchen, everyone would grab their plate from the kitchen where Vincenzo had already plated everything and head out to the table.

If the younger workers arrived late, they got a stern look from Vincenzo over his glasses. He would size up if they were fit to work for the evening, asking why they were late, had they been out partying the night before? And so I could see that some things were the same all over the world. Aldo and Marco would check the wait staff for dress code and hygiene and update them on the menu and any specials for the evening.

The group had been through a lot together, and it felt like another type of family. They teased each other and bantered through the meal throwing out the usual Italian expressions for everything, including swear words. As I was the newest member of the family, sometimes they would forget that I was there and might understand what they were saying, so they would stop and look up at Vincenzo and then at me to see if I was reacting. They were men, I expected this. I especially enjoyed when we got to taste a new dessert or dish that Vincenzo was creating for the menu.

Aldo had trained as a sommelier and was always bringing in new wines. He loved it when I was interested in tasting a new wine to go with the dishes Vincenzo created. I got to know and taste most of the wines from the region this way. Vincenzo never had much of a taste for wine, but I enjoyed it very much.

After we finished eating, we all had a strong coffee and gathered our strength for the long evening's work. For me, this included prepping the tables, sweeping the polished terra-cotta floors, cutting the giant loaves of Tuscan bread, checking the wine glasses, calculating the bills, and drying wine glasses until around midnight.

The restaurant was an elegant one, the kind that you might go to for a special occasion, like a birthday celebration or to make a proposal of marriage. It had little coves in every corner where diners could have a little table to themselves. And it was theirs all night long. People would come from all over the region to eat Vincenzo's food and experience the incredible ambiance that was found here. I will never forget one night as I was prepping to open. Aldo opened the door to the restaurant and a very stylish couple walked in.

The woman glanced over at me and said, "Oh, you must be one of the owners, it's nice to meet you."

I looked surprised and greeted her, "Thank you, it's so nice to meet you as well. I am Vincenzo's wife." She looked at me with a surprised expression, eyebrows up, as if I was some exotic creature standing in front of her.

Aldo looked at me and said, "Yes, you are part owner of this restaurant now too, you are married to Vincenzo."

It was the first time I realized that this was now a part of who I was as well.

The experience of helping Vincenzo gave me a whole new look at the incredible and difficult work that it took to run a restaurant. Owning a restaurant, being a chef, or working in a restaurant seems so romantic and fun; however, it is more work than anyone can imagine. By the end of each night, I was usually so tired I could barely walk and my feet would hurt so badly that I thought I might not make it across the square to our apartment. The stamina needed to do this every day was something else.

Each night, I would watch Vincenzo in the kitchen. He had laser focus on the food that was being prepared. He almost seemed to be directing an orchestra. Each dish had to be perfectly created in the correct order, with the others in the kitchen moving in perfect harmony to his direction. He personally checked each dish as it went out through the kitchen doors to make sure it was perfect. And if the dish was returned to the kitchen not completely eaten, he wanted to know the reason why, just to make sure that each person was truly enjoying their experience at his restaurant.

Each table's order was perfectly timed for each course, so that there was time to enjoy the wine and meal, as well as the company around the table. If something went wrong, he was fierce with himself and the workers, even yelling and throwing things across the kitchen to make his point. Everyone took it in stride. They knew that he expected perfection.

Most of the staff that worked with him in the kitchen had little or no training. He was the one who taught them everything. During the nonservice times and less stressful times, he was an incredible teacher and formed real friendships with the guys he worked with each day.

This time spent in the kitchen was the first time I witnessed the person he became at work. His alter ego was tough and demanding. Yet if I walked back to see how things were going, he instantly changed into the gentle man that I knew and loved. He always told me not to worry, that he would never get upset with me like that. I told him that he better not, or I would kick his ass. Well, I said that with the playful but stern look that I had learned from the women in Italy as they warned their husbands to behave. He would just smile at me and give me a kiss and send me back out to the wine glasses. I would just shake my head in disbelief.

On a busy night, we would finish up the evening service around midnight and walk across the square to our little apartment. He was always hungry, so our tradition was to have grilled cheese (or simply toast as the Italians say) and perhaps a gelato before dropping into bed around 2:00 a.m. At home, he loved anything that I cooked for him, so this was easy. Sometimes I would make focaccia or pizza as well, but his favorite was grilled cheese toasted to the point where it was almost burned. Comfort food made by the one you love was the most important thing to him.

I could see that the real world of being a chef and owning a restaurant was not all glitz and glamour like the cooking shows we see on TV and in the movies. The real picture is that it is physically demanding, with little pay and no time at home. As one of the owners, they always paid their workers first, then paid themselves, and it was very little. The reality was that people truly respected him as an artist and talented chef, but I started to wonder if it was all worth it. I had fallen in love with this man, but could I survive this lifestyle?

As I got to know all of this, I realized that he was always going to be in the restaurant working when everyone else was celebrating the holidays. This included Easter, Christmas, and everything in between. He rarely had time to travel to see his friends and family in Abruzzo, and we only had Sundays for our time to get away together.

We talked about it a lot and he always said, "This is the career I have been given, so it is my job to do it well, even if it means sacrifice." He added, "I really don't know any other kind of life. This is how it has always been for me."

From the time he was a teenager, he had been training and working in kitchens. He did not miss what he never had. However, I understood that maybe together we could have more of a life together, but I was not sure how we could manage to achieve it for him (and us).

Even though he was so busy each day with his work, Vincenzo was a true romantic. This was one of the qualities that made me love him so much. In the first few months after our wedding in Tuscany, he started a tradition of bringing me a bouquet of three roses on the tenth of every month to celebrate our anniversary. I knew that he could not easily escape the busy restaurant to get me flowers, so it was sort of a surprise to me that each month such lovely flowers would arrive. Some days, I would wake up to find them waiting for me on our little kitchen table. Other times, I would return from shopping or a walk to find them carefully placed in a vase near my desk.

In Italy, a bouquet of flowers was treated like a true treasure, not like the cheap supermarket bouquets you find in the States. Each bouquet was carefully arranged with various greens and very long stems on each flower. It is also important to give only an odd number of flowers in the bouquet, which was why he usually brought me either three or five flowers. The bouquet was usually wrapped in beautiful paper that changed with the seasons and tied with lovely ribbons. I always felt like it was such a pity to take it apart to place the bouquet in the vase.

One day I was curious enough to ask him how he got the flowers each month.

He looked at me with a clever smile. "You really want to know?"

I insisted, "Yes, they are so beautiful, where do they come from?"

Vincenzo just smiled and said, "Well, they come from the flower vendor near the old cemetery."

It was common to see flower vendors set up near the cemetery so that people could purchase the flowers they wanted to place on their loved one's grave each week. The woman who sold the flowers got to know Vincenzo well, and eventually he told her that the monthly bouquet was for his wife (who was still living). She took extra special care to make the bouquets even more creative and unique each month. She would even put sunflowers in the arrangement when she had them. The tradition of the anniversary flowers has continued to this day, and Vincenzo tells me that he will never stop bringing me flowers.

19

Yet Another Wedding Celebration in Abruzzo

I had no idea what we were thinking, but we decided to have a little wedding dinner celebration in Abruzzo close to Christmas for Vincenzo's relatives who could not travel up to Tuscany during the summer for the wedding. Understand, this started out as a casual conversation with his mother who does not understand the word little.

Within about two months, the celebration had grown into a breakfast, formal wedding Mass, dinner, and dancing. It was way out of control and I had no way to stop it. Vincenzo's mother, Concetta, was planning everything; we did not need to worry about a thing. Well, I was worried. We would get frequent updates about this on the phone with his mom.

Vincenzo would insist that we did not want anything grandiose, and she would reply, "Don't worry, it's just a little party."

The venue for the party was a local hotel that was made to look like a castle. It had just a few rooms to stay, with a restaurant and large spaces for events. We booked a room there so we could have some privacy during the week of Christmas and during the celebration. We arrived a couple of days early to do a few errands prior to the party. We had no idea what we were in for. Concetta had a list of things for us to do literally every minute of the day leading up the party.

We started with picking out the confetti almonds for the event. We went to a local shop that specialized only in the production of the specialty almonds—famous from the area right in Abruzzo—Sulmona. We tasted and searched and finally decided on a variety of almonds with various chocolate coverings and colors.

Later, we had dinner at the restaurant of the castle to taste the various courses that were planned for the celebration. We also had to decide the table assignments and themes (we decided to name the tables according to the American states). At the last minute, we arranged to also have a DJ playing music so that people could dance as well. This was really for Vincenzo's father and family as they loved to dance and celebrate in a very traditional way. I was hesitant to add this, because I knew it was costly, but in the end it was worth every penny.

I had no idea what to expect, and I had no idea how much all of this was costing, and I was starting to panic inside because I knew that his parents did not have much money and we did not have much income either. Once again, I got the impression that no one seemed to be concerned about this but me.

Our other errands consisted of traveling to various bakeries for each collection of traditional sweets that had been created for our party, including about a dozen private homes where cousins and aunties had been assigned (or offered) to make items for the breakfast or the sweets after the dinner party. Vincenzo traveled over a mountain one hour each way to retrieve crepes filled with prosciutto made by his aunt Cristina that were to die for.

I have never seen so much food in my entire life. All of these items were either arranged in the spare salon at his parents' house or delivered to the restaurant for the party. Concetta and Angiolino were all abuzz with activity during these three days, along with anyone else who had been assigned duties.

Vincenzo's grandfather Nonno Vincenzo was quietly paying attention to all of this and secretly planning his outings as well. He would quietly come down the stairs for a little TV watching and dinner around 6:00 p.m. and then head up the stairs to his room early in the evening to retire. He had even picked out a new shirt to wear with his suit for the wedding dinner.

Occasionally, I would make eye contact with him, and I could see a little twinkle of approval in his eyes. He only seemed to show this to me. Vincenzo always said, "Nonno Vincenzo really loves you. He knows you are special, he does."

The day of the celebration arrived, and Vincenzo and I got busy dressing for our day of celebrating. It was winter, so I had picked out a classic black dress with a long sweater coat that was black with hint of a design of gray roses woven into it. I put on my strand of pearls and put my hair in a half-updo myself. Vincenzo had on black pants, a black shirt, and a tweed coat that looked nice, but casual.

We kissed each other good luck and said in Italian to each other at the same time, "Forza e coraggio" which means, have strength and courage. We both would need these two things along with a heavy dose of patience to get through the day.

As we were winding up the mountain road, Vincenzo's phone rang and it was his mother. "Where are you? You're late. We are all here waiting for you. It is starting."

We just shook our heads and kept trudging up the road. As we arrived at his family home, there was barely enough room in the driveway to even park. Cars were parked every which way like only Italians can do—in a big pile so that only one person at a time could actually leave the event easily without having to ask the person behind or on top of them to go and move their car. It was an art form that I never understood.

As we walked in the door, we were greeted with a loud "Auguri" or congratulations. Everyone had gathered in their tiny kitchen and were patiently waiting for us to walk through the door. One of the men grabbed a bottle of prosecco and popped the cork as loudly as possible. Cheers went out and everyone started in on the feast in front of us. The tradition of having a little bite to eat before the ceremony was well under way. We were not even having a ceremony, but a Mass to honor our nuptials that had taken place earlier in July.

As I glanced at the group of family members, I only recognized a few familiar faces. It was going to be a long day for me, especially trying to greet everyone and understand the heavy dialect that most people in the room were speaking. Vincenzo's mom was deep in conversation with a couple of ladies and was explaining the menu for the lunch we had planned for later. She eyed us as we walked in with a combination of pride and a bit of scolding at the same time, for our late arrival.

I realized very quickly that this day, this celebration was as much for Vincenzo's family, extended family, and friends as it was for us. So much of what we had in front of us for the day was not really what we wanted, but we felt a strong sense of what tradition dictated that we do. Even now, as I look back, I realize the traditional celebration of our wedding in this way was very important to his parents and grandfather.

As I looked around the house again, I recognized a few aunties and uncles, cousins, friends, and neighbors. Everyone was eating, chatting, and catching up. We walked through the house and greeted everyone. A few people handed us cards during this time, and I could see that a few gifts had been assembled on the side table. Some of the gifts looked big, which worried us as we had such a tiny apartment and had not requested any gifts.

We took time to enjoy a few of the traditional foods prior to leaving for the Mass as well. I remember trying Vincenzo's auntie's crepes filled with tuna salad, and a taste of a little sandwich that was part of a giant tower of a sandwich, called panettone gastronomico with many layers of bread sandwiched with various meat and cheese fillings. It was an ingenious way of serving to a larger group. You started cutting from the top down, with each layer revealing new fillings separated by a top and bottom layer of bread.

There were platters of meats, homemade sausages, local cheeses, and green olives. And the sweet items: I could see traditional bocconotti (little shortbread cookies filled with chocolate or pistachio cream), little sponge cake sweets that looked like peaches, coconut/ricotta balls, and the sise delle monache (a meringue-like sweet, with three peaks that looked like it had three breasts).

After an hour or so of greeting everyone and eating, we all got in our cars and drove down the mountain to Roccascalegna for the Mass service to be held that day in our honor. The church was decorated for Christmas during this time and had the altar pieces with a baby Jesus in a manger featured in the front of the church. Vincenzo's mother had arranged special flowers for the day, including sunflowers paired with roses to keep with our wedding theme from Tuscany.

The service was really touching and included guitar music and sung in English by a few of his cousins. They had been working on the song for a while and were excited to be singing for us.

We left the church after Mass, and I could see that Vincenzo was talking to his brother and father about something special. His brother got in the car and drove us out of the village. As we approached a spot in the road where his cousin's house is located, everyone stopped. We got out of the car and

Wedding Mass in Roccascalegna; in front, Sheryl and Vincenzo; in back, Concetta and Angiolino.

could see that his cousin and family were all waiting for us to arrive. They flanked either side of the road together with other family members and were holding a strand of wide white ribbon across the road.

As we approached, his cousin handed us a scissors to cut the ribbon, together. As the ribbon fell to the ground, everyone cheered and wished us well. This was a traditional way of recognizing our marriage as a couple with Vincenzo leaving the fold of his family to be with me.

We got back in the car, with JP driving us, and in a train of cars filled with friends and relatives, we trailed down the

Cutting the family ribbon after Mass.

mountain together—honking and flashing our lights the whole way. Those we discovered along the way greeted us with smiles and waves.

Now, as we headed in the direction of the castle for our late-afternoon lunch and celebration, we looked at each other with little smiles and kept encouraging words along the way.

Vincenzo looked at me, when I asked, "So, it's almost over, yes?"

He smiled and replied, "It's only just beginning."

We arrived at the hotel and castle where we were staying as everyone was starting to gather. Even though it was December, the day was sunny and warm. We approached the stairs of the castle where the lunch and celebration was getting started and someone announced, "The bride and groom are here."

The manager of the event handed us each a glass of prosecco and had us wait out on the terrace and not enter the salon where the lunch was to be held. He wanted us to have a grand entrance. We were then draped with long, heavy robes to wear into the room—sort of like royalty entering. I had no idea what was going on, but I just went along with it.

We entered the room to music that sounded like the arrival of the king and queen. Everyone toasted us with their prosecco, and we were led to the wedding table—the table with the label Minnesota. I could see that the round tables were filled with family and friends all waiting to celebrate with us. And so our lunch began.

Vincenzo and Sheryl with wedding cake in Abruzzo.

The "little lunch" Vincenzo's mother had planned was over the top. It was not little, light, or anything like that. In fact, our lunch was eight courses including crostini, two kinds of pasta, a meat course and a fish course, a three-tiered cake with fire crackers on it, and a lemon-sorbet-prosecco drink called a sgroppino to top it all off.

In between courses, we greeted everyone in person by making the rounds at all of the tables where the guests gave us envelopes of congratulations and cash. We danced, we toasted, and we had a great time. At one point, I remember being out on the dance floor with Vincenzo's father, and we were dancing to a traditional Italian accordion song. I looked over and saw Nonno Vincenzo dancing like he was light as a feather floating around the room. This is a man who normally used a cane to walk, spoke in a whisper because of throat cancer, and never showed much emotion. He was smiling from ear to ear as he led one of the cousins in a dance like I have never seen. Everyone clapped and watched as they finished the dance together.

Looking back, it was a memory we all treasure. Nonno was dancing his last dance and I think he knew it. He died one month later peacefully in his sleep.

Around 10:30 p.m. I thought my feet were going to fall off, so I took off my shoes and was dancing barefoot on the dance floor.

Vincenzo's mother was so upset when she saw this and exclaimed, "Oh my God, you are going to get a sore throat now for sure. Put your shoes back on."

Her belief was that bare feet drew in the cold from the floor, which traveled directly to the throat and made you sick. I thought to myself that I would gladly accept the potential of a sore throat over feet that could not walk for days if I stayed in my shoes. Earlier in the evening, I had asked the manager of the event to turn on the fan or air in the room because it was so hot I thought I might faint.

Sheryl and Angiolino dance at the wedding celebration.

It could not have been more than five minutes of lovely cool air movement when Concetta grabbed the back of her neck dramatically and exclaimed, “What is that, air? We can’t have this. I will get sick for sure from the air entering the back of my neck.”

So the air was turned off immediately. This was just the beginning of my understanding of her traditional beliefs of how cold and air bring on illness. This belief is still quite prevalent in the culture, especially in southern Italy.

After the meal and dancing were over, the traditional sweets came out around midnight. There were platters and platters of cookies and cakes and traditional items both sweet and savory, along with coffee and traditional digestive liqueurs such as Nocino, Montenegro, grappa, and others to help digest all of the delicious food we had indulged in all day. As we said goodbye to everyone, we had a special gift from us to them, a little decorated Christmas tree and a sachet filled with confetti almonds with a little ribbon noting our wedding date.

The next day, we slept late and went back to Vincenzo's house and had lunch and opened wedding presents and cards. We had tons of food left over from the day before, and Concetta made a big pot of pasta with her famous tomato sauce. A few of the relatives stopped in for coffee and cookies and a chat to see how we were all doing. I noticed the day before that many people had brought packages of sugar and coffee along with their cards and gifts.

I thought it was strange and asked about it. "Why all of the coffee and sugar?"

Concetta replied, "This is another of our traditions; we take care of each other. Celebrations of weddings and funerals take a lot of resources, the top ones being sugar and coffee, so everyone always pitches in."

As we were talking about the event in the days before and after, I remember being so worried about the cost of the celebration. Vincenzo and I had very little money, and his parents even less. How would we ever pay for such an expensive day? Then I realized, as we opened each card, how we would pay for it. Each family generously gave us money in order to cover the cost of the wedding. His relatives had paid for our celebration. This is another tradition. The celebrations are extravagant, even if you are poor. However, each guest comes with the expectation to help pay as much as possible to help the family celebrate in a way that only Italians can do—with great passion, generosity, abundance, and exuberance.

Another of the old traditions from Abruzzo is to also hold a serenata. Typically this is done just prior to the wedding or in the days immediately after the wedding. A serenata or what we might call a serenade is planned in secret to surprise the bride with love songs, waking her in the night as she sleeps.

Vincenzo and I had returned to his parents' home a few months after we celebrated our Minnesota wedding for a family visit and to pay our respects to his grandfather's grave as we had missed his funeral. The days were always full, and we would typically fall into bed around midnight and easily go into a deep sleep.

The time of this visit was March and it was quite cold, so on this night, I had on my flannel pajamas, and we had just fallen asleep. I thought maybe I was dreaming when I started to hear music and singing. I tried to sleep through it, thinking it really was just my dreams. However, as the music got louder and more real, I opened my eyes and thought, this music is here below the window.

I nudged Vincenzo who was already sleeping soundly. He seemed annoyed that I was waking him up. I asked him, "Do you hear it? It's music."

He opened one eye, then the other, and groaned, "Oh no." There may have been a few swear words inserted as he realized what was happening.

I insisted that he tell me. "What is happening?"

He said, "Oh God, it's a serenata. We'd better wake up."

I slipped out of bed and opened the shutters to look below us. I could see a group of people with their coats and hats below the balcony. One I recognized as his cousin with a guitar. I was so excited. We were being serenaded. The song was a traditional one with very lovely words. Vincenzo also got up and came to greet everyone from our window. When they finished the song, I clapped and blew them kisses.

They yelled up to us, "Let us in, it's freezing out here."

Even if it meant I was now wide awake, I turned to Vincenzo and asked, "Now what?"

He rolled his eyes a bit and said, "Oh, this is only the beginning of the night."

I threw on another fleece top over my pajamas and headed down the stairs to the kitchen where everyone had gathered. Vincenzo's parents were still fully clothed and looked at us with a twinkle in their eyes. They had been planning this surprise for days and had been up since we had gone to bed getting the house ready for the party. It was a tradition for the bride and groom to invite the group of singers in for prosecco, spaghetti, and sweets after the serenade.

The group of cousins came in followed by neighbors and friends. Soon, the entire house was full with around fifty people. The prosecco was opened followed by more singing and celebrating. Vincenzo's mom had two big pots of water on the stove to cook the pasta. She also had a batch of her homemade tomato sauce ready that we all loved. The table was prepared and we all sat around and ate spaghetti and celebrated until the early hours of the morning. I took a picture of the clock when we finally had cleaned up the kitchen and headed back to bed. It was 4:30 a.m.

As we fell into bed again, I said to Vincenzo, "Wow, your family really does know how to celebrate a wedding." He just shook his head, said something about Italians being crazy, kissed me, and we both dropped dead into a deep sleep until about noon.

20

And Finally the Below-Zero Minnesota Wedding

I can't believe that we planned three weddings within six months, but we did. It was January now and once again we were headed across the ocean toward Minnesota for a few weeks. We were to celebrate a small wedding ceremony in my little Lutheran church in the countryside.

We wanted to keep this celebration simple, but meaningful. We did need to apply for our marriage license, which was incredibly easy compared to the process for me in Italy. We spent about fifteen minutes at my local courthouse where Vincenzo just had to show them his passport to verify who he was, and we were done with the application.

I remember him looking at me in astonishment as we got back in the car as he asked "Tutto qui? Giá fatto?" (That's it? It's done?) I responded, "Si, giá fatto!" (It's already done). What a contrast to the paperwork and many trips to the government offices in Italy. This was better than fine, it was great.

I was so happy that Emma had asked if she could come and attend our Minnesota wedding. She was to join Vincenzo's brother in Rome to fly to Minnesota together a few days before the wedding. Emma was then ten, and she already knew what she wanted. She was our little cupid, and she had my heart forever as her second mom.

In the days prior to our third wedding day, I was nervously watching the weather. January winters can be brutal in Minnesota. I was hearing a forecast for minus-20-degree weather for the day of our ceremony. When I brought this up to my parents, they told me not to worry, people will come.

Gian-Piero and Emma had arrived a few days earlier and were enjoying the novelty of the snow and cold. We went out exploring each day to show them my home, which at that point felt more like Antarctica. They loved the trips to see the famous place where I had worked as a nurse for many years, Mayo Clinic. We wandered the hallways and eventually made our way to the historic bell tower of the Plummer building where a carillon plays songs every hour each day.

As we climbed the stairs to the top of the tower, we found the man who plays the carillon. I had arranged for a private tour and access to the outside of the bell tower in order to see the views of Rochester and Mayo Clinic. It was so cold that day, but the sun was shining brightly. As we ventured out, the music he played was perfect for the day, he was playing "That's Amore." We have a great photo shot of all of us standing in below-zero temperatures outside the bells of the Plummer building. Later, we found the local Starbucks and warmed up with a decadent hot chocolate. Both Emma and JP are obsessed with Starbucks, so this was a highlight for everyone.

The day of the wedding arrived, and we traveled the few miles to my little family church near my parents' home to get ready for the ceremony. Earlier that day, Mom and Emma and I had our hair done for the special day. Emma looked like a little princess with beautiful curls framing her face. Gian-Piero was there as the best man for Vincenzo, and my friend Ann was my matron of honor. We had invited a small group of family and friends to join us. The church was still decorated for Christmas with a large tree near the altar and flowers along the pews—the perfect setting.

For this ceremony, I carried a simple little bouquet of red roses this time. We had decided to add a little diamond to my wedding ring as we celebrated our Minnesota wedding. The diamond had been my grandmother Alice's. It was set originally in a necklace that she had received from my grandfather as an engagement present. She had given the necklace to me just a few months before she died. I treasured this always and was so happy to add this special stone to my wedding ring. The diamond was placed in between the two intertwining hearts of my engagement ring. When I showed my father the ring and told him what I had done, he got tears in his eyes. I was so happy that he loved it.

The ceremony was traditional with the exchanging of vows and rings. Vincenzo was so nervous during the ceremony that he kept leaning over and kissing me. I know that he was worried about saying his wedding vows in English. He had been practicing for weeks. When the moment came for him to say that he wanted to take me as "his wife," instead he said that he would take me as "his husband." He had been practicing the word husband for so long that it just came out all wrong.

As this happened, everyone in the church went very silent, as if trying to absorb what he had said, even with his Italian accent it was obvious. Then I looked over at JP who recognized what he had said. He was looking down and shaking his head as if to say, brother, you really screwed this one up. We could not help but start to giggle, all of us. Everyone in the audience joined in as well.

The pastor asked if we wanted to start over with his vows and he got it right this time. Finally, the pastor said, "NOW, you can KISS the bride." And we kissed and laughed and ran down the aisle to the reception area, which was attached to the church.

My mom, aunts, and cousins had planned a traditional Minnesota wedding reception. This included Norwegian treats like lefse and krumkaka and little appetizers. Vincenzo had requested that Mom make his favorite, her BBQ sandwiches, so he was in heaven.

Our cake for this wedding was a deep, dark, red velvet chocolate cake with cream cheese frosting. We had brought our Italian traditions also to this wedding with little red and gold almond confetti candies and a present for each couple who attended. This time it was a little pizza cutter with the word LOVE on it. I thought it was absolutely perfect.

The reception was short as people were worried about getting home in the below-freezing temperatures. I think a few people actually left their cars running during the ceremony in order to keep their cars warm enough to get home later. It was one of those nights where you felt like your nose and eyes were frozen the minute you stepped outside.

Despite the cold, the third wedding was done, and we had officially celebrated with everyone.

The next day, we woke to the most beautiful hoarfrost on our windows that covered everything in the countryside. The designs on the windows were so intricate and artistic and the trees seemed magical all covered in white. Vincenzo, Emma, and JP had never seen this effect of frost. We even ventured outside after lunch to take a wedding photo with my dad's antique Ford Model T. We wanted to replicate a photo that I remember with my dad's parents, Grandma Alice and Grandpa Norman Ness, on their wedding day so many years ago.

After all three of our wedding celebrations, I could not help but reflect back to my grandma Alice and how proud she would be that I had been so strong and pursued my dream. I kept my maiden name of Ness through all of this as it is not tradition to take the husband's name in Italy. I have to admit, I was a bit relieved to keep my simple (easy to spell) Norwegian name.

That last night in Minnesota, Vincenzo and I cooked spaghetti alla carbonara for our family and celebrated with some Italian comfort food on such a frigid night. This is a very traditional Roman dish and one of Vincenzo's specialties. Everyone loved getting a little taste of Italian food before we left for our honeymoon.

Spaghetti alla Carbonara

4 ounces pancetta (cubed)
4 large egg yolks
4 ounces pecorino cheese (grated)
Salt and pepper to taste
15 ounces paghetti pasta, cooked al dente
Coarse salt (for the pasta water)
Additional parmesan cheese for grating over the top prior to serving.

Fry the pancetta in a nonstick sauce pan until well cooked (crispy). Take off heat, cool for a few minutes and place the pancetta in a large pasta bowl. Add the eggs and cheese and mix together with the salt and pepper. Set aside.

Bring a large pot of water to boil over high heat. Salt the water well with 2 tablespoons of coarse salt. Cook the spaghetti pasta according to the directions, until it is al dente.

Add the cooked pasta to the egg mixture and mix together quickly. The warmth of the pasta will create a custard-like sauce from the egg and cheese mixture. Serve warm with extra cheese. The secret chef ingredient is to add a spoon or two of the pasta cooking water to the mixture if it gets too dry.

Serve by grating additional parmesan cheese over the top with a drizzle of olive oil. Serves 4.

The next day, Vincenzo, JP, Emma, and I all piled into the airport shuttle and made our way to the Minneapolis airport. We knew that Vincenzo's brother, JP, loved Chicago and especially loved the Chicago Bulls and Michael Jordan. We had arranged a big surprise for him with tickets to see the Bulls play in a few days.

The flight to Chicago was short and we settled into our hotel rooms. My younger brother and his wife and kids joined us by car as they lived close to Chicago. So we celebrated the first few days of our US honeymoon once again with our family. We explored the city in the freezing cold and sunshine. We went to the top of the Willis Tower and stood together on the glass balcony, took funny pictures in front of the silver bean, and ate and drank our way through the city for three memorable days.

21

California Honeymoon with a Touch of Cinnamon

After our days in Chicago, JP and Emma got on a flight back to Rome while Vincenzo and I flew to San Francisco. This was finally going to be our true honeymoon. Together. Just the two of us. Alone.

We were so looking forward to this time away to relax and enjoy. The trip actually had a very funny start. I had mentioned to my mom that I missed having cinnamon in Italy. I could not easily find it in the stores. So, for a little present, she had given me a larger tin of her favorite cinnamon to take back to Italy. I had it packed in my checked baggage on the trip to California because we were leaving from there directly back to Italy.

We arrived in San Francisco and retrieved our bags. I noticed that when I put my bag down, a light red dust came off it. I thought perhaps it had gotten dirty in the transfer. As we settled into our hotel downtown, Vincenzo placed my bag on the rack and opened it. All I could hear was swearing in Italian.

I looked inside, but all I could see was a dark red dust covering every item in my bag. At first I had no idea what had happened. Then I remembered. The cinnamon. It was a new container that was made of tin, so I figured what happened is that security found it and was curious about what was inside. They must have opened it and then just tossed it back in my bag.

I was furious. I don't think that Vincenzo had ever heard me swear so much in his life. This time, I think I taught him a few new English words. He tried to calm me down and all I could do was cry. The cinnamon dust was covering all of my clothes and every item I had in the bag. I had no idea what to do. I decided to just close the bag and keep on the clothes I had traveled in for our romantic dinner I had planned for the evening.

As we passed by the front desk, I asked where the closest laundromat was located, and they told me there was one just a few blocks away. I looked at Vincenzo and said, "Guess what we are doing first thing in the morning?" He just smiled and said that all would be fine.

We walked out to enjoy the evening stroll and were anticipating a romantic dinner together at Scala's Bistro. We arrived and were seated at a little corner table reserved for us. I had mentioned that it was our honeymoon when I made the reservation. The server greeted us and arrived shortly after with two glasses of prosecco. Things were looking up. They were, that is, until he tipped his tray and the entire glass of prosecco landed on top of Vincenzo. We could not believe it. The only thing we could do was laugh and say that it must be "good luck" for us to have this start to our marriage. We had one more reason to visit the laundry.

The next morning, we took my bag and rolled it up the steep hills of San Francisco about five blocks to the laundry. As we walked in, I could see that Vincenzo was impressed.

He gasped, "All of these machines are available for anyone to do laundry?"

He was fascinated by this idea. I told him that we should pick two to three machines and start loading the clothes. We washed the items twice to try to get all of the cinnamon dust out. Some of the clothes were permanently stained, and the bag smelled like cinnamon for a couple of years. From that moment on, we referred to our honeymoon as the "cinnamon moon" instead. We finished up by early afternoon and went out exploring the city.

We had three days in San Francisco to visit as much as we could fit in. It was cold, rainy, and windy in these January days. We walked Market Street and went to the Ferry Building market and got items for a picnic lunch. We took the cable cars up and down the streets. Vincenzo had so much fun experiencing the city. He said that it was just like the TV show he used to watch when he was a kid, The Streets of San Francisco. I had no idea that shows like this were dubbed and broadcast in Italy early on.

We took a selfie in front of the Golden Gate Bridge and traveled to the beach for lunch. We also had lots of downtime, sleeping in and napping together. It had been a very busy and stressful six months. We were ready to settle in as husband and wife and to a quiet life together.

One day, we took the BART up to Berkeley as we had reservations for lunch at Chez Panisse. On the way, I explained to Vincenzo that the restaurant was famous and the chef, Alice Waters, had been a big influence on the slow food and farm-to-table movement of sourcing local organic ingredients for her restaurant many years prior. I knew that he would love the traditional and simple way that the dishes were created and presented. We enjoyed a lovely lunch together and soaked in the ambiance of the unique restaurant. I picked up a signed copy of her cookbook and stashed it away for my collection back in Italy.

Vincenzo and Sheryl at Chez Panisse.

After three days in San Francisco, we rented a car and drove down the coast to Monterey. Here we had splurged and rented a hotel room over the waters of the bay near Cannery Row. It was absolutely beautiful, with a fireplace and a large soaking tub for me to relax in each night.

We found a wonderful seafood restaurant down the road called the Chart House that we loved so much, we went every night. It had stunning views of the bay and felt a little like Italy as they made us feel welcome to stay as long as we liked.

They discovered that Vincenzo was a chef and so by the last evening, we had probably tasted every item on the menu. Vincenzo was in heaven because it was mostly fresh fish.

One of my favorites was the cioppino, or fish stew. It was one of the best I had ever tasted. They even created a special menu for our last night with our names, the date, and the menu we had chosen. I think we still have it in a keepsake box somewhere. During the day, we went exploring the rocky beaches and ocean views of Big Sur and Carmel by the Sea. At this point, I could see that Vincenzo was enjoying exploring America. California remains one of our favorite places to visit whenever we have the opportunity.

22

Layers of Beauty and Culture

As we settled back into our quiet life in Italy, I grew to appreciate the layers of beauty evident in the horizon each day. The views from our little village were like a canvas that changed colors and scenery on a regular basis. Sometimes, as I would walk out of the village to go for a long hike in the countryside or leave in the early morning to wait for the bus to travel to Siena for the day, I would look up and around and just stand in amazement. There were days when the clouds would be so low to the ground that they seemed to be covering everything around the village. As the fog would lift, the mountains in the distance would come into view, but not before I got to experience the clouds lingering between the valleys and drifting along as if we actually lived in the clouds.

Imagine walking out beyond the walls of the village to see the world unfolding around you each day. I loved watching the colors of the hills of olive groves and grapevines as they changed with the seasons. Starting brown and dead-looking in the winter, a vibrant green in the springtime, and then becoming a darker green, violet, and gold in the late summer and autumn. The trees and grapevines were planted in every nook and cranny of the countryside, some of them still terraced to make the best use of every bit of land. The color of the countryside came to life with little stone homes made from brick and limestone that had been patched together over the years. Each one set off from winding one-lane country roads that only the wild boar roam.

Picture ancient umbrella pines that tower above the homes and villages and cypress trees that line the medieval roads and surround ancient noble castles in the distance. Deeper in the horizon, I could see the purple shadows of the Tuscan mountains along with the lower Crete Senesi, where clay for the traditional terra-cotta is harvested and travertine is mined.

The horizon also included not only the sights but the smells of the countryside. As I would walk at various times of the year, I would smell pine, cypress, sulfur, figs, smoke, and a mixture of woody, musky air. It was like the earth was sending me healing messages with the sights and smells all around me. I felt surrounded by beauty and love, and I could never replicate this anywhere else I visited.

As with the layers of beauty in the Tuscan horizon, I found that the layers and connections I made with the people of Italy were so different than the connections I made on a daily basis back home. Italians are loud and passionate and will tell you exactly what's on their mind. I had to get used to this level of frankness in my daily life. If I walked out and seemed sad, the people around me noticed and asked what was going on. If I was happy and smiling, they smiled with me. Italians can take twenty minutes to say hello and another twenty minutes to say goodbye. They don't only get to know you on the surface—they want to know who you are on a deeper level. We held regular conversations about art, history, foods, traditions, music, and poetry at all levels.

I remember talking with a new friend, Norah, whom I met during a visit to a nearby castle one weekend. She greeted me with warm brown eyes and a friendly smile and asked me what brought me to Italy. She talked about what she loved about this country and was so proud of the history, culture, and traditions. Norah, who is originally from Argentina, is married to an Italian. She went on to study to be a sommelier so that she could explain the traditions of winemaking in Chianti.

With her, I felt a deep connection to the traditions of Italy and the people. Norah was one of my trekking companions, and frequently we would hike together on Sundays for the entire day and come back with great memories of the places we discovered.

One winter, I got an invitation from three local men who wanted to work on their English skills. Normally this might seem a little strange, but Lorenzo, Enzo, and Beppe were regulars at Vincenzo's restaurant and I knew them well. The men were all in their late fifties or early sixties, and all had led interesting and colorful lives. Their playfulness and curiosity about life in general was so refreshing.

We agreed that every Wednesday evening they would stop in our little apartment and we would read and interpret English poetry together for an hour or so. They would arrive as I was finishing work for the evening. They would always laugh at me as I would be working away at my little desk in the corner, typing with my wool finger gloves on because it was so cold in the house. The first time Lorenzo walked into our little kitchen and pulled up a chair around our wooden kitchen table, he looked up and around like he knew the house well.

"This was my grandparents' house at one time. How I love these old wooden beams on the ceiling and the memory of my grandmother cooking Sunday dinners for our family here," he said, closing his eyes as if he were remembering the smells of her cooking. "They had all three levels, not just this one. I remember coming here as a boy. This part of their house was the kitchen and dining room."

He went on to explain that the house was later sold and made into the three separate apartments that exist today. I felt like it was an honor to have this knowledge of the people who had lived in this cozy place before we did. At one point in the evening, Lorenzo got up, walked to our back window, opened it up, and started singing to the countryside. He had a beautiful voice that was so uninhibited. I wondered if he had done this as a child with his grandparents. Soon the other two joined in singing with him. It seemed that they, too, understood that he was paying homage to this place that was once owned by his family.

What struck me about these three men was their ability to be happy, and playful, yet serious in moments when appropriate. The poetry we read together was complicated and deep even for me to read and interpret the meanings in English, so we had a good laugh many times as I made up a story about what I thought the poetry meant. As we read together, they would ask me to help them with pronunciation and meaning. They kept a notebook with words and meanings as did I for new Italian words. Many times, I asked them my questions about new Italian words I heard them saying as well. Each time we connected, I learned so much from them about the Tuscan dialect and traditions.

They loved talking about politics and comparing Italy to America. They told me about the culture of the politics in Italy. This was during the time when Berlusconi was the leader of Italy. Every day, there were different stories about his influence and shenanigans in politics. They explained why so many people had to do business "under the table" because with such a high tax rate, it was difficult to make a living. However, these higher taxes also allowed everyone in the country to have free health care and other public assistance programs, so in a way it was important, but still difficult to manage for most people.

One day when they were with me for the evening, I asked about the mafia, as I was curious about this part of the culture. I asked if they knew anyone who was connected to the mafia. They just looked at each other and laughed. They explained that in Tuscany, there were many people who were considered the "soft mafia" with landlords who asked for payoffs and favors, and people with money still holding the majority of the power over most dealings even in the area where we lived. The more property they owned, the more control they had of the market and could charge the highest rent possible to the people in the area. This was not much different than the rest of the world.

When I told them to elaborate, they mentioned the owners of the building that Vincenzo and his partners rented for the restaurant space. They told me that the two men who owned the building owned much of the property in the village next door and other areas. They just shook their heads. This had me a bit worried. It was also common for someone to get a position or a job because of a connection rather than their skills or experience. It was more about "who you know" than "what you know."

Next, I asked about the priest of the village as I had gotten the impression that he also held a lot of power. And I noticed that he drove a Mercedes and lived in one of the best apartments in the village.

"Of course, while it may not be the same as the mafia, the church holds a lot of power in Italy," they said. This is normal. All of the money that the little bar I call the "church lady bar" makes goes back to the coffers of the church and the priest. He can do whatever he likes with it. These conversations were showing me the reality and many dark layers of the local culture as well as the beauty. It was eye-opening. I had so many questions to ask Vincenzo.

Vincenzo arrived later that evening after finishing up at the restaurant and had a lingering conversation with the group. He was so comfortable with them around our table, he pulled up an extra chair and sat down, patting each one on their backs. As I mentioned our conversation about the local mafia, he just looked defeated.

All he could say was, "They have us all by our balls in one way or another."

The three men exploded in laughter and agreement. This expression told me everything. I asked, "Well, now I'm curious. Do any of you have connections?" They all looked at each other as they considered their response.

"We all know someone who is connected," Vincenzo replied. "Around here, it helps to have connections to good people, like my friends in the police force and the mayor who love my food."

That was the response I was hoping to hear. The three men agreed. Beppe said, "Why would anyone not love Vincenzo? He gives us sustenance and a smile practically on a daily basis."

Lorenzo added, "I would be a lot skinnier than I already am if I did not have Vincenzo's food to eat when my wife is not here during the week. Sometimes I forget to eat. I might even starve to death."

This time his smile told me that it was true; the restaurant was an important place to all three of these men, as was Vincenzo. I had to admit, sharing his talent for creating good food did have a certain power over people. One that was legitimate and above the table—and at the table, to be exact.

23

An Ancient Sorority of Women

Being a woman in our little village was a bit like being in the middle of a strange sort of ancient sorority, with the average age of the women around seventy-five. Many of the women had lived in the area all their lives, so this place was theirs. I got to know a few of these women well during my time living in the village.

Nara

Let me introduce Nara. She was like the queen of the sorority and was born in San Gusme. Her house was an apartment in the main square, previously part of the palace back in the 1300s with a beautiful Juliet terrace overlooking the square. Nara usually was up at around 7:00 a.m., and I could tell because she would pull open her old metal shutters, which were always closed at night. While her little stovetop Moka coffeemaker was boiling her morning coffee, she would water her geraniums in the window boxes on her little terrace. She then started the laundry for the day, which later would be hanging out on her terrace or from her window clothesline.

The ladies of San Gusme sharing the bench.

Next, Nara would go down to her stoop on the lower level in her housedress and sweep away any pigeon feathers, dust, or leaves that had settled on her doorstep from the day before. Sometimes she would scrub the steps with a mop and soak them down with pails of water thrown from the top down. Beware, if you were walking by, she was hard of hearing and would soak you if you happened to be standing or walking close by.

Her next move was to get dressed and go to the church lady bar and do her morning shift making and serving cappuccino and brioche, or whatever the locals were having for breakfast.

She was always in a traditional dress and cardigan sweater with buttons, with panty hose and nice shoes. Her hair was perfectly coifed as each week she would go to the hairdresser for her weekly appointment, as did most ladies her age.

At the bar, she was in her element. She would catch up with the local gossip, or start the local gossip, and also sweep and clean the bar in the morning. This bar was organized by the local church. Everyone who works there volunteers their time, with the profits going straight back to the church. Visitors could buy everything from potato chips, grappa, wine, and coffee, to bus tickets and ice cream. This is where everyone would hang out to watch the soccer matches on TV and play cards outside in the summer. There was a large back room where the kids could play ball, dance, and watch movies together.

At around noon, Nara would finish her shift at the bar and walk with her shopping bag to the local grocery store. As Nara entered the store, she greeted Signora Brogi and surveyed the store like a hawk looking for the best options to eat for the day. Signora Brogi patiently awaited her order.

The transaction might sound something like this. Nara would say, "Do you have fresh asparagus?"

Signora Brogi retrieves her best bunch of asparagus and hands it to her.

"Let me see it," she says as she grabs it out of her hand. "No this will not do. How about zucchini?" As she inspects it, she seems satisfied. "Okay, I will take that. I want to make a risotto today. How about your fruit, what is good? I need some good apples to make a cake for my nephew who is coming to visit. Which ones are good for a cake?"

Signora Brogi advises her that the yellow apples are the best for cakes.

Nara regards her for a minute as if to verify this in her mind, and then nods, "Oh yes, you're right. I'll have six of them. But give me only the good ones." As if she never trusted her to do this in the first place.

Once finished, she steps outside with bag in hand. Other women from the village enter and greet her with smiles and kisses.

I could see that Nara carried some sort of unspoken authority and respect. I think that perhaps her family had money and power in the village at one point. This was also evident from her apartment, which is one of the most prestigious locations in the village.

After shopping, Nara would go over to the bench near the main door of the village with her shopping bag to sit and wait for the bread to arrive. Every day, except Sundays and holidays, fresh bread arrived around noon. The bread was still baked in the Tuscan tradition, fresh every day from another small village about thirty minutes away.

Nara knew everyone and had an opinion about everyone, as only she could have. She also could be very critical in her opinions and people tolerated it. However, when she walked away, I could see that they would whisper about her and say that she was arrogant. I even heard one woman say, "Just because she was born and baptized here does not give her the right to be so mean to everyone."

In my years living in the village, I got to know Nara better. She was our neighbor in the square and lived directly above the restaurant. This meant that we had to be friendly and kind to her, which is not too hard for me most of the time. She was kind to me, accepting me into the village and greeting me every day. She also approved of our geraniums that I placed in the flower boxes on our terrace to make sure that our house matched the beauty of hers for the festivals, which are hosted during the summer and fall months.

Nara was the first person to call me "the Americana" followed by "the chef's wife," and later she called me a version of my name, Cielo, which means sky, instead of Sheryl. Not many people from the village could pronounce my name because it is not at all a traditional name known in Italy. Most importantly, it did not end with a vowel, so they usually added any vowel that they saw fit to work with my name.

After shopping, Nara would walk back home to prepare lunch for herself, usually a pasta or risotto. She would check on her laundry and turn on her TV to watch the local news. She was a bit hard of hearing, so I always knew what was happening without having to turn on my TV. After lunch, like most everyone in the village, she would take a nap and rest for at least an hour.

Sometimes I would wander out during this time. The village was totally empty and peaceful as everyone was inside resting. This was my time to observe and just enjoy taking everything in. Around 4:00 or 5:00 p.m. (or later in the hot summer months) everyone was back outside for the evening passeggiata, or walk, and another chat.

Nara was out and about for this every day. This is when the children would be playing ball, running, and playing games together, and the teenagers would hang out at "the rock" in the vineyard directly behind the village or go to get a gelato or soda from the church lady bar.

Dinner started later, usually around 8:30 or 9:00 p.m. Everyone, including Nara, would go inside to eat dinner. In the summer months, the villagers would go back outside later in the evening to enjoy the cooler air. At around 11:00 p.m. or midnight, everyone would tuck in for the night as I could hear their nighttime greetings to each other, saying, "Buonanotte," as the heavy doors of each home clicked closed and San Gusme would become silent for the night.

Life in Italy had a beautiful rhythm to it, like a piece of music, starting out quietly, building to a middle crescendo, then quiet again until the big finish at the end. For me observing all of this as an outsider, it felt as if the locals would dance to the music and their voices were like songs. They would walk arm in arm together catching up and had a closeness that Americans would never dare to show. I loved this. When they would talk, their entire body got involved, from the gestures, to the voice inflections to the facial expressions. Sometimes, they did not even say words, but instead sounds that have meaning. It took me a while to figure out what they all meant, but it was fascinating to observe and learn.

Dina

Dina is another one of San Gusme's matriarchal women. She was always up each morning, catching up with all of the residents, making sure that everyone was okay. She usually asked questions like, "Where are you going?" and "How are you doing today?"

Dina also took care of her two grandchildren every day after school and most of the weekend as their parents worked. Dina always made sure that one of the elderly women of the village, Maria, had enough bread and food and whatever she needed for the day. She also provided daily company and someone to talk with.

Dina was someone with endless energy. Each year during the Festa del Luca, she would be on her feet cooking and helping for hours on end. In the morning, she was up early to start cooking in her house again for the next day's food. Like most of the women in the village, Dina's husband had died a few years before, so she now lived alone. However, she always had her village family that she cared for and that cared for her in return.

One day, Dina slipped and fell and broke a bone in her foot. She was in the hospital for five days after her surgery to repair the break, and then traveled home by ambulance to her apartment in San Gusme. Her apartment is one level, but to get to it were three flights of stairs with no other option. A couple of the men from the village took her up the three flights of stairs to her apartment.

Her accident caused a major stir in the usual order of things in San Gusme. Now, Lucia, Dina's daughter-in-law, was bringing Maria bread and food and making sure that she was okay for the day. Even Gianni, the owner of the market in town, made sure that he delivered food and bread when she needed it. The care of the grandchildren was shared among family and friends in the village as well.

It was so powerful to see how everyone took responsibility for making sure that this family unit was taken care of, as well as all of the people that Dina cared for. Everyone made plans to help Dina and make sure that she had food and everything that she needed while she was recovering.

Dina had a bright window to look out and survey the happenings of the village. People would yell up their greetings, and she would wave out the window with a hearty hello. At times, Mariano, one my neighbors who is young and very strong, would go up and carry her down the three flights of stairs so that she could sit on the bench at the church lady bar and catch up with her friends. He carried her gladly and with no hesitation or hint that this was not anything other than the usual. Dina was just a tiny little lady and Mariano was all muscles, so he made this look like it was a piece of cake.

Even though Dina was tiny, she had one of the loudest and mightiest voices in the village. This is an amazing example of the love, care, and concern that everyone had for each other in this tiny, medieval village.

Lina

Lina lived her entire life in the village. She shared an apartment just outside of the walls with her husband. I called it the Gusme burbs. It is a small little suburb of houses and apartments that are more modern than those within the walls of the village.

Lina was around eighty and still worked her shift at the church lady coffee bar every day with Nara. She colored her hair a bright red, which is the color most women her age colored their hair. She had a bright smile, when she would show it, which was not too often. She usually walked around with a broom in her hand because she did not like to use a cane. Sometimes I would imagine that perhaps she was a witch with special powers in disguise (una strega).

Lina was a true leader when it came to cooking for the festivals and dinners that were held in the village. She was like a Master Cheftress for the recipes like the pasta sauce with wild boar and ribollita soup. Both of these dishes are traditional Tuscan peasant food and are still served when the village held festivals in the summer and fall. Tuscan people had long been known as mangiafagioli, or bean eaters with the tradition of including white beans in many of their dishes. One day, I joined the ladies in the communal kitchen that was in the village, helping to make ribollita soup for a dinner for the local carabinieri (police). I walked in and greeted everyone and asked if I could help out.

They all looked at me with surprise, and Lina tossed me an apron, saying, "Here, you can chop the celery."

So, with a very dull kitchen knife and a wooden cutting board, I chopped and cleaned celery for about three hours until my hands were sore. During these hours together, the ladies of the village kept busy, chopping and peeling vegetables for the traditional soup. All the while gossiping and laughing with each other. They all tried to include me in the conversation, each time struggling with my name, followed by laughing at each other because they all called me different names. However, I did feel as if I had joined the ladies club and was slowly being accepted into their circle, which was important.

Every thirty minutes or so, Lina would check on our progress and add our vegetables to a huge kettle that was simmering on a large heating element on the floor of the kitchen. She was using one of the largest wooden spoons I had ever set eyes on to stir the soup. The vegetables were all fresh and looked wonderful. There were carrots, celery, onions, leeks, tomatoes, zucchini, kale, and white beans that had been soaked overnight. When I think back on all of the time it takes to chop and make the soup, I wonder if the time spent together while prepping and making the soup was just as important as the end product, the actual soup. Perhaps this was another important aspect of the recipe. The fresh local ingredients and the communion of the people interacting to create it.

At the end of the cooking, it was traditional to add stale bread to the soup, which made it even heartier and more delicious. The bread would dissolve into the soup and become a part of it—making it thick and hearty. This was true Tuscan cooking from years of the tradition of using fresh vegetables in season and not wasting a thing, including any stale bread that was left over. The soup was usually served with a nice drizzle of local extra virgin olive oil over the top. At one point, I stopped chopping and asked her if she had the recipe written down anywhere.

Lina just shook her head and wagged her pointer finger at me. "No, no, that is not necessary, it is all here," as she pointed to her head. She checked and stirred and tasted until all of the ingredients were just right and then gave us the signal that we had chopped enough of each ingredient.

After this experience together, each time I would see Lina, she would give me a warm smile and we would chat a little about the weather or my travels, or the happenings of San Gusme. I frequently would go to the church lady bar in the afternoon to buy bus tickets or ice cream. She always reminded me when there was a festival to prepare for, and I would try to pitch in and help out.

After the first experience, I brought my own knife and cutting board. I felt like I was part of the village traditions, steeped in deep history. But I always wondered where the other young women were. Who will carry on these traditions and remember the recipes? I worried that the history and traditions would be lost to the younger generation.

Ribollita Soup

¼ cup extra virgin olive oil
1 medium onion (chopped)
2 leeks (chopped)
2 cloves garlic (minced)
4 stalks of celery (chopped), and it's okay to also include a few of the celery leaves chopped as well
4 medium carrots (peeled and diced)
4 small zucchini (diced)
4 medium potatoes (peeled and diced)
2 15-oz cans cannellini beans
4 medium tomatoes (diced, seeds removed)
2 tablespoons tomato paste
6-8 cups (2 quarts) vegetable stock (Keep warm on the stove next to the soup pot.)
3 cups fresh Tuscan or black kale (chopped, use only the tender leaves, take out the middle stem)
3 cups fresh spinach (chopped, use only the tender leaves, no stems)
½ loaf crusty white bread (sliced)
Olive oil and parmesan cheese for serving

Place the olive oil in a large Dutch oven or large stock pot over medium heat. Sauté the onions, leeks, and garlic for 3-4 minutes. Add the carrots and potatoes. After each vegetable, add a ladle of vegetable stock. Next add the zucchini, kale, and spinach. Add in the remaining broth. Let simmer for 1 hour and 20 minutes.

Now, add the beans, tomatoes and tomato paste. Stir well and let simmer for 10 minutes.

Sfumata (Oil Infused with Aromatic Herbs)

1 cup olive oil
1 head of garlic (cut in half)
4 fresh rosemary sprigs (leave intact on the stem)
4-6 sage leaves
4 bay leaves

Place the oil in a small saucepan over medium heat. Add the garlic, rosemary, sage, and bay leaves and warm until it starts to simmer. Take off heat and pour the oil over the soup (pour over using a strainer to remove the garlic and aromatic herbs).

Lay out the sliced bread on a sheet pan and toast them in the oven (425 degrees) 5-6 minutes until lightly browned.

Next, layer the bread with the soup in a large, deep casserole dish. Alternate layers of bread and soup until you have used it all. Let sit until ready to eat. After soaking in the soup, the bread dissolves and becomes the hearty part of the soup. The longer this sits, the better the taste. You can place this in the refrigerator and take out a portion at a time if you like.

Just before serving, place the soup back in the stock pot and warm again until boiling. If the soup is too thick from the bread, add more water or broth to thin.

Ladle out into soup bowls and top with grated parmesan cheese and a drizzle of olive oil.

This soup is delicious after a few days as well. This makes 6-8 servings.

Recipe note: Tuscan kale (also called lacinato or black kale) can be found in the fresh greens area of most grocery stores. It's important to use only the tender leaves and remove the center stem prior to chopping the kale.

The recipe is Vincenzo's version of ribollita soup, as he also made it often in the restaurant. When I asked him about the specifics of the recipe, he also responded as Lina had, indicating that it is created all with your eyes looking to see how much of each vegetable is added, with equal parts of each one, depending on how many people you are serving. We have since recreated this at home, with me checking and noting the amounts so that the recipe can be passed along. As with many of the recipes, ribolitta takes fresh ingredients and time, but is so worth it in the end.

Tosca

Tosca was perhaps one of my favorite people in San Gusme. I felt a deep connection to her because she was a bit like me, quiet and inside herself, showing her feelings and emotions only after she got to know you. She lived on the very top floor of the old palace in the square, which required going up four flights of uneven stone steps, which she did several times a day when she carried wood up for her fireplace or if she went out to get bread or go to the market.

She had also lived in San Gusme forever. Her husband died many years ago, and, more recently, she lost her son who died suddenly as well. Every day, she would walk out the village doors and down the long path to the cemetery to visit their graves and pay her respects, many times with a little bouquet of wildflowers in her hands.

Even though she was shy, Tosca was out every day, catching up with the locals as she waited on the bench for the bread to arrive. She would frequently take bread crumbs and other treats and leave them on the wall behind the village for the stray cats. The children of the village all knew her as well, giving her ample hugs and kisses when they saw her.

Vincenzo always called her Toschina, meaning little Tosca. He would check in with her frequently in the winter to make sure that she had enough firewood and that she was keeping warm and safe. When anyone asked how she was doing, her favorite expression in Italian was "insomma," which translates to "not great, but not bad either."

When I looked into Tosca's eyes, I could see it all. The pain, the loneliness, and sadness were all there, mixed in with a lifetime of joys and experiences. I loved to find Tosca out on the bench during the day and just sit and be with her. She never required much attention—and very few words if any. However, I always knew that we were having a conversation between our hearts.

Sometimes when it was cold weather, we would snuggle in on the bench and I would reach for her hand while we talked. I loved to bake biscotti or scones and bring a few to her as an expression of my care for her. In Italy, food equals caring, so she understood this from me. I was always amazed at her resilience and strength.

Lavender Ginger Biscotti

½ cup unsalted butter (room temperature)
¾ cup sugar
1 large egg
1 tsp. vanilla extract
¾ tsp. baking powder
¾ tsp. sea salt
½ lemon (zested)
2 tsp. dried lavender flowers (crushed between your fingers)
8 ounces white chocolate (chopped)
4 tablespoons candied ginger (finely chopped)
½ cup roasted almonds (whole)
2 cups all-purpose flour

Preheat oven to 375 degrees.

Cream together the butter and sugar. The mixture should be light yellow and smooth. Add the egg and beat well. Next add the vanilla extract, baking powder, and salt. Mix well.

Zest the lemon and add to the dough. Add in the almonds, candied ginger, lavender flowers, and white chocolate chips. Mix well.

Add the flour 1 cup at a time, mixing well. You may need more or less flour depending on the humidity. The dough should not be too sticky. You should be able to handle it with your hands without sticking.

Separate the dough into three equal parts and form three logs of dough that are about 1½ inches wide and 10-12 inches long. Place on baking sheet that is covered with parchment paper.

Bake at 375 degrees for 10-12 minutes. The cookies should be light golden brown.

Let cool for about 5-10 minutes.
Reduce oven heat to 350 degrees.

Place the cookie logs on a cutting board and cut into individual slices about ½ inch wide (like slicing bread, except don't use a sawing motion when cutting, use a sharp knife and cut in one motion down through the cookies). Place the cookies back on the baking sheet with one side down. Bake again for 8-10 minutes until they are just slightly brown. Cool on a wire rack and place in airtight container.

Recipe note: If you would like to experiment with different ingredients, add dark chocolate, grated orange zest, and chopped almonds instead of the ginger and lavender. Or try other nut and chocolate combinations, such as hazelnuts and dark chocolate, pistachios, dried cranberries and white chocolate.

VILMA

Vilma had a strong presence in the village as the wife of Giancarlo and a grandmother. She was out early each morning in her back garden tending to her garden and chickens. Her grandchildren, two little girls, were a big part of her life. She would frequently take care of them before and after school and was always in the kitchen cooking when not out in the village square as they played and enjoyed being kids.

The two girls would often set up camp on the outside grounds of the church near our apartment with their blankets, dolls, and dishes. In the summer, they even featured a little market where you could buy treasures that they had collected.

I loved getting to know Vilma early on in my time in Italy. She was one of the first ladies to welcome me to the village family. She always had a smile and would help me with recipes and fresh herbs from her garden when I asked for them. I would frequently sit out on the bench with her as she entertained her grandchildren.

Vilma was an Italiana inside and out. She was direct, to the point, and always told you exactly what was on her mind. At the same time, she could switch to being kind and gentle and was always helping someone else out when they needed her. She had a voice so loud you could hear it from the other side of the village. This came in handy when she was trying to locate the kids and call them in for dinner. Her heart was as big as can be, and she will always have a place in my heart as well.

I eventually became less shy with the sorority of women in the village. As the months went on, I would frequently take a break from working in the evening and go out and squeeze in on a bench with two or three of the women as they were gossiping. I think they enjoyed this as well. Someone new to join in the conversations.

They mostly did not understand what I did for work, so much of the time, they asked me questions about this: "What do you do all day in the house all alone?"

I explained, "I'm a nurse and a medical writer."

They exclaimed, "A dottoressa," meaning a female doctor or professor.

I went on to explain, "I write textbooks and design courses for nurses to learn. I also write documents for patients to understand more about a health problem that they have."

They just looked at me in wonder, one of them saying, "You do all of that from your computer?"

Then I went on to explain how I used Skype for meetings with my colleagues back in the States and others whom I was working with. They could hardly believe it. I'm not sure what they thought of me before this, but after this conversation, I received more sincere looks and felt a sense of respect from them. Sometimes I would even get nurse questions if someone wanted advice about a sore toe or other symptoms they were having. I really loved knowing that they felt close enough to me and trusted me to reach out like this.

24

The Men of San Gusme

nteresting characters all—the men of San Gusme have long ties with their history of living in the village.

Vezio

Vezio, the tailor, is about eighty-four and still working in his shop every day, except Sundays. He has worked so hard as a tailor that his back is curved from bending over the sewing machine. If you walked into his shop, his eyes would light up as he greeted you with open arms and any local news that he felt he needed to share.

If you looked around his shop, you could see the antique sewing machine that he still used and the old cutting table with what seemed like years of scraps of silk and wool that all have a story. People traveled from all over the area to have him create designs for them. He made custom dresses and suits and was also the primary person who sewed the traditional robes, drapes, and decorations for the religious processionals and celebrations that take place within the village. Vincenzo once left him a pair of his chef pants to hem and did not get them back for months. Perhaps the more complicated the project, the more interest Vezio had in the work.

His pride is the ancient church in the village, which was from the fourteenth century. If you asked to see the church, Vezio was the one with the key. He would take you on a tour of a lifetime, giving you all of the details of the church, the altarpiece, crypt and artwork with hundreds of years of history. Vezio was the caretaker of the church and watched over her like a beautiful treasure. He regularly cleaned the floors and dusted the benches, gathered flowers for the church altar, and made sure that it was ready for any festival or special ceremony.

Once I asked him about the old villa that sits empty outside of the village. I frequently walked past the villa and overgrown gardens and wondered what it must have been like years ago. Vezio's eyes lit up like the sun, and he settled in to tell me the story of what the villa was like when he was little.

"Oh, I remember when I was about ten years old, my parents would let me go and play around the villa," he said, adding, "They were descendants of the original family who built the villa in the 1400s." He smiled at me as he understood my love for the history of this place.

"Go on, please," I said.

"I remember that the children all had their own maid and nanny. They would take a picnic down to the pond and eat off of silver plates. I always thought it would be more fun to be in my place, because they could not get dirty in their elegant clothing, but I could. I'd run off and dream of what it might be like to live there just for a little while. I always thought I had it better because I was free to wander and do what I wanted without someone watching over my every move. What fun I had." He was smiling from ear to ear.

He went on to explain that the villa had such incredible gardens, sculptures, and fruit trees that it seemed like paradise. As I would walk around the stone walls that surrounded the overgrown gardens, there were places where someone could sneak in and take a peek at the beauty of the grounds, even as they were now, abandoned and wild. I loved imagining what it must have been like in the day when a noble family had once lived there. I thought it was so fantastic that Vezio had experienced it as a child and had given me a little glimpse into what it was like.

Vezio's routine was to take his afternoon coffee at the restaurant. He would arrive, sit down at the family table near the kitchen, and someone would immediately start making a coffee for him. He would sit and casually fill in Vincenzo and anyone else present on all of the local news and gossip as he sipped on his coffee. He had eyes like an eagle and noticed everything that happened in the village. I knew that whenever I needed an update on news, I would just head over to Vezio's shop to say hello, but leave at least thirty minutes to talk, as that is the minimum amount of time needed to get all of the news. In the summer, if you brought him an ice cream, he was forever grateful, smiling from ear to ear as he accepted the gift. Still a child at heart.

Remo

Remo is a local man who was now in his mid-eighties. He still went to work every day in his local cantina selling Chianti wine, vin santo, and olive oil. Remo was busy especially in the summer when tourists wandered through San Gusme. If you were curious, you would find Remo sitting at his little desk in his blue work coat checking the books for his wine and oil business. If you poked your head in, he would come out and greet you with a smile and a welcome. When you looked into his eyes, you could almost imagine the life that he lived. Remo's cantina had huge old chestnut barrels that he still aged his Chianti wine in. In the back of the cantina are the large terra-cotta vats with the latest olive oil just waiting to be tasted.

I especially loved to taste the new olive oil just after the harvest each year. New oil is celebrated and treasured by everyone in Italy. In November or December when the olives are harvested, I would wait for the first taste of new oil from anyone who was willing to share it. New oil is bright green and opaque, with a wild fruity and spicy flavor. I would describe it as a grassy, herby taste with overtones of black pepper. As the oil would age, it would become more clear and mellow with more fruity tastes like banana followed by a spicy, peppery aftertaste. Many times, Remo's wife would grill bread over the wood fire, with olive oil drizzled over it, followed by a healthy sprinkle of salt. Bread and oil, pane e olio—one of my favorite ever tastes from Italy. I also loved to make bruschetta with fresh tomatoes, basil, and olive oil. It is like a taste of pure heaven.

Tomato Bruschetta

3-5 fresh tomatoes
Olive oil (extra virgin)
Salt
1 clove of garlic
3-5 sprigs of fresh basil leaves (torn into small pieces)
1 loaf of Italian bread or French baguette (sliced)

Slice the fresh tomatoes, reserving the seeds. Add to bowl and drizzle with olive oil (enough to just cover the tomatoes). Sprinkle salt to taste and stir together. Add the torn fresh basil leaves and let sit for a few minutes.

Next toast the bread slices in the oven at 425 degrees (or on the grill) until just brown, around 5-6 minutes. While the bread is warm, rub the garlic clove over each side of the toasted bread. Spoon the tomato, basil, and oil mixture over the top and serve.

Serves 4.
Recipe note: When making tomato bruschetta for a larger group, estimate one tomato per person and adjust the rest of the ingredients accordingly.

Remo's olive groves and grapevines sat just outside the village. The land had been in his family for generations. His father built the cantina in San Gusme in the early 1900s. Remo spoke with a very heavy Tuscan dialect, so it took me a few years to really understand everything when he spoke to me. I frequently would stop in with my Chianti wine jug and an empty bottle for olive oil, and he would provide me with some of my favorite local treasures.

He would always tell me that the best way to really taste the olive oil was to make spaghetti with oil and parmesan cheese or what was called pasta bianca. This featured some of the simplest ingredients of the land of Italy. Pasta made with local wheat, fresh green and spicy olive oil, and aged parmesan cheese. Everywhere in Italy, traditional recipes are those that are made with just a few simple, local ingredients.

Remo's cantina was just a few doors away from our little apartment, so he was our neighbor. Sometimes I would just stop in to say hello if I was walking by and saw that he was sitting at this desk. One day, he told me a story that I will never forget.

Remo was a child during World War II. The German troops occupied San Gusme during the war because of the strategic location, offering the walls for protection and the view of the surrounding countryside. Remo told me that he used to sneak out of the village on his bicycle and take food into the countryside where he knew a few members of the allied troops were hiding out—English soldiers. During this time, the Germans would frequently come around to each house and check to see if anyone was hiding soldiers or helping them. Remo told me his family helped provide a bicycle to an English soldier who was able to escape the area and ride to a train station about 70 km and eventually return to Rome. He said that the allied troops had taken Rome back at that point and the soldier was able to eventually return home safely.

That same soldier later wrote Remo's father a letter after the war thanking him for the help they had provided. Remo still has that letter framed in his office. Allied troops eventually liberated San Gusme from the Germans by busting through one of the stone entrances to San Gusme with their tanks. The people of the village never repaired that entrance to the village, and that is why to this day, you can still see the outline of the damage that occurred from the tanks. The people say that it will remain this way forever to remember the war and how they were saved by the allied forces.

As I got to know Remo, I could see that his health was declining. One day I noticed that he had a cut on his face and some bruises. When I asked him what happened, he said that he had been in a little car accident. After this, the doctors had told him he could not drive anymore because they thought he had a little stroke. This did not slow him down much at all.

Every Wednesday, instead of driving into Siena to go to the local market to check on his business accounts, he would instead take the bus. Some days, we would ride the bus together into Siena. One day, he asked if I wanted to have a cup of coffee once we got to Siena and I agreed. I got off at the stop he liked and hiked uphill for six blocks into the city. Normally I preferred the stop that had the escalator that would take us uphill into the city center. He told me that he never took the escalator, he liked walking instead. It is the same attitude that may well be his secret to living well into his eighties.

He took me to his favorite coffee bar where everyone greeted him like the old friend that he was. His farmer friends were all there waiting for him to arrive. They had a little wink in their eyes today as he arrived with this blond American woman. I have to say I felt like I was with a celebrity. We had coffee together and then he went on his way to connect with the other local farmers to find out about the olive and wine commodities. He probably had this routine for sixty years or so.

He once showed me a photo of how his father would transport Chianti wine into Florence with large horse-drawn wagons piled with bottles strategically placed. He still had many of the older-style green hand-blown demijohn wine jugs that back in the day would have had straw woven baskets around them.

As Remo and Vezio aged within the walls of the village, they passed along their wisdom and history to the younger generation. Men like Giancarlo and Lorenzo who had also lived most of their lives in the village were there to carry the baton to the next generation.

Giancarlo

Giancarlo, the protector of the village, was out each day surveying what was going on in all aspects. He regularly hunted in the woods just outside the village and knew every inch of the land, birds, and animals that roamed it. He also participated as a volunteer fireman for the region. Every year, the fire and ambulance rescue would bring their helicoptors and equipment to San Gusme for practice drills. Giancarlo was frequently on call during the hot, dry summers when the fire risk was high.

For me, he personally rescued me many times when I would forget my key in the house as I was out chatting with the ladies on the bench below our terrace and the outside door slammed shut in the wind. Giancarlo and his ladder were there to get me back in. He also killed what seemed like the most evil looking insect I ever came across one day as I was padding out from the bed to start my morning.

I looked down on our terra-cotta floor and saw a big black insect about five inches long with legs like a cricket and wings like a grasshopper. I shot out the door in my pajamas and slippers to see if Giancarlo was in the area. He and Vilma lived just a few feet down the village. I found him quickly and tried to describe what I saw.

He just got a big smile on his face as he said under his breath "must be a diavoletto." I knew what that word meant: little devil. I thought it was the perfect word for what I saw. He quickly retrieved a broom and ran up the stairs to find the beast. I was close behind him, but not too close. With one swipe, the insect was dead and thrown out of the apartment onto the central square.

By this time, Vilma and their grandchildren were out in front of our apartment to check out just exactly what all the fuss was about. They all agreed that it was a terrifying looking insect. From that day forward, I always referred to Giancarlo as my cacciatore, or hunter.

Lorenzo

Lorenzo, with his long family history of living in the area, is carefully preserving the structures and heritage of his family home. He and his wife, Daniela, have transformed a corner of San Gusme where they have lived for years to a traditional garden and space to admire the countryside views. During the local wine festival, they host a special art event where local artists can showcase their pieces among the beauty of the nature around the village. He has preserved a family cantina with antique farming and harvest equipment with a collection of treasured wines from the family vineyard.

Recently, Lorenzo restored a large family apartment into three unique apartments that visitors can rent while they are exploring the area. Look for Borgo San Gusme if you are searching for this bed and breakfast gem while visiting the area. Together, they have formed a thriving partnership keeping the history and people of the village moving forward.

25

The Girl on the Train

One day during the first year of living full-time in Italy, I decided I needed to get out and explore more on my own. I planned to take the train to Florence to spend the day. I told Vincenzo I would be fine navigating my way alone. I wanted to be independent using public transportation as much as possible. I took the local bus from San Gusme that arrived at the Siena train station.

I purchased a round-trip ticket from the ticket counter and sat in the little coffee bar and had a cup of coffee prior to leaving. The Siena train station is small, with only four main tracks, so I was not too worried that I would have a problem finding the track to catch the regional train to Florence. I glanced at the timetable listed on the board and it said that the train to Florence would arrive on track 1 in twenty minutes.

As I glanced at track 1, I noticed that there was a train already waiting there. I wondered if the train could be here this early. In my experience, trains in Italy are hardly ever early or even on time, so I was doubtful.

As I was standing there contemplating if I should get on the train, I noticed another woman standing nearby who seemed to be doing the same thing. I sensed that she was approachable and maybe even friendly, so I asked her, "Is this the train to Florence?"

She replied, "I think so, but it is early." I noticed a little smile of doubt, like I had thought. "Why so early?" she added. We laughed together and she quickly switched to speaking in English. She could tell that I was an American from the accent, and she could see my relief as she started talking. I apologized for my terrible language skills, and she reassured me that it was okay. We both got on the train and I asked her if she wanted some company on the way to Florence. I was normally very shy, but for some reason, I felt like I should connect with this woman.

We started talking as the train departed Siena and made its way to Florence. The regional train was very slow and stopped at many little villages along the way. It was great to have company for the ninety-minute train ride into the center of Florence. I learned that Stefania was a kindred spirit. She worked in the field of medical research for a pharmaceutical company in Milan. When I told her that my background was also science-based, and that I was a nurse from Mayo Clinic, she was thrilled to hear about the work I had done during my career, which included research.

I mentioned that her English was fantastic, and she said that she speaks in English on a daily basis for her job. She also lived in Hawaii and Boston for a period of time with a boyfriend who was American, with Italian roots. That had ended when she decided that she did not want to live in America, mostly because she missed Italy too much.

We talked nonstop during the trip to Florence. I shared that I had just moved to Italy a year prior and that it was for love. When I told her the story of meeting Vincenzo, falling in love and deciding to move to Italy, her big brown eyes were wide and warm with surprise. When I asked her why she was visiting Siena, she told me that her boyfriend was from Siena and that she had just been with him for the weekend and was traveling back to Milan for the week.

The ninety minutes flew by, and as we arrived into Florence, we shared our phone numbers and email addresses. I really knew in my heart that Stefania would be an important person in my life from that day on. We often connected when she was back in Siena for day-trips to the thermal springs or outings to Florence, Pienza, or Cortona.

One of my most fond memories I have of Stefania during my time living in Italy was a girlfriend adventure together about a year or so after we originally met. She and I connected in Siena, and I jumped in her little car with my bag for the week trip to her beach house on the Mediterranean. As we traveled north, I could see the landscape changing with steep mountains in the near distance.

Stefania had a family house in a beach village called Focette. The house is nestled in a residential area that is surrounded by towering umbrella pines with the beach just a ten-minute walk away. We planned to go to the beach during the last week of August. Most Italians take the entire month of August off and flock to the beaches because of the heat in the summer.

This was my first time experiencing this idea. Imagine, an entire month of vacation. This idea would never work in the US. We found her favorite pizza place and had dinner late after we arrived. The whole feel of the place seemed to be back in time a bit. Next to the pizza place was a coffee bar with a bakery. She told me that she would regularly bike down in the morning for fresh pastries and a newspaper. I peeked into the windows of the shop next door and could see that they sold traditional linens and household items. I could not wait to explore this place more in the daytime.

We arrived at the beach house and dusted off the covers of the furniture and opened up the shutters and patio doors to a terrace shaded by magnolia trees. She showed me the bedroom where I would be sleeping, and I could sense the layers of family history in the house. I could see her mother's robes, slippers, and sundresses still in the closet. I found vintage wool blankets and cotton bed coverlets from years past.

I knew that her mother had passed away a few years previous and that she and Stefania had been very close. I understand that these items still remaining in the house were important family treasures for her to keep. Stefania told me of fond memories of spending her summers here when she grew up.

For me, the beach house seemed frozen in time. I saw matchbooks from restaurants and old journals, family pictures, and memories everywhere. We cleaned the kitchen together and plugged in the refrigerator and got settled in for the five days together. We explored the markets for local produce and cheese. I remember slicing into an heirloom tomato that was large enough for us to eat for two days. The instant it was sliced open, green, herbal tomato scent filled the kitchen. We also had fresh mozzarella cheese, crusty bread, and big leaves of fresh basil to partner it with. Stefania had brought a bottle of her favorite olive oil from Siena. I had a couple of bottles of my favorite Chianti Classico from the vineyard of Felsina near Castelnuovo Berardenga.

Every day, we would plan out our adventures. The first day was beach day. I will always remember the little bicycle that she had for me to ride. It must have been circa 1970 because it had the banana seat and curved handlebar style that I had always wanted. There it was, just waiting for me to live out my childhood dreams again. We loaded our bags with towels, sunscreen, and a picnic lunch for the day and headed out on our bicycles to the beach.

The beaches are just breathtaking in this area, with white sand and clear blue water. In the near distance, we could see the white streaks and pockets of marble that looked like snow in the Apuan Alps where Carrara marble is mined.

We arrived at the beach and got settled into our reserved area with an umbrella and two lounge chairs. Italians know how to enjoy the beach. The same area had changing rooms and a café where we could get a cold drink, snacks, and ice cream. We had a great view of the sea in front of us, with the mountains behind us. Every time I looked around, I thought perhaps I was in a dream. We took a long walk, had a swim, ate our picnic, and spent the afternoon either napping or reading with intermittent dips in the sea. The Mediterranean water was clear and warm.

It got very hot in the afternoon, so at one point I went into the little café and found a treat that is still one of my favorites in the summertime—Coppa del Nonno, which translates to "Grandfather's cup." It is a soft, creamy, frozen treat that combines coffee with ice cream and a little chocolate that is served in a little espresso cup. Instead of drinking hot coffee, this was the perfect alternative and a nice pick-me-up after a day of swimming and lounging.

Coppa del Nonno

1 pint heavy whipping cream

3 eggs (separated)

½ cup sugar

¼ cup strong brewed coffee or espresso

¼ cup cocoa powder

1 tsp. vanilla extract

½ tsp. sea salt

Start by whipping the heavy cream until it is just starting to get thick (around 2-3 minutes). I use a stand mixer. Set aside.

Place the egg whites in a bowl and whip well until they form soft peaks and are starting to get shiny. Set aside.

Next, mix together the sugar and egg yolks until they are creamy and well mixed, around 1 minute. Add the espresso, cocoa powder, vanilla, and sea salt and continue to mix well for another 20 seconds.

At the end, in a large mixing bowl, use a whisk to mix together all three ingredients until they are well incorporated.

Place the creamy mixture into a freezer-safe container and freeze well, about 3-4 hours. Scoop out the cream into individual cups to serve. Store remaining cream in freezer until ready to use.

Each day, Stefania and I had a new adventure planned. We went to the beach nearly every evening to walk and watch the sun set. We laughed and talked like only girlfriends can do together. One day, we took the little trolley to the neighboring village, Forte dei Marmi or the "Marble Fort," which is where tourists find stunning villas and people who seemed like royalty and the rich and famous, but incognito.

On the way, I could see everyday life unfolding in front of me. There were ladies out with their market baskets, kids riding their bikes, men getting their hair cut at the barber shop, and people in and out of the little coffee bars enjoying their morning coffee. Forte dei Marmi has a large outdoor market every Sunday. This area is famous for cashmere and linens. We had a great time looking and making a few small purchases at the market.

Another day, we took her car and drove to the marble mountains of Carrara. This was a spectacular day for me as I love geology and rocks in general, but to see where the famous Italian marble is mined was a special gift for me. We traveled all the way to the top of the mountain to a little village called Colonnata, which is famous for two things, marble mining and lardo di Colonnata. This is the same area that was the source of the marble for Michelangelo's David in Florence.

The settlers of this village have long been involved in working in the marble quarries. Even from the beginning, it was a village where the slaves lived. The quarries are still busy with miners, but the old techniques have been replaced by modern ways. Stefania had a great conversation with an older woman as she was hanging out her laundry for the day. She recounted that she remembered when they transported the marble down the mountain using logs and ropes to roll or drag the large pieces to the bottom.

Lardo di Colonnata is a delicacy only found in this area. Lardo is bacon fat that is cured with rosemary, salt, and other spices for months in large vats of marble from the area. It is typically served sliced very thin over toasted bread from the area. The fat basically melts into the bread and is absolutely delicious.

I purchased a couple of packages to take home to Vincenzo. He has a fantastic recipe that he serves in his restaurant with potatoes, lardo, and rosemary and pecorino sauce. It is a baked potato tartlet that consists of tender potatoes that have been baked with slices of lardo surrounding it and plated with a pecorino sauce over the top.

POTATO TARTLET WITH BACON AND ROSEMARY

2 pounds baking potatoes (russets are perfect)
2 tsp. salt
¼ cup olive oil
6 slices of good bacon or pancetta (diced into small pieces)
1 tablespoon fresh rosemary (chopped)
Spray oil
16 additional slices of bacon or lardo (thin sliced).

Preheat oven to 400 degrees.

Prick the potatoes with a fork in a few places and place the potatoes on a sheet pan. Bake the potatoes for one hour. Remove from the oven and let them cool for 20 minutes. Cut the potatoes in half and scoop out the potatoes from the skins. Place the potatoes in a large bowl. Next, use a ricer to rice the potatoes. If you don't have a ricer, you can mash them by hand with a potato masher.

Add the salt, olive oil, diced pancetta, and rosemary to the potatoes and mix well.

Spray eight individual 6-ounce ramekins with spray oil. Take one slice of bacon or lardo and drape it inside the ramekin. Place the second piece of bacon in the ramekin crossing the first piece. The edges should fall over the side of the ramekin. Spoon the potato mixture into the ramekins until full. Fold the bacon (or lardo) slices up and over the top of the potato mixture.

Place the ramekins together on a sheet pan and bake in the oven at 400 degrees for 15 minutes. Remove from the oven and turn over onto a plate so that the potato tart falls out onto the plate.

While the potatoes are in the oven, make the cheese sauce to go over the potatoes.

Cheese Sauce

12 ounces heavy cream
14 ounces pecorino cheese (grated)
4 sprigs fresh rosemary (chopped fine)

Warm the heavy cream over medium to low heat on the stove until the milk starts to steam. Lower the heat to low and continue to warm for another minute. Add the pecorino cheese and continue to warm another minute. Stir well. Remove from heat and serve over warm potatoes. Serve with fresh rosemary and a drizzle of olive oil.

Recipe note: You can find lardo at specialty shops, butcher shops and some grocery stores. Ask about it at the meat counter. Any kind of bacon is a good substitute. If you are unable to find pecorino cheese, you can substitute parmesan cheese.

As each day passed by, I felt like I had a glimpse of Stefania's life growing up in this area. We talked about little things and very deep subjects. Stefania has a similar sense of curiosity about life in general and I love this about her. The fact that she was sharing this place with me was a beautiful gift. In the end, I felt like we were sisters, telling a few of our stories from our past and revealing secrets and future dreams with each other.

She is an only child, and I have two siblings that are brothers, so we both felt like we connected on a sisterly level. We have enjoyed this close bond that we have together and frequently plan time together to connect and catch up where we left off. It's strange, but we prefer to have our time together as just the two of us. Vincenzo knows that when I plan time with Stefania that it is important "sister time" so he totally respects it.

Stefania and Sheryl.

26

Health Care, Illness, and Superstitions

Traditional beliefs were entwined with modern beliefs when it came to health care and medicine in Italy. For me, as a nurse and a researcher of cultures, it was fascinating to learn how health care was delivered as well as the strong beliefs about health and illness in Italy.

In San Gusme, the village doctor came to the walk-in clinic three times a week for two to three hours. If you had a medical problem or needed a prescription, you could simply go to the clinic and sit and wait for your turn to see the doctor. There was no appointment secretary to call and no receptionist to receive you when you arrived. Instead, you walked into a tiny little office that was situated just on the outside of the clinic, with farmland and vines surrounding it, to find the handful of chairs in the narrow entrance filled with the local elderly or a mother with a sick child all waiting to see the doctor.

One day I arrived to ask about a prescription that I needed to renew. As I arrived, I looked around to see if there was a place to sit, and I wondered how the whole experience would be that morning. Vincenzo had come with me this first time to show me the protocol of waiting for a visit with the doctor. Here is how it goes.

Just after I arrived, another elderly woman from the village arrived. She looked around and said to everyone, "Who was the last to arrive?"

Everyone pointed at me and said, "The Americana." This way, she knew whom to go in after. This was the only way to keep track of the schedule of people waiting to see the doctor each day. So then, I wondered, when was my turn?

Vincenzo was reading my mind and asked the group, "Who was last before Sheryl?"

One of the ladies spoke up and said, "That's me."

And that's how we discovered where I fit in the order that day.

We had waited about seventy-five minutes and it was about my turn to go in to see the doctor, when he bolted out of his exam room with his black bag in hand and said to the group, "I need to leave to make a house call."

He offered no other alternative or opportunity for anyone to protest. We all needed him for one reason or another. I could not believe it.

The entire waiting room let out a collective groan and one by one began to leave the waiting area, giving up for the day. Perhaps to return the next time the clinic was open, or, if more urgent, they would travel to the neighboring village on the next day to find the doctor where he was.

The doctor served this village and the surrounding villages. He made his rounds during the week to tiny little offices like this one in each village. On my first visit, he registered me into his computer and later I was given my health care card for Italy. To me, the socialized medicine system was a mystery. I had never experienced it firsthand.

If you had something serious occur and needed to be in the hospital or go to the emergency room, your care really depended on where you lived. The cost of the care was free or cost very little. We lived near Siena, where there was a teaching hospital with most of the specialties.

If you needed a routine scan or exam, you were put on the list for the next available, which could be as much as a year later. You also had the choice of paying a little more out of pocket to go to a private clinic or office to have tests and scans completed. The cost was a fraction of the cost in the US. If you needed a prescription, you paid on a sliding scale according to your income. So, we usually paid nothing, as Vincenzo's salary was so little in those days.

Along with traditional science and medicine, most Italians held superstitions and traditional beliefs about what makes a person sick. This fascinated me. I had realized that one of the biggest fears of Italians is to catch a bad gust of wind, or un colpo d'aria, which can cause a variety of maladies such as influenza, sore throat, neck pain, and stomach problems. Even worse, if you are warm and sweaty, and catch a gust of wind, you could possibly catch pneumonia or worse.

My mother-in-law especially lived with this belief daily. I learned that it was vital to wear a protective undershirt in the winter to protect myself from the cold. A warm scarf and hat would also protect a person from any ill effects from bad air entering my body. I had noticed that Italians always wore scarves, and I thought it was such a beautiful fashion statement and started to do the same during my time living in Italy. Little did I realize that the scarf served a double purpose, along with being a beautiful accessory, a scarf was worn to prevent them from getting sick from a cool breeze.

This is one of the primary reasons why Italians fear air conditioning and open windows. Of course, being a nurse, I would try to explain to anyone who would listen (over and over again) that being exposed to fresh air does not cause sickness; perhaps a virus in the air could be the problem, but a cool breeze in the summer, no. They would just look at me and shake their heads, waggle their fingers at me indicating that I was wrong for sure on this point. After a while, I stopped trying to correct them and just went with it.

Over time, I discovered many other beliefs and traditions that remain from long ago. Again, the past meets the present. Here are a couple of stories from spending time with my husband's family in Abruzzo, where the old traditions are still very much present even today.

I frequently wear shoes or sandals without socks. The first time my mother-in-law noticed this, she seemed to panic. She told me that if she went without socks and shoes, she would instantly have a sore throat.

This was just the beginning of a long history of my mother-in-law asking me, "Don't you feel cold. Aren't you afraid you will get sick?" All because of my bare feet in my sandals, or bare shoulders, or an exposed neck region, and so on.

On our visits in the summer, Vincenzo and I would take his parents shopping or out for errands. It is very hot even in the mountains of Abruzzo, but the air conditioning is never used in the car when we have them with us. Instead the windows are only cracked a bit for a little air, and we all arrive at our destination sweaty and cranky—all for the fear of catching something from a bad wind.

In the south, some people still believe in the evil eye and a sort of curse that others can put on you and make you feel sick or have a headache. In fact, Vincenzo has a strong belief in the evil eye and frequently would ask his father to take the curse away if someone had given him the evil eye. The evil eye could be given to you primarily out of envy or jealously.

The first time I realized this phenomenon was when Vincenzo and I were visiting his family home. We had been out for a little walk, and during that time, we meet an old friend of his from many years back.

His friend said something like, "You have a very beautiful wife."

I noticed that Vincenzo instantly became nervous and anxious. We chatted for a short while and returned to his parents' home. As soon as he walked in the door, Vincenzo searched out his father to ask him to check to see if this person had given him the evil eye. I was astonished at what I was hearing.

I watched as his father took his wedding ring off his finger and make a sign of the cross on Vincenzo's forehead two or three times. He then took the wedding ring and placed it in a bowl of water with two kitchen spoons crossed on the top of it. Next, he placed a couple of drops of olive oil into the water. He watched as the oil stayed in one place and did not disperse.

He declared that Vincenzo was safe. No evil eye this time. No curse had been placed. If the oil had dispersed into many parts in the water, this would have meant that he did have a curse. If that had been the case, Vincenzo's father would say a special incantation in dialect to ward off the evil spirits.

As I witnessed this, I was in shock and disbelief. I did not know what to say or think about this. Since that time, I have come to accept this belief as very real for him and don't question it. And it is a habit of mine to frequently go out of the house in a cold breeze and forget my scarf. He always looks at me like I am crazy to do this. If I happen to get a sore throat, stomach ache, or a cold, it is always blamed on my exposure to the bad air.

I also discovered that number 17 is considered the unlucky number in Italy, not 13 like it is in the US. I learned this the hard way when I originally suggested that we get married on the seventeenth of July. I actually thought Vincenzo was going to stop breathing when he heard this.

He looked at me and said, "Do you want to bring us bad fortune? Absolutely not on the seventeenth." His eyes were wide with fear and disbelief.

Thank goodness I had a backup plan for July 10, so that was how our wedding date was originally chosen. All to avoid a day of bad luck. I would agree that we had a memorable day filled with fortune and love.

27

Daily Life, Daily Bread

Bread is essential to life in Italy. If you don't have bread, you can't eat. This is serious business. The ladies of the village waited patiently every day (except Sunday) for the little white van that arrived around noon from the neighboring village of Ambra. At first, I had no idea why everyone was out chatting and catching up in the square every day at the same time. I always thought that it was just the time to gossip and catch up with each other in the morning. However, one day I discovered what they were all really waiting for.

As the bell tower of the village would ring out the noontime song, everyone, especially the ladies of the village, anticipated the arrival of the little bread van, and people would start to queue up near the place where he stopped, just to make sure that they were able to get their favorite bread.

If someone was sick or not able to go get their bread for one reason or another, it was always a priority to make sure that someone else picks up the bread for that person and delivers it in person. Sometimes I would see a bag of bread hanging on the fence near a driveway as I would take my walks each day. I also noticed that bread was delivered at times to people in upper-level apartments by a little basket lowered down with a rope tied to it so that the bag of bread could be placed in it. The person would carefully pull it back up to their apartment to retrieve the bread.

The breads from Tuscany are made in the traditional manner and baked in a wood-fired oven—the crust thick and smoky and crunchy with the inside delicate and chewy. The breads come in many shapes and sizes and are named after what they look like: ciambella (donut), guanciale (pillow), ciabatta (slipper).

In most of the small villages in Tuscany, the bread is still made without salt. The history behind this is that during war times and in the early days, salt was heavily taxed. It was during this period that people started to make bread without salt. Because of this, the bread does not have a lot of taste on its own. However, it can be transformed into a wonderful vehicle to eat other delights such as the traditional prosciutto, salami, mortadella, and pecorino cheese. And, of course, to fare la scarpetta, or clean up the delicious sauces left on your plate.

Bread is used fresh or stale, and it is never, ever wasted. In fact, stale bread is reflected in many of the traditional Tuscan dishes as a primary ingredient, such as panzanella, pappa al pomodoro, ribollita, and polpette. There are even Tuscan folk songs about bread and these dishes.

Daily bread is important also because a slice or two of bread is always found beside your plate at each meal. The bread is used as a second utensil to push the pasta onto the fork before eating and to sop up every bit of sauce that remains on the plate at the end of the meal.

Honestly, I am not sure that people would be very comfortable eating a meal without bread. It would just seem wrong. In fact, I often heard the ladies of the village talking about the topic of bread. Especially if the bread delivery will not take place one day, such as a holiday. They always made sure that they had an emergency backup plan for bread.

FOCACCIA

3 cups all-purpose or bread flour

1½ cup warm water

1 packet active dry yeast (about 2 tablespoons)

1 tsp. sea salt

1 tablespoon sugar or honey

2 tablespoons olive oil

In a large mixing bowl, mix together the flour and salt. Next place the warm (not too hot) water in a small bowl and sprinkle the yeast, followed by the sugar. Let this sit for 5-7 minutes (or longer if needed) to allow the yeast to bloom. Add the olive oil to the water, yeast, sugar mixture and then mix into the flour with a spoon. You can also use a mixer with a hook attachment, but I keep it simple and stir for 5 minutes with a spoon.

The dough should be a bit wet, so keep adding water if the dough has too much flour. Cover the bowl with a tea towel and let sit in a warm place for 2-3 hours.

Preheat oven to 425 degrees.

Next, place the dough in an oiled round or rectangular baking pan (or two, depending on how thin you press it out and your toppings). Form into the shape and size you want with oiled fingers.

I would sometimes leave it quite thick (about an inch or so high), and it would create a bread that you can use for sandwiches. A thinner pressed dough (about ¼ inch high) was pefect as a main dish, like a pizza. Cover and let rise again for about 45 minutes.

Topping

Olive oil

2 tsp. sea salt (or more to taste)

2 tablespoons fresh rosemary

For a traditional focaccia, push indentations throughout the dough with your fingers (wet them first). Drizzle extra virgin olive oil over the dough and sprinkle sea salt and chopped fresh rosemary.

Bake in oven at 425 degrees for 25 minutes or until bottom crust is crisp and top is golden brown.

Recipe note: I usually put a pan of water on the very lowest part of the oven to create a steam oven, which makes the bread moist inside and crisp outside. This recipe also adapts well to toppings to make a white pizza, such as sliced pears and pecorino cheese, topped with pistachios and honey, zucchini flowers and mozzarella, cherry tomatoes and oregano. Experiment with your favorite toppings.

28

For Whom the Bells Toll

It did not take me long to realize the unique closeness that was present among the people in the village. Each day was like a piece of music or art shared with each other, perhaps even an opera. Relationships were intertwined; everyone had a deep history connected to this place. Their dance was filled with passion and joy, balanced with elements of life's challenges.

Everyone knew their part, so I was trying to see how I could also join in the dance. San Gusme had around 250 people living within the walls of the village. Most of these were families with roots going back centuries. I once read that the vineyards around the village had a history of belonging to one of the most illustrious families of Siena, the Piccolomini.

The village was a fort that had for years been a strategic outpost meant to serve and protect the larger village of Siena in the days when the major cities of Italy would fight each other for land and power. They knew how to protect the village, their land, and each other. It was instinct that taught them that they needed each other to survive. Even today, that instinct remains alive and well. They carefully regard each other with a mixture of love and respect, with moments of tragedy and hardship.

The elders of the village were mostly respected and held in high honor. I could see that the elders checked in with each other. They had grown old together and took care of each other. Each day, they wandered out into the village square after their morning chores or as they walked the children or grandchildren to the little school bus. They would stop in and have a coffee, check on the weather, finish the laundry and hang it out if the weather was cooperating, do a little gardening, and then take a midmorning break.

Many times, if they could not get out, the ladies would talk to each other across the piazza from window to window while hanging out the laundry. Most times, the conversation was focused on the food they were preparing for their families and getting updates on children and grandchildren.

When one person could not get out for shopping or to get bread, another would offer to help. I witnessed daily the love and care that they had for each other. Sometimes it was a gentle kidding or joke that brought a smile to their faces. Other times, it was a simple greeting, kisses and simply sitting on the bench together and catching up on the daily and weekly happenings.

This care and tradition of being with each other was passed down to the children and teenagers as well. They helped each other with homework and chores and then celebrated together watching a soccer match or running to get a gelato or bag of potato chips from the local church lady bar. It was tradition that brought them together and the bond was strong, even today.

The elders would organize any local events, with the ladies cooking for the village celebrations, and then men doing the heavy lifting, such as putting up decorations, getting the church ready, assembling the stage for a concert, and lending a hand in the kitchen, mostly with the wine, coffee, and grappa as a meal was completed.

In the evening, everyone was back out for the passeggiata (stroll) to catch up on the day's activities. The children would be out playing and laughing in the summer months until midnight. The ladies would be sitting on the bench, as many as four to five on a bench, sitting together as closely as possible, something you might never witness in the US, gossiping and catching up on the daily activities.

The men were usually playing cards together or watching a soccer match on the TV at the local bar or Circolo. One day, I heard the bell tower chiming a song I had not noticed before. I had just returned from my afternoon walk and was taking in the sunshine sitting on the bench just outside of the village. The sound was sad and reverent at the same time. It played over and over again for about thirty minutes. I noticed that everyone seemed to be anxiously checking with each other.

I could hear them all saying, "Who is it?" and "What had happened?"

As I watched from the bench outside the square, I could see that everyone was gathering in the main piazza to discover more. So I followed them in and observed from afar. Someone had died—that's what the song from the bell tower meant. One of their own was gone. Everyone was hugging; some were crying and passionately talking about what had happened.

This was the first time I had witnessed the traditions of a death in the village. An elder, Siri, had passed away in the night. Her daughter had gone to check on her when she did not answer her calls and had discovered her dead. It was a sad, but expected death. Siri was in her nineties and had lived a long life within the walls of the village. She had been born in the same house that she had died in. As she grew old and frail, people helped along the way.

Her family lived close by and checked on her, but others in the village also had helped her stay in her home until her death, bringing her bread and groceries, medicines when she needed it, taking her out for walks, getting her to the bench to sit, and making sure that she was warm on winter nights.

A life lived like this was something that seemed like a treasure to me. It was how life should be lived, at home, among friends and family, and simply not waking up one day with a peaceful death. In a way, the village was celebrating the circle of life by honoring her in this way.

A few days later, a funeral was held in the little church in the village. A procession with family and friends took place with another round of church bells marking the event. Later that day, I could see the family still gathered in the village. Siri's grandchildren were playing with others, running around in the spring weather, and asking for ice cream and treats as the night went on. Life went on, and so did the village.

29

Speaking with Passion—and the Hands

I learned quickly, especially in my relationship with Vincenzo, the importance of connecting not only with words, but also with facial expressions, hand gestures, and other body language. Passion is the one word that I can use to describe how Italians communicate. Also, they are very good at reading each other's mood immediately because of this. I am intuitive this way, so I immediately was drawn to the traditions of the way Italians communicate.

I took every opportunity to observe what happens when people were communicating; however, I had a lot to learn. It was fascinating to understand the power of communicating with all of these aspects occurring at the same time—the spoken word, facial expressions, and gestures.

Italians top the charts with their ability to passionately speak about anything and everything from the weather, the pasta dish they had for lunch, to the local gossip and happenings. Once I had a better understanding of the words, I could fully grasp the deep meaning of the words used in conversation. For example, if one of the local ladies was describing what she was planning for lunch or dinner, the details and descriptions were amazing. Pasta made fresh from their favorite auntie. Sauce from tomatoes that they had stashed away in jars from last summer's harvest. All served with their favorite cheese from the neighbor, including bruschetta made from local bread toasted and served with their own olive oil.

Many times, the conversation would dive deeper in the state of the olive harvest that year and the way the new oil tasted. Words like fruity, peppery, spicy, buttery, smooth, and grassy were used. One conversation about lunch might take twenty minutes or more.

I also learned that sometimes what people said and what they meant were two different things. Italians could be brutally honest with each other, telling them exactly what their opinion was. Other times, they seemed to be playing a game with each other, with words that were said, but without actual intention. Here is an example.

Vincenzo has a huge circle of friends and family. So each time we would go for a visit to his family in the southern part of Italy, we would do our best to try to see everyone. It was an unending circle of coffee, lunches, sweets, dinners, and late-night conversations. I noticed that even as we would say our goodbyes to each one, there was a promise of some sort to return again before we left. At first, I wondered how we could ever do this. Then, I realized that he was just using words to indicate how important the person or family was, in saying that we would try to see them again soon.

The Italian language itself is fascinating. We lived in the middle of Tuscany, so the language spoken here was considered the true Italian language first documented by Dante. As we traveled around the country, I observed that each area had a different dialect and incantation, or kind of musical way the language was spoken.

The northerners were influenced by the neighboring countries, so sometimes their words sounded German or French. Venetians spoke a dialect mostly unknown to any other region. Southern Italy had many different dialects, with Rome, Naples, and Sicily being drastically different. They all had different expressions as well, especially how they expressed everyday words, and especially swear words.

The thing that most interested me were the hand gestures and body language. At first, I thought everyone was angry with each other. Voices were strong and loud, with so many gestures that I had no idea what to interpret. Gradually, I figured most of them out, and even found myself starting to use a few.

The best way to understand these are to see them. However, I will attempt to describe a few here:

- The index finger wag: No, I am not doing that. Don't even think about it.
- Index finger to the middle of the cheek as you push in and turn it slightly back and forth: Delicious, I can't even stop eating to tell you how good it is.
- Hands together in a prayer gesture: I pray, stop busting my balls about this.
- Hand motioning with your fingers pinched together from the nose out to indicate your nose is growing: Like Pinocchio, it's just a little lie that I'm telling you.
- Both hands palms facing to the back, motioning from the bottom up and close to the body: Describing a person who hangs onto their money, or is cheap.
- One hand stiffly hitting on their teeth with their index finger first: This is hard, through the teeth.
- One hand grabbing the other upper arm muscle in a swift motion as the arm moves into an L-shape with the hand making a fist: Screw you.

- Making the sign of a horn with the index and little fingers up: Someone just said something I am worried about, so to ward off the bad luck or evil eye, the sign of the horns is made.
- Index finger making a circle forward or backward: See you soon (forward) or see you later (backward).
- Both hands motioning down with your palms facing up and flapping: What more do you want from me?
- Both eyes looking from side to side quickly with a serious face: Now I am angry, so get out of my space.

Communication is such an important aspect of our daily lives, and even more important when the language being spoken is not your mother tongue. I had learned early on in my experience to pay attention not just to the words spoken, but also to little expressions, and odd sounds that are made along with the body language. It's a trio of communication that goes together to form a special meaning. Many of these unspoken expressions are too difficult to explain with words. These sounds are not words at all, but when you hear them, you know exactly what is meant. If you ever have the chance to visit Italy, just sit, listen, and watch a conversation among the people. You will not be disappointed.

30

The Beauty and Balance of Life in Tuscany

As I settled into my life in the village, I enjoyed getting out to explore the countryside on a regular basis. Sometimes I would take off on my own, and other times my friends Stefania or Norah would join me. I remember the first time I visited Italy, it was to hike with my friend Ann through the villages of Tuscany. I think this is probably another time when my past and present collided.

My friend Ann and I had hiked through the little villages right around where we now lived in Chianti. I remember us starting out our day looking for the adventure of what we would see and experience in the countryside—wild poppies, yellow broom, and the first glimpse of wheat in the fields. Each day would end with us heading straight uphill to our destination village for the day, with time to explore the alabaster artisans in Volterra, the towers of San Gimignano, Colle Val d'Elsa, Monteriggioni, and Siena.

I could not believe that Tuscany was now my home. I knew which paths offered a few of my absolute favorite things, like the lavender bunches, rosemary, fig trees, sunflower fields, and vineyards. All of these delights were within a short walk from our village. I frequently returned from my walks with little treasures for the house. I loved bringing back fresh rosemary or a bunch of wildflowers or sunflowers. It was hard to believe that all of this was available to enjoy.

I especially loved the old cypress trees that lined the ancient roads and felt as if they would welcome me into their world for a while. I could smell the fragrance of the grapes as they ripened in the sun, the clay as it baked in the warmth of the long hot afternoons, and the fresh scent of pine from the trees as I would pass by. In the late summer and fall, the rolling hills of wheat became golden light, and in the quiet winter months as the olive trees and vines were quietly sleeping, they were greener than Ireland and offered a glimmer of beauty against the cool weather and short days.

Living in Italy, I cherished the days at home where I was able to balance my work and life for the first time in my life. I would start my day writing for work, a quick lunch break followed by a lovely hike just outside the village. Vincenzo would come home from the restaurant for an afternoon break around 3:00 p.m. As the only chef and part owner of a restaurant, it meant that he worked every day for around twelve hours. His only day off was Sunday.

So when he had his afternoon break, we took advantage of the time. We took long naps together, did our shopping, and always had a cup of coffee together before he returned to work. This was also my time to finish my work in the evening. I loved being able to cook with fresh ingredients, bake items from scratch again, and enjoy the real taste of fresh fruits and vegetables in season.

After we were married, we applied for my official paperwork to live in Italy, called a Permesso di soggiorno. This was relatively complicated and difficult to achieve as well, with more visits to the government offices in Siena and background checks to make sure I was not a criminal and that Vincenzo and I were indeed officially married. After a few months, this was also completed and I was officially a resident of Italy. This came with great benefits, like healthcare coverage, but it also came with a challenge. Within one year, I had to convert my driver's license to an Italian one in order to continue to drive legally in Italy. Italy did not recognize a US driver's license as the signs and laws were different in Europe.

I started studying to take the driver's test and realized it was going to be a big challenge for me. I had been driving off and on for the entire time I had lived in the country and understood the signs well. But it was all of the little regulations that I did not understand. The test was written and driving, just like in the US. I even enrolled in driving school, which was held in a neighboring village in Chianti. The funny part was that, to attend class, I would drive on one of the curviest, most challenging roads I had ever experienced, parallel park the car on a hilly, narrow street (nothing was flat there). I would walk into class while most of the students (with an average age of eighteen) looked at me with such surprise. I could sense the questions in their looks. What does she think she is doing? She drives here? Why is she in school?

I would usually joke with the instructor that if I could manage to arrive to driving school each week safely, he should just give me my license because it was one of the most difficult tests of my skills yet. I regularly would meet herds of bicylists or dodge local drivers who seemed to be playing chicken all the way to class. Italians love to drive down the middle of the road and will quickly move to their lane on the right just before meeting an oncoming car. The first time I experienced this, I think I saw my life flash in front of me.

When I mentioned my difficulty to others, they had great suggestions for me. "Why not just get a black market license from Naples? I have a connection. All you have to do is pay. It's about the same as what you would pay for a legal one anyway." What? I could never do that. I really only wanted to be able to drive short distances to other villages in the region anyway.

I eventually gave up on the idea and would take the bus and train to get from place to place or asked Vincenzo or my friends to drive me if I needed help. The trains are fantastic and can get you from place to place very quickly. They do vary, with the regional trains moving slower and stopping in every little village along the way, to the ultrasleek and fast bullet trains that can get you from Rome to Florence in less than two hours.

Giving up driving was hard for me because I loved my independence. If you do travel to visit Italy, I would not recommend driving if at all possible. The main highways are usually filled with semitrucks and the cities are crowded and confusing. In Italy, the trains are designed for people, and the main highways are used heavily for commercial transportation. The exceptions are the rural areas where you can find a more peaceful driving experience. The only danger might be a wild boar that wanders out on the road at night.

Parking is also a major challenge anywhere you go. Most places that you might visit have very little space to park your car, so you end up shimmying your car into an open spot any which way that it might fit and hope and pray that when you are ready to go home, you can actually get your car back out of the spot again. Italians are famous for double parking, parking on the sidewalk, sideways and any way that they can possibly find a place to put their car. Many people use a scooter or motorcycle to get around and frequently will dodge between other cars as traffic is moving or when stopped.

Stop signs are a suggestion, with people stopping only if they actually see someone approaching. Roundabouts are everywhere, even half roundabouts which are really confusing. The most important thing is to make sure you keep moving along because, if you stop, you are in big trouble. It seemed like maybe Italians are born with these skills. They have some of the most defensive driving skills I ever witnessed—always expecting the other person to do exactly the opposite of what is expected. Traffic signals are not clear or placed in the same obvious location that we are used to. And directional signs are not always present. You may never find the name or number of a street or road, but as long as you know the next city you are traveling to, that is the most important thing to know. The one thing I did understand: all roads heading south really do lead to Rome eventually.

Each summer, for our anniversary in July, Vincenzo and I would take just a couple of days together and return to the castle where we celebrated our honeymoon. This little piece of heaven was only thirty minutes from where we lived, so it was an easy drive to get there. We stayed in a different room each time—discovering the unique treasures and designs that Salvatore had uncovered or created in each room. The pool was there and waiting for us to enjoy during the hot, hot days of July.

Sometimes I would bring Vincenzo's favorite cheesecake along and we would share it with Salvatore and Antonio. At this point, they felt like old friends. Vincenzo was crazy for Nutella, so I had created a special recipe for him that included cheesecake with a top layer of ganache with dark chocolate and Nutella. It was something special, and so very decadent that I only made it once a year.

For these two days, we pretended to be tourists in Italy, lounging by the pool and going to our favorite restaurants in the evening. It was such a nice getaway. I felt like we were lucky to have the opportunity to do the things that most people only get to experience once in a lifetime.

Nutella Cheesecake

Crust

1½ cups chocolate wafer cookies (crushed) or graham cracker crumbs
¼ cup sugar
½ cup melted butter

Preheat oven to 375 degrees.
Combine the crumbs, sugar, and butter and mix well. Pat into a 9- to 10-inch pie plate or tart pan. You can also use a cheesecake pan, but it is not needed with this recipe. Bake for 6-8 minutes. Remove from oven and let cool.

Reduce oven heat to 350 degrees.

Filling

24 ounces whipped style cream cheese
4 ounces mascarpone cheese
¾ cup sugar
2 tsp. vanilla extract
3 large eggs
1 tsp. lemon or orange zest (optional)
½ cup Nutella (optional)

In a large mixing bowl, blend the cream cheese with the mascarpone and sugar until well blended (use a hand or stand mixer). Next add the vanilla, eggs, and lemon zest and mix well until creamy and smooth.

Assembly

(Note: When I make this for Vincenzo, I start by warming the Nutella and spread it on top of the crust before adding the cream cheese mixture.)

Next add the cream cheese mixture and spread to the edges of the crust. Bake the cheesecake for 55 minutes until the top is slightly browned. Remove from oven and cool on a wire rack.

Chocolate Nutella Ganache

¼ cup whole milk

¼ cup Nutella

½ cup dark or semisweet chocolate chips

½ tsp. sea salt (optional)

½ cup chopped pistachios, roasted almonds, or other favorite topping

Warm whole milk in a small saucepan until it starts to steam. Take the milk off the heat and add Nutella and chocolate chips. Stir well until chocolate is melted and the mixture is creamy. Add sea salt to taste.

Spread the ganache over the top of the cheesecake and top with ½ cup of pistachios, almonds, or other topping.

Place in the refrigerator to cool well. Chill covered for at least 6 hours prior to serving.

I also loved to escape from my work some days and get away with a friend to explore the local area whenever possible. Vincenzo's work schedule was crazy, and he did not mind that I would occasionally take a day-trip to visit a new area or one of my favorite spots with friends. Some of my favorite outings were day-trips to Cortona to walk in the village perched high above the vines and olive trees of Umbria. Cortona was home to many little artisan shops, so it was delightful to peek in and explore the pottery, jewelry, and art that was being created.

Siena was the biggest city that was close by, so I would frequently take the bus with the ladies from the village to do some shopping or meet a friend for lunch. If it was a Saturday, many of them would go in to have their hair done for the weekend and do some shopping. Wednesday was market day in Siena. Sometimes I would go and explore the larger market and especially loved trying the local foods it had to offer.

I discovered my favorite little places to shop and have tea, most times with my friend Stefania if she was in the area. One of my favorite shops included Toscana Lovers—Artigianato Toscano on Via delle Terme, where you could find artisan pottery, linens, and household items made by locals. Another that I loved as it featured artisan leather goods was Cuoieria Fiorentina on Via Malavolti.

I also loved going into the Consorzio Agrario di Siena on Via Pianigiani. This is the farmers association of the province of Siena and has a fantastic selection of all things only produced in the area. I would shop for local bread, cheeses, and honey here. You could also have them make you a panino to eat as you explored Siena for the day.

It was comfortable for me to wander the streets and then head in the direction of the Piazza del Campo to sit by the fountain and take in the sights and sounds of the city. Siena started to feel very familiar. I loved checking out the little restaurants and cafes as well. A few of my favorites were Osteria Nonna Gina, Osteria Boccon Del Prete, and Osteria Le Sorelline.

Stefania and I would always end our day in Siena with a cup of tea and a treat from one of the little shops in Via dei Rossi as I would walk back to the bus stop to return to San Gusme. I was finally getting comfortable in this unique and beautiful city that initially felt so complicated and a bit closed to me.

I also would occasionally take the train from Siena to Florence and meet Stefania or my friend Elisabetta for lunch. It was so wonderful for me to have girlfriends who loved to explore their homeland with me. Elisabetta was a local woman who is one of the best guides I have ever met. (You can find her on TuscanyTrotter.com.) I got to know her because of the private travel planning work I had done with my friends. She showed my own family Siena while they were in Italy for our wedding. She took such good care of them.

After this, we became close friends and adventurers together. Elisabetta would occasionally call me and invite me to join her for an outing for the day. She would take me in her little Fiat 500 and off we would go. She showed me Pienza, which is famous for pecorino cheese, and Montepulciano, well known for wine. Both Elisabetta and Stefania loved to go to the local terme as well, so I joined them to have a relaxing day in the warm pools. This was a big treat for me.

Sometimes Stefania would come to San Gusme for a long hike, and we would finish the day with tea and my homemade strawberry and white chocolate scones at my apartment. We usually had a lot to catch up with, so it was a nice way to spend time together.

Dried Strawberry White Chocolate Scones

5 tablespoons cold butter (cut into small pieces)
2 cups all-purpose flour
3 tablespoons sugar
1 tablespoon baking powder
½ tsp. salt
½ cup of dried strawberries
1 lemon (zested)
½ cup white chocolate (chopped)
1 cup heavy cream

Preheat oven to 425 degrees.

Mix together the flour, sugar, baking powder, and salt. Add the cold butter and mix together with your fingers, forming a crumbly dough.

Then add the dried fruit and white chocolate. Mix together just to incorporate the ingredients. Next pour in the heavy cream and stir together to form a sticky dough.

Make into a ball of dough (it will be very sticky). With flour-covered hands, gently flatten out dough on top of a piece of parchment covered with a little flour until it is about 3/4 inch thick. Use a round biscuit or cookie cutter

(about 2-3 inches round) to cut out each scone and place on cookie sheet covered with parchment paper. You can also create two smaller circles of dough and simply cut the scones into 10-12 triangles with a sharp knife or metal dough scraper.

Brush the tops of scones with a little milk or cream and sprinkle a light coating of turbinado or coarse sugar over the top. Bake for 12-14 minutes at 425 degrees, until golden brown on the bottom.

Recipe note: Experiment with combinations of your favorite dried fruit such as cherries, blueberries, currants, or cranberries. You can also add a different flavor by using orange or lime zest.

I felt I was living a dream for sure. I also became very familiar with the neighborhoods and piazzas of Florence. When I would spend the day in Florence, I would wander around the Straw Market, or Mercato del Porcellino, featuring the little statue of the pig not far from the Piazza della Signoria. In the winter, I would wander over to a chocolate shop called Vestri that had unique handmade chocolates and other treats.

I especially loved the area of Santa Croce where there were fewer tourists, and the little narrow passageways let me discover something new every time. I knew where to go for my favorite focaccia at Cantinetta dei Verrazzano as well as my favorite gelato shop, Gelateria Dei Neri. With my gelato in hand, I would walk across the Ponte Vecchio or old bridge, showing its strength and endurance still today as it survived the wars of years past. This is still the place where lovers and friends meet to sit and reflect on the sites of the river Arno.

Many times, I would hike up to the piazza Michelangelo and take in the 360-degree views over the city with the Duomo and all of Florence below. In the days before Easter and Christmas, Santa Croce square is host to open-air markets with local cheeses, wines, sweets, and other artisan items.

I often wondered how long this incredible life adventure would last. I knew that it probably would not be forever, but I wanted to enjoy every minute of every day in this beautiful country.

About a year after we were married, I was excited to host a Thanksgiving feast for our Italian friends. Italians are curious about this tradition, especially because it involves a huge feast of traditional foods. It had been a few years since I had been home to visit my family during Thanksgiving, and I realized how much I missed this tradition. I started planning a Thanksgiving feast with Vincenzo helping me.

The first thing we had to do was to find a turkey. Next, decide on how many people would fit around our table in our small kitchen. We eventually found the turkey from the restaurant supply that Vincenzo used for the meat for his restaurant. It was safely stashed in the freezer of the restaurant for now.

I made a list of all of the dishes I wanted to prepare for the day: roast turkey, mashed potatoes, gravy, stuffing, green beans, salad, bread, pie, and whipped cream. I wanted to have it all. We invited eight of our friends to join us on a Sunday afternoon in late November and hosted the feast. I had arranged the table with every plate and glass we had. The table actually took up almost the entire living space we had, so it was tricky to get around the chairs to even greet everyone.

I had to ask Vincenzo for a few plates from the restaurant as we did not have enough for the dessert. The friends we had invited seemed to be honored and also thrilled to have the chance to experience this special holiday. As they arrived, I could see the anticipation in their eyes. They came with flowers, wine, and chocolates to add to the celebration. This was the kind of holiday they loved. It involved friends around the table and hours of eating good food. This kind of occasion made me infinitely happy inside.

Vincenzo had put the turkey in the oven of the restaurant because it would never fit in our little oven we had in our apartment. He had roasted it with a chestnut, sage, and apple stuffing that I had made earlier. He placed carrots, celery, and onions on the bottom of the pan to give the gravy even more flavor. I think it was one of the best turkeys I had ever tasted.

We passed around dish after dish and enjoyed each one. The local Chianti wine from Castello Brolio was a perfect match for the feast. We finished the meal with a green salad made with dried cranberries and walnuts. Then came warm apple pie with fresh whipped cream. This was followed with espresso and a little chocolate treat that had been placed at each setting.

Per the Italian tradition, I placed grappa and vin santo on the table to help us digest our feast. We made toasts to each other as new friends, and Vincenzo and I thanked each and every one for the love and support they had given both of us over the past two years.

After everyone had gone home, I looked around our little kitchen and felt such joy. It was a beautiful mess. I kissed Vincenzo and hugged him extra tight and thanked him for helping me cook, even on his day off. We washed dishes and cleaned until around two in the morning. As we dropped into bed, I thought this was one of the best Thanksgiving celebrations of my life. I will never forget the happiness and pure joy I felt in my heart that evening.

31

The Mother's Day Cake Contest

As I grew comfortable with my life and our little apartment, I enjoyed reconnecting with my love for cooking and baking. I had earned how to cook and bake with my mother growing up on the farm. We frequently had to cook for our own family as well as farm hands who would help out my dad. It had been years since I had the time to cook and bake the way I had always wanted to.

Mom taught me how to make simple dishes that everyone loved, as well as cakes and cookies. I always had a plan to bake something new every week because I knew that I could share it with friends and neighbors. Emma would frequently stop by in the evening, and we would bake together. Many times, she would stay for dinner as well. It was during one of these evenings that we were talking about the Mother's Day cake contest.

It was early May and each year the ladies of the village would celebrate Women's Day (or what we call Mother's Day) with the *gara della torta* or cake contest. I had entered a cake the year before, but it had not won a prize. Someone mentioned to me later that everyone thought Vincenzo had actually made the cake, not me, so even if my cake was good,

I would not be allowed to win because they thought I was (in essence) cheating.

I could not believe it. Even though I insisted that I really had made the cake, no one believed me. I had been thinking it would be fun to make a cake again this year. So Emma and I decided to make the cake together and that she would take it to be entered into the contest. I felt that if Emma took the cake to be entered, we might have a better chance to win a prize. It was well known that one particular woman from the village frequently won the prize. This seemed to be a given. However, the cake was not always the best one. I had tasted it before.

Emma and I planned to make a chocolate cake with a decadent ganache frosting. This is a cake I knew everyone loved as I had made it for dinner parties and birthday celebrations here in Italy. I planned for the middle layer to feature a local homemade red currant jam topped with thin sliced fresh strawberries. The top and sides were frosted with the most delicious chocolate ganache that I had learned to make from my mother. I finished off the cake with slices of fresh strawberries, red currants, and blueberries arranged in a circle around the edges. It looked like a circle of hearts.

The entire village prepared for the day with the men setting up round plastic tables and chairs in the main square with red flower accents on the table. Any woman who wanted to bring a cake or dessert could enter into the contest. The entries were brought into a special room where they were registered and given a number. This was serious business.

On the registration, you had to list the ingredients in the cake and the name of it so that they could put it on the ticket next to the cake. People come from the neighboring villages and purchased a ticket that allowed them to have a taste of five different cakes. After they taste, they vote for their favorite with a voting card. They sit outside together in the square and enjoy the cakes along with coffee or tea and compare ideas on who made what cake.

When we finished the cake that morning, I sent Emma out to deliver the cake. I wanted her to be the one who was recognized for the cake this year. We were both excited about the possibilities. Our cake was absolutely beautiful, and I knew that it tasted good because I had made it many times for friends' birthdays over the years.

Later, I stopped out in the square to purchase a ticket and try a few of the cakes. I could see that there were many enjoying our cake and asking who had made it. The women of the village and their families were all there making comments and speculating about who might win this year. I could hear them talking about the usual winner, and how she usually stacked the votes with members of her family and loyal friends. But, really, how many times did she need to win?

Vincenzo stopped in on his afternoon break that day and asked me how everything was going. I told him our plan and he just said, "You will never win the contest. The same woman always wins. That is just how it is."

With this thought, I felt a bit defeated and decided to take my afternoon walk. I had a peaceful walk in the countryside, thinking to myself that I was certain nothing would come of this year as well, and as I was returning, I was greeted by Emma who had the biggest smile on her face.

"We won, we won." she said. I ran up to her and gave her a big hug. She showed me the handpainted plate and bouquet of flowers that they had presented to her as the winner. I was so happy. This was a fun moment for both of us, even if no one ever knew that I was behind the cake. We had won the Mother's Day cake contest as a team.

Chocolate Mother's Day Cake

Cake

2 cups all-purpose flour

1 tsp. baking soda

1 tsp. baking powder

½ tsp. salt

1 cup unsweetened cocoa powder

1 cup boiling water (you can also use a combination ½ cup hot water and ½ cup strong coffee to add flavor)

2 cups sugar

3 large eggs

¾ cup (1 ½ sticks) unsalted butter, room temperature, cut into small pieces

1 cup buttermilk (if you don't have buttermilk, add 1 tablespoon lemon juice to whole milk and stir well)

1 tsp. vanilla extract

Preheat oven to 350 degrees.

Spray two 9-inch round cake pans with 2-inch-high sides with nonstick spray. Line bottom of pan with parchment paper rounds. Spray parchment paper with nonstick spray. Dust pan with flour, tapping out any excess.

Mix together flour, baking soda, baking powder, and salt into medium bowl.

Add the cocoa powder to separate medium bowl. Pour 1 cup boiling water over cocoa; whisk to blend.

Using hand or stand mixer, beat sugar and eggs in large bowl until light and fluffy, about 2 minutes. Add butter to egg mixture and beat until blended. Beat in cocoa mixture. Add buttermilk and vanilla; mix to blend. Add dry ingredients and beat on low just to blend. Transfer cake batter to prepared cake pans.

Bake cake for about 35 minutes or until toothpick inserted into center comes out clean. Cool cake in pan on rack.

I like to make the cakes one day in advance so that they are nice and cool when I assemble the cake.

Filling

16–18 ounces of seedless raspberry or black currant preserves
2 tablespoons Chambord liquor (optional)
¾ cup fresh strawberries (thinly sliced) or raspberries (cut in half)

Warm seedless raspberry or black currant preserves over medium heat in a saucepan.

Optional: Add 2 tablespoons of Chambord liquor and mix well.

Remove the cake from the pans and place one of the cakes flat side up on a serving plate. Spread the warm preserves over the top. Place thin slices of fresh strawberries or sliced raspberries over the top.

Place the second cake flat side down on top of the filling. Press lightly.

GANACHE FROSTING

¼ cup (½ stick) unsalted butter

1 tsp. vanilla extract

¾ cup heavy whipping cream

½ cup sugar

5 ounces dark chocolate, chopped (60-70 percent)

¾ tsp. sea salt

Make the chocolate ganache by warming the heavy cream, butter, and sugar over low to medium heat in a small saucepan. When the cream starts to bubble, remove from heat and add the dark chocolate. Stir well. When the chocolate is melted, add the vanilla and sea salt and mix well. Set the ganache aside to cool for 10-15 minutes. After the ganache has cooled, top the cake with chocolate ganache frosting and decorate with strawberry slices, raspberries, and blueberries. Cool well in the refrigerator prior to serving.

Recipe note: This cake is stunning decorated with white chocolate curls placed all over the top and sides as well. The contrast between the black and white is beautiful. To make the curls, use a larger bar of white chocolate that is room temperature. Use a potato peeler to gently peel off thin sections of the chocolate.

32

The Italian Dinner Party

Our little apartment in San Gusme frequently became the site of regular dinner parties. I had a circle of friends whom I originally met because they spoke a little English. I instantly found that it was so nice to be able to speak my mother tongue as I was doing my best to also learn Italian.

Vincenzo and I only spoke Italian at home as he did not speak English at all, so this was how I learned the language so well. However, I soon discovered that my circle of friends wanted to get together with me to speak English for their practice as well. I also learned that they had a passion for food like I did. It was not hard for me to enjoy their company as they are all such interesting people.

I worked from home, so when I had time in between writing, I loved to cook and explore the unique local ingredients. About once a month, our group would plan to get together and cook. Sometimes we cooked based on themes or other cuisines. One of my favorite dinner parties was the night we made French crepes together. Everyone was to arrive around eight to start cooking together.

I was curious about how to make crepes from a friend of mine, Gwen, who is French. She brought over her well-seasoned crepe pan, and we started to experiment with a couple of recipes we had. Her recipe was from her mother, so it was very traditional and absolutely delicious. After about an hour, we got the hang of it. Just about that time, the rest of the group of friends arrived with their treasures in hand and we kept making crepes until around 1:00 a.m.

One thing I learned is to never expect a dinner party to start when you schedule it. Italians arrive in their own time, which is notoriously thirty minutes to an hour later than you tell them. Friends brought local wine, vin santo, cheeses, ham, and Nutella. I had already thought of making dessert crepes, so I had dark chocolate, fresh whipped cream, strawberries, and bananas ready for the dessert.

I never sat down that entire night, but just kept on flipping crepes with their orders coming in from my little square table in the middle of our tiny kitchen, where they had all pulled up a chair and started enjoying a glass of wine. Each person took turns alternating making crepes with me and then eating them, followed by making more crepes and eating again. We made cheese crepes, ham and cheese crepes, Nutella crepes, dark chocolate crepes, both with either strawberries, bananas, and/or whipped cream on them. It was so much fun.

Vincenzo arrived home around midnight, just in time to eat a Nutella crepe and help me clean up the kitchen, which lasted until the early morning hours. To this day, every time I find my handwritten recipe for the crepes we made that night, I see evidence of cheese and Nutella on the pages, and I am flooded by the fun memories of this night together.

If you have never made crepes, it is good to have a practice run so that when you are ready to entertain others, you have the technique down.

Crepes

2 cups all-purpose flour

1/3 cup sugar

4 large eggs

2 cups whole milk

1/2 cup melted butter

Place the flour and sugar in a mixing bowl and stir well. Add in the milk, butter, and eggs and stir to incorporate the ingredients. The mixture will be slightly lumpy. Place the bowl with the batter into the refrigerator and let sit for an hour. The resting time is important, don't skip this part.

To make the crepes, warm a small nonstick crepe pan or griddle over medium heat. When the pan is warm, add a small pat of butter for the first crepe. Spread about 1/4 cup of batter on the pan at a time. Working very quickly, pick up the pan and tilt it so that a thin layer of the batter covers the entire surface of the pan. Once you start to see bubbles forming on the top of the batter, flip it over and cook the other side until brown. Once your crepe pan is hot, this will be around 1 minute per side.

Serve crepes filled with your favorite fillings, such as Nutella, chocolate, bananas, strawberries, whipped cream, or ice cream. Be creative and have fun.

Recipe note: Savory crepes can be made with this same recipe, just leave out the sugar. Fill savory crepes with cheese and ham.

My friends and I did our best to get together on a regular basis to share good food together. One of these times, I tried to organize a potluck party where everyone brought a dish and I had them all on a side table (set up American style, organized with the plates, utensils, and napkins first followed by the various dishes that everyone had brought). I tried to explain that you should pick up a plate and then move through the line to choose food that you wanted to eat, then sit down at the table to eat it.

I had made focaccia with zucchini flowers as well as a plate of local pecorino cheese topped with fig jam that I had made that summer. Others brought fennel and apple salad, local salumi (salami), and a frittata with potatoes and ham. They all got so excited about the food table that they all ended up standing around the food table budging in to try all of the foods. There was no orderly movement through the items on the table, just standing around dipping into each dish and placing items on their plate.

We lost track of each other's wine glasses as usual, and everyone had a wonderful time. Everyone talked at once with conversations around and through each other. They all said that the American potluck was a huge success. They never did find the table to sit at until later when we had coffee and grappa to digest our feast and compare notes on the various recipes. Here are a few from the night that I remember.

Fennel Apple Salad

2 apples, thinly sliced, keep the skins on for color (I love Fuji apples for this.)

2 bulbs of fennel, thinly sliced (take out the hard inner core of the fennel)

½ cup extra virgin olive oil

½ tsp. sea salt

1 lemon (juiced)

4 ounces parmesan cheese (shaved into thin pieces)

Slice the apples and fennel thin with a mandolin or knife. Place in a serving bowl and mix in the lemon juice, salt, and olive oil. Shave the parmesan cheese over the top and mix well. Serve immediately.

Ham and Potato Frittata

4 tablespoons olive oil
½ onion (diced)
3 large peeled potatoes (sliced thin)
10 ounces ham (diced into small cubes)
10 large eggs
¾ cup whole milk or heavy cream
Sea salt and black pepper (to taste)
6 ounces Gouda cheese (grated)
2 tablespoons fresh parsley (chopped)

(Note: You will need to use an oven-safe sauté pan for this recipe as it goes in the oven to finish.)

Preheat oven to 375 degrees.

In a 10- to 12-inch sauté pan, heat the olive oil, onions, and potatoes. Add sea salt and black pepper to taste. Sauté for 8-10 minutes until the potatoes start to get tender and cooked. Next add the diced ham and warm for another minute.

In a separate bowl, beat the eggs well so that they are yellow and creamy. Add the milk and stir well. Pour the egg mixture over the potatoes and ham and cook for the first 5 minutes on the top of the stove over medium heat. Sprinkle the cheese on the top and place the pan in the oven to finish cooking for another 8-10 minutes.

Remove from oven when the top of the eggs starts to brown and the cheese is melted and bubbling.

Remove from the pan, finish with fresh chopped parsley, and let cool on a large serving plate. Serve room temperature in small triangle slices.

Needless to say, this experience of hosting a potluck taught me a lot about the fact that Italians really don't understand how to stand in line for anything. Everything is a group affair with very little order to it, in fact it seemed to me, the more chaotic it is, the better. This is evidenced by just about everything I noticed in Italy. There was no orderly line to get coffee, but instead a herd of people all budging in and trying to get the attention of the bar owner for their orders. The food vendors at the markets have crowds around them, never a line.

I had to learn how to be more aggressive for everything I did in Italy. The art (and science) was to take note of when you arrived compared to the people who were already there, versus those that arrived after you. When you knew it was your turn, you budged in and spoke up. It was an unspoken rule everywhere in Italy.

It was during one of our dinner parties when I realized that I had gone the entire night without speaking in English to anyone. This was probably two years into my experience living in Italy. Frequently, during our dinner parties, we would switch from Italian to English, to French followed by Italian as the night went on.

I was so excited to finally think that I had understood most of the conversations that took place that evening (except some of the French). I was finally getting more fluent and brave as I made conversation outside of my security of speaking (poorly) for so many months with Vincenzo. This felt so freeing to me. As I became more comfortable, I did my best to speak regularly with the ladies of the village and even sit with them in the evenings on the little benches in our piazza to catch up on the local gossip.

33

Living between Two Worlds

It had been almost four years living in Italy when we had to make one of the most difficult decisions ever. Vincenzo's restaurant was struggling financially more each year. Because the restaurant was located in such a remote part of Tuscany, it had long periods of quiet in the winters and early spring. The building rent was so high along with all of the fees and business taxes. It was crushing them. This was happening to many people with a business in Italy, and it was sad to see.

He and his partners tried everything to keep it going, but we understood that each year that they were in business, things seemed to be getting worse instead of better. It was tragic and sad to see such a beautiful restaurant struggling to survive. It was even more difficult for me to watch Vincenzo suffer.

At this same time, I knew that my parents might need me to be closer as they grew older. Each year that I was away, I could see they missed having me close to them. Mom would seem so sad when we would Skype because I was so far away. We had always been close, so it was hard also for me to be so far away from my family. I had nieces and nephews that were growing up fast, and I was missing out on this time with them as well. I was torn between two worlds.

I was also getting increased pressure with my job to be back in Minnesota. I had been working remotely for a few years, but now the payroll tax laws had changed, and I was being asked to pay taxes also to Italy for having my home office out of the country. We could not afford to do this, and my salary is what was keeping us alive financially. I was also working as a freelance medical writer in the evenings and on the weekends.

We both felt like we worked so much, we never had time to be together and enjoy what we had. It was a paradox that was hard for me to reconcile in my mind. I wanted to keep living in Italy, but all of the practical reasons were stacked against me.

Therefore, we decided that we needed to make a plan for Vincenzo to exit the partnership and leave the restaurant. As we told his partners, their disappointment was palpable. They wanted to keep trying, keep going even though the chance of making the business work financially was obviously not going well. We devised a two-year plan to start working on paying off our portion of the debt and transitioning to a life back in Minnesota.

I knew now that I had to prepare to leave a place that I loved. I would have just one more year in Tuscany full-time. I treasured every moment of every day and started to capture photos of everything I could. I wrote about my experiences for this book and explored the traditions and recipes I loved with even more urgency. We kept our traditional Sunday evening dates, each week going to our favorite pizzeria, always ending the night sharing one of our favorite desserts, tiramisù.

Tiramisù

1 cup sugar
3 eggs (separated)
8 ounces mascarpone cheese
1 cup of espresso or any strong coffee
2 tablespoons liqueur (such as brandy or chocolate liqueur such as Godiva)
24 savoiardi (ladyfingers)
¼ cup cocoa powder

Start by beating 3 egg whites with 1/2 cup of sugar. Beat until the mixture is shiny and white and forms stiff peaks. This will take 5 minutes or longer. You should be able to turn the bowl practically upside down and the egg whites will stay in the bowl. I like to use a stand mixer for this.

Next, mix the 3 egg yolks with the remaining 1/2 cup of sugar and the mascarpone cheese with a hand mixer. Mix until well incorporated.

Gently, add the egg white mixture to the mascarpone cheese, folding in with a spatula so that the air from the egg whites keeps the mixture fluffy.

Mix together the espresso and liqueur in a shallow bowl. To assemble the tiramisù, start by spooning a thin layer of the

mascarpone cheese mixture into a 9 x 9 pan. Dip the ladyfingers into the coffee just briefly (1 second on each side is the secret to not getting them too soggy) and line up next to each other on top of the mascarpone cheese. Continue with ladyfingers until the entire pan has a layer of ladyfingers.

Next, add half of the remaining mascarpone cheese mixture to the top of the ladyfingers, and continue to layer on espresso-soaked ladyfingers on top of this second layer. The top layer should end with the remaining mascarpone cheese. Tap the pan slightly to settle the cream well.

Place in refrigerator for at least 1 day. Dust the top of the tiramisù with cocoa just prior to serving. Cut into nine squares or scoop into individual dishes to serve.

Recipe note: Tiramisù translates to "pick me up" in Italian. You can find savoiardi (ladyfingers) in the cookie or coffee section of the grocery store. It's best to use the traditional kind, not the softer ones. Marscapone cheese can be found in the specialty cheese section of most grocery stores. You can also serve this with fresh berries, finished with a chocolate-covered coffee bean or dark chocolate shavings. Cocoa is the traditional way that this dish is finished in Italy. This recipe doubles well placed in a 9 x 11 pan.

Even though I knew I had to say goodbye and it would be painful, I could see that Vincenzo seemed relieved to have a plan for a better life. For this I was happy. I wanted him to be successful in his work, but also to have time to enjoy our life together. I loved the idea that we could celebrate holidays together without thinking about the restaurant and working all of the time. I thought of this new transition as an opportunity for him and hoped that, eventually, we might still be able to have a few months in Italy each year. I had no idea how we could do that, but I kept this in my mind as the ideal arrangement.

As the weeks passed, Vincenzo and his partners made their plan to sell the restaurant. The economy was so difficult at the time, they did not expect to gain anything from selling. This move was really meant to get out from under the weight of the high rent and expenses of running the business.

The restaurant was eventually sold and transitioned to new owners. We planned a last dinner together with all of the partners and their families, along with a few regulars from the village. We ate and shared memories and stories late into the night. This was in January, so the restaurant closed for the winter, but for Vincenzo he was saying goodbye to an old friend and a dream.

We traveled back to Minnesota for a few weeks as we usually did for the winter break and enjoyed catching up with family. Everyone was excited to hear that we would be eventually moving back to Minnesota. We did a cooking class at a local restaurant again and everyone loved the idea that someday Vincenzo would bring his love and skills for Italian cooking to Minnesota. We started working on the painful process of getting Vincenzo's green card, which we knew would take awhile. We had one more year, as he wanted to help his partners make the transition to managing an existing restaurant in Siena.

I stayed in Minnesota for a few more weeks to work, and Vincenzo traveled back to Italy to open the new restaurant that was housed in a hotel in Siena. This was the plan that the partners had discussed. One more year of working together as partners and then Vincenzo would be officially out of the business arrangement. I started to think about where we might live when we transferred back to Minnesota. It made the most sense to live in Rochester. I planned to start looking for houses when I returned later that summer.

The year that followed was a difficult one. We cherished every moment that we had in Tuscany, realizing that we were saying a long goodbye. We celebrated with friends and tried to fit in everything we could. I started to pack up the items that I knew I would want to have in Minnesota with us, and other items that we could store at Vincenzo's parents' house with the idea that someday we might be back in Italy.

During this same year, Vincenzo's father learned that he had lung cancer and started to have treatment. It was devastating news for the family. During our summer visit, I could see that he was not doing well. I knew too much about this terrible disease. I knew that his time was now limited. I could not help but take as many pictures as I could of Vincenzo with his father as they worked clearing the olive trees and did the little things together.

We treasure these memories now as it was two years and he was gone from this earth. I remember the last time I saw Angiolino as I visited him in hospice.

I reached down to kiss him and say goodbye, and he whispered in my ear, "Be careful." Angiolino was a man of few words, but for me, I knew this meant "take care of yourself and love Vincenzo."

I replied, "I will always love him and take care of him. Don't worry."

Angiolino passed away a few weeks later with his family around him. His death made our transition even more difficult. However, we knew that we both would have good opportunities moving back to Minnesota. We bought a house, Vincenzo got his green card after about fourteen months, and we made the move back to Minnesota in 2015. I started working as a medical writer full-time, and Vincenzo brought his chef skills sharing his passion for traditional Italian cuisine with the people of Minnesota.

One of our absolute favorite pasta dishes that we make here for family and friends is Pici Cacio e Pepe, or pici with cheese and pepper. It is what I consider to be Italian comfort food. Pici pasta is a very thick, long pasta that is traditionally made fresh in the region of Tuscany. It is a bit like a thick spaghetti. I have discovered a few sources to order pici here in the US; however, I always include as many bags of pici pasta as I can fit in my suitcase when we travel back and forth each year.

Pici Cacio e Pepe

14 ounces pici pasta (you can also use bucatini pasta as a substitute if you are unable to find pici)

Coarse sea salt for pasta water

6 ounces pecorino cheese, grated

2 tablespoons fresh ground black pepper

Extra virgin olive oil (for cooking and for serving)

Additional grated pecorino cheese for serving (2 ounces)

Boil water in a large pasta pot. When boiling, add 2 tablespoons coarse sea salt and stir well. Next add the pici or bucatini pasta and cook according to the directions on the package. This will vary depending on the thickness of the pici pasta.

While the pasta is cooking, place a large sauté pan on the stove over medium to low heat. Add ¼ cup of olive oil, grated cheese, and black pepper to the pan to warm slightly. Stir as the cheese is melting. Once the cheese starts to melt, take the pan off the heat.

When the pasta is cooked to al dente, use a strainer or slotted spoon to transfer the pasta to the sauté pan with the cheese and pepper. Place the pan back on medium heat and mix well for about another minute until the cheese coats the pasta well. The secret chef ingredient is to add a spoon or two of the pasta cooking water to the mixture if it gets too dry.

Serve with a drizzle of olive oil and additional grated pecorino cheese.

Now, Vincenzo is the one learning a new language and adjusting to American culture. He loves exploring traditional American foods and living the dream of freedom and opportunity in America. We love to partner together doing private cooking classes, private dinners, and events. My love for the art of cooking makes us the perfect team to do this together. Our dream is to continue to grow a little business that gives people a vintage, old-school look into what it's like to enjoy and understand the history and traditions of Italian life with heritage recipes and traditional cooking.

For now, he also has a job making fresh pasta and other dishes for a local Italian restaurant in Rochester. He has brought a little taste of his traditional cooking to the Midwest. His fresh pasta dishes, tiramisù, and the recipe for his mom's fried cheese balls have been rocking the menu at Terza Ristorante since it opened in 2015. We enjoy traveling back to Italy at least once a year to catch up with Vincenzo's family and our friends in Abruzzo and Tuscany. We miss them all so much. We hope to eventually have the opportunity to spend a few months each year in both worlds.

This year, more than ten years have passed since my visit to Italy that changed my life. I thought that this was the perfect time to finally write the story. In the three years that have passed since we moved back to Minnesota, much has happened. Lina was called home by the bells, and the economy continued to touch San Gusme and other villages in the area. The little market in San Gusme closed, and new owners have opened the restaurant. Slowly, the people of Italy are healing and growing stronger, especially with the strength of the locals as well as the younger generation.

If you visit the area, be kind and gentle with the village and the people. You may have the opportunity to meet Lorenzo and stay at Borgo San Gusme, walk on the country roads and see the tall cypress trees and wander out through the vines and olive trees near the village. Stay in the Castello delle Serre with Salvatore and Antonio and dance on the top terrace of the Tower Room. Spend the day at Rapolano Terme taking in the healing waters with the locals. Drink the wines of Tenuta di Arceno, Felsina and Castello Brolio. Visit Castlenuovo Berardenga and have a coffee or gelato with Silvia at Bar Centrale where we had our first date. Shop the open-air market on Thursday and take the narrow, curvy road all through Chianti to visit the many little hilltowns and villages that remain untouched by time.

For me, I will always have the incredible memories of the experience I was so fortunate to have. There are times when I still can't believe that it all happened. Vincenzo and I are happy and thankful each day because we are together. Emma still loves to visit us at Christmas time, with a week of baking cookies, eating my mom's Swedish meatballs, drinking tea, and catching up with her Minnesota family. I am indebted to have met Pam and Sam who originally showed me their true Italy and introduced me to their family and San Gusme. I am forever grateful that I listened to my inner spirit and followed my heart to Italy and discovered love in a Tuscan kitchen.

Drawing of La Porta del Chianti Restaurant.

About the Author

Sheryl Ness was inspired to become a nurse by her father's mother, who was one of the first formally trained nurses of her time. Sheryl has a master's degree in Transcultural Nursing from Augsburg College in Minneapolis. She works as a clinical editor for Elsevier based in Rochester, Minnesota, and where she worked for thirty years as a nurse at the Mayo Clinic.

Her interest and love for the appreciation of cultures has been a strong influence in her life and inspired her to travel to other areas of the world—always curious for knowledge from cultural traditions of places and how this influence defines a person's world.

Sheryl and her husband, Vincenzo Giangiordano, now live in Rochester, Minnesota, where he prepares traditional Italian cuisine as a chef for specialty restaurants. Together, they present Italian cooking classes and events as well as host private dinners.

They would love to hear from readers. Share your stories, try the recipes, invite them to come and cook with you, and send a note if you want to be in touch at:

loveinatuscankitchen@gmail.com.
Follow on Facebook @loveinatuscankitchen.

Sheryl and Vincenzo live
and work in Minnesota.

Made in the USA
San Bernardino, CA
27 June 2018